The who's who of

DOCTOR WHO

The who's who of
DOCTOR
WHO

A WHOVIAN GUIDE TO FRIENDS, FOES, VILLAINS, MONSTERS, AND COMPANIONS TO THE GOOD DOCTOR

Cameron K. McEwan, the creator of *Blogtor Who*

with illustrations by Andrew Skilleter

Race Point
PUBLISHING

Race Point
PUBLISHING

A division of Book Sales, Inc.
276 Fifth Avenue, Suite 206
New York, NY 10001

ISBN: 978-1-937994-70-9

Cover/Chapter Opener Images:
Space Nebula Background © photodune/clearviewstock
Armageddon Background © photodune/Galaxia Studio
David Tennant © REX USA
Peter Capaldi © Getty Images
Matt Smith © BBC Photo Library

Editorial Director: Jeannine Dillon
Copyeditor: Paul Simpson
Picture Research: Danielle Rhodes
Designer: Caroline Wong
Cover Designer: Maru Studio (Sophie Yamamoto) and rocketdesign (Shingo Kikuchi)

Printed in China

10 9 8 7 6 5 4 3 2 1

TABLE OF CONTENTS

THE DOCTORS

....

As a Gallifreyan with two hearts, the Doctor chose his name at a young age after staring into the Untempered Schism. The name, a promise he made as a Time Lord, was a notion he lived for throughout his personas (well, apart from the one that broke the promise—but let's not talk about that guy yet) as he helped hundreds, nay, thousands of civilizations throughout the universe and across all of time. We surely wouldn't be here if it weren't for him. In the following pages, you'll find details of all eleven Doctors so far and what makes them the men they are, as well as an indication of the many beings they've met along the way.

THE FIRST DOCTOR

Initially mysterious, aloof, and somewhat dangerous (not to mention bad-tempered), the First Doctor was a well-dressed elderly individual with a preference for Edwardian style. While he was quick to anger and saw humans as somewhat inferior at times, his outward bluster hid a heart of gold, a passion for justice and a strong moral core, not to mention a well-veiled sense of humor.

The old man spent some time living in London, Earth in 1963 with his granddaughter, Susan. The young girl attended Coal Hill School and came to her teachers' attention thanks to her erratic behavior. Ian Chesterton (see COMPANIONS) and Barbara Wright (see COMPANIONS) were prompted into investigating her home life, discovered not only the Doctor, but also the TARDIS, disguised as a British Police Box in a scrapyard in Totter's Lane.

After the teachers had forced their way into the TARDIS and discovered its secret, the gruff, aggressive alien revealed that he and Susan were self-imposed exiles from their home world, and wanderers in the fourth dimension. Fearing that Ian and Barbara would expose them to the authorities, the Doctor rapidly put the TARDIS into time-space flight, without any planned course.

They traveled back to the year 100,000 B.C. and the unlikely traveling companions found themselves involved in a tribal power struggle between cavemen, desperate to discover the secret of fire, abducting the Doctor after they saw him smoking a pipe, lit with a match. During their attempts to flee to safety, Ian prevented the Doctor from euthanizing an injured caveman.

The TARDIS then took the quartet to the irradiated forests of Skaro and the Doctor's first encounter with the Daleks and the Thals. Curious about a city they had spotted, the Doctor deliberately sabotaged the TARDIS to justify further excursions. As they eventually learned, centuries after a deadly radio-active war, the two species on Skaro, the Dals and the Thals had both mutated. The Dals had become Daleks, creatures dependent on mobile, armed casings; the Thals were now peaceful, humanoid bipeds. In a bid to prevent the Thals' genocide by the Daleks, the Doctor taught the peace-loving race that sometimes they must take up arms to defend themselves. A malfunction with the TARDIS in flight caused the crew to turn against each other. The Doctor, mistrusting the human interlopers, took extreme

action, drugging Barbara, and accusing her and Ian of sabotage. When all was revealed to be caused by the TARDIS warning the crew of danger, the Doctor apologized for his actions, realizing he had misjudged his companions.

After an encounter with Marco Polo, and a quest to recover the lost keys of Marinus, the Doctor found himself at odds with Barbara about changing human history when they arrived inside an Aztec temple. He also ended up accidentally engaged to an elderly Aztec lady, Cameca, after inadvertently courting her by sharing a drink of chocolate. A meeting with the Sensorites, nearby space neighbors of the Ood (see ALIENS), revealed more about the Doctor and Susan. They had some telepathic abilities, and the Doctor currently had one heart; Susan also described their home world, with its burnt orange sky

and silver-leaved trees.

After being caught up in the events of the French Revolution, the TARDIS crew returned to Ian and Barbara's home time, but miniaturized due to an error with the TARDIS. All microscopic life was a threat as they battled for survival. Two hundred years later, the Doctor and his friends again faced the Daleks, who had conquered the Earth and planned to mine out its magnetic core. During this struggle, Susan fell in love with freedom fighter David Campbell. Sensing she was torn, the Doctor deliberately locked her out of his ship, letting her begin a life he could not offer her, as a woman not a girl. Heartbroken, the Doctor left his granddaughter behind, with just Ian and Barbara for company. A visit to the planet Dido saw the Doctor encounter the wreckage of a starship and its two survivors, including Vicki (see COMPANIONS) left alone by the crash. The TARDIS crew, in particular the Doctor, adopted Vicki, taking her along with them. After a bawdy visit to Nero's Rome, and a meeting with the Zarbi and Menoptra on Vortis, the Doctor attempted to avoid the politics of Richard the Lionheart's court. He also proved remarkably resistant to interrogation when captured by the Moroks, after the TARDIS jumped a time track and landed on Xeros.

Soon afterward, the TARDIS was chased through space and time by a Dalek execution squad. A robotic duplicate of the Doctor was created by the Daleks, but they were not aware that the makeup of the TARDIS crew had changed. When Ian and Barbara realized that the Dalek time-space craft represented an opportunity to return home they said farewell to the Doctor and Vicki. However the travelers weren't alone: on the planet Mechanus, astronaut Steven Taylor (see COMPANIONS) had stowed away aboard the Ship.

Arriving with a bemused Steven on the coast of England in 1066, the Doctor met another of his own race other than Susan for the first time. The Monk intended to alter human history by supplying advanced weaponry to the Saxons on the eve of the Battle of Hastings. An encounter with the Drahvins offered little rest before the Doctor became embroiled in the fall of Troy at the hands of the Greeks, which resulted in Vicki opting to leave the TARDIS. Steven was injured and the Doctor departed with handmaiden Katarina aboard ship, the first companion to die while traveling with the Doctor. Katarina chose to activate an airlock sending herself and mad killer out into the vacuum of space. Space Security Agent Sara Kingdom helped the Doctor and Steven battle the Daleks but she also died, aged to death by the Daleks' time-destructor weapon. The death toll left the Doctor visibly moved by the end.

A return trip to Paris, this time during the 1572 massacre, revealed the First Doctor's uncanny resemblance to the Abbot of Amboise. As the bloodshed rose, the Doctor and Steven departed, landing in 1966. Clearly affected by all the recent deaths he'd witnessed, Steven walked out on the Doctor, leaving him alone, in a reflective mood, realizing that none of his traveling companions understood why sometimes he could not act, and that he could not still go home to his own planet. However, the presence of an approaching policeman resulted in Steven returning to warn the Doctor, unaware that the TARDIS has also been entered by a young girl Dodo Chaplet (see COMPANIONS), who had mistaken it for a real Police Box. The Doctor, Steven and Dodo made two visits to the Ark around the year 10 million A.D., but then the Doctor vanished from the control room of the TARDIS. The Celestial Toymaker, an immortal being, forced the Doctor, Steven and Dodo to engage in a series of deadly games. The Doctor won after demonstrating an ability for mimicry, and impersonating the Toymaker's voice at a crucial moment.

In agony from toothache, the Doctor arrived in Tombstone, Arizona, in 1881, only to find himself mistaken for Doc Holliday and caught up in the infamous events at the O.K. Corral (and also at odds with the gun-driven culture of the time). On an unknown planet in the far future, Steven elected to remain behind and help rebuild the society after the Doctor destroyed the technology used by the apparently civilized Elders to exploit others.

Returning to London in 1966, the height of the "Swinging Sixties," the Doctor became involved in a plot by super-computer WOTAN to use the newly built Post Office Tower to enslave humanity. During a visit to a nightclub, the Doctor was shown to be out of touch with vernacular dialogue. Back in her own time, Dodo elected to leave the TARDIS, and asked sailor Ben and secretary Polly (see COMPANIONS), who had helped the Doctor defeat WOTAN, to return her TARDIS key to the Doctor. They barged into the Police Box, and were whisked away into space and time.

After taking his new companions to seventeenth century Cornwall for an adventure with pirates and smugglers, the Doctor arrived at a South Pole base in 1986, as a planet, identical to Earth, was approaching the human home world. An army of cybernetically-enhanced humans, the Cybermen (see ALIENS), inhabited Earth's twin and began to drain Earth of its energy. However, defeating the Cybermen took its toll on the Doctor's health, and a confused and weakened old man journeyed back to the TARDIS, collapsing on the floor of the control room. In front of an astonished Ben and Polly, his features begin to glow, and soon, a new and very different man was lying before them.

This wasn't the last time that we saw the first incarnation of the Doctor. The First Doctor was briefly removed from his timestream by the Time Lords during Omega's attack on their home world. However they were unable to bring him fully into the Third Doctor's timestream, due to failing power reserves, so he could do little more than advise, expressing little regard for the appearance of his two future incarnations, or their intelligence.

He was removed from his timestream another time by Time Lord President Borusa, and brought to the Death Zone of Gallifrey, where he was reunited with an adult Susan, and his Second, Third and Fifth lives.

THE SECOND DOCTOR

The second incarnation of the Doctor displayed a very different energy to what had come before. Seemingly a lighter, relaxed, witty, scruffier, bumbling individual, beneath was a clever, calculated, brave and strongly moral figure.

Initially Ben and Polly doubted this was the Doctor in light of the somewhat strange references he made to his past life, but after an encounter with the Daleks on Vulcan—where the Doctor was recognized as their mortal enemy—they accepted this was the same man. Shortly after this, during a trip to the highlands of Scotland, after the Battle of Culloden, the Doctor was joined by his most faithful companion, Jamie McCrimmon (see COMPANIONS). After an encounter with the survivors of Atlantis, the Doctor faced the Cybermen on the surface of the moon—the first of many meetings with the deadly foes for this incarnation of the Time Lord.

A visit to an unnamed Earth colony in the future, spurred by the image of a giant claw seen on the TARDIS scanner, brought the Doctor into his first encounter with the deadly, crab-like Macra (see ALIENS). Returning to Heathrow, Earth, in 1966, the TARDIS team faced a shapeshifting race of aliens known as the Chameleons, who were infiltrating society by taking over comatose human bodies. On discovering that the date of their landing was identical to the day when they left London with the First Doctor, Ben and Polly opted to leave their journeying days in the TARDIS behind them.

When the TARDIS was stolen, the Doctor and Jamie were led to a Victorian-style shop where the antiques appeared a little too modern. Run by Edward Waterfield, it was soon revealed as a trap set by the Daleks. The Doctor and Jamie were transported back to 1866, where they met Waterfield's daughter, Victoria (see COMPANIONS). After traveling to Skaro, the Doctor learned that the Daleks, led by their Emperor, wanted to spread "the Dalek factor" throughout human history using the Doctor's TARDIS. In the final battle, Waterfield was killed, and the Doctor promised to act as a guardian to Victoria, who joined the TARDIS crew.

On her first journey with the Doctor and Jamie, Victoria found herself on Telos, the lost second home world of the Cybermen, where the last few remaining cybernetic survivors were in deep, cryo-hibernation. During a brief lull during the attempt by the human Brotherhood of Logicians to forge an alliance with the Cyber Controller, Victoria mourned the loss of her father, and the Doctor comforted her with a rare talk about his loved ones, revealing himself to be around 450 years old.

When they traveled to Tibet in 1935, the Doctor explained that he previously visited the Detsen Monastery some three hundred years earlier and taken a Ghanta bell for safe keeping. The Doctor was accused of murder by Yeti hunter Professor Travers, and when fearsome, robotic Yeti attacked the monastery, the Doctor was horrified to learn that his old friend, Master Padmasambhava, was still alive after three hundred years, and was now possessed by a disembodied force, the Great Intelligence, who was controlling the Yeti.

With the Intelligence defeated, the Doctor and his friends met the Ice Warriors (see ALIENS) for the first time. As a scientific team battled to hold back the effects of a future ice age in Britain, the frozen, partly cybernetic body of a native Martian was discovered, which had been trapped in the ice for millennia. When revived, he identified himself as Varga and began to retrieve his comrades from their ship. The Doctor became caught in a crossfire of cultural misunderstandings, resulting in the destruction of Varga and his crew.

Enjoying a holiday on the beaches of twenty-first century Australia, the Doctor was attacked by a would-be assassin. This was a case of mistaken identity: The Second Doctor was a double for Salamander, a dictator within the United Zones Organization. The Doctor and his friends agreed to help bring down the megalomaniac, but this meant that Salamander discovered his resemblance to the Doctor. In a last ditch attempt to escape, Salamander tried to steal the TARDIS, but he was blown out into the Time Vortex.

The Doctor arrived back in London deep within the Underground system and learned that the Yeti had reappeared, forty years after their first encounter. Working with Professor Travers, the Doctor helped the British Army, including a Colonel Lethbridge-Stewart, to stem a deadly web-like fungus spreading throughout London, and defeated the Great Intelligence—which once again escaped.

After the TARDIS materialized above the North Sea in the early 1970s, the Doctor, Jamie, and Victoria became involved with an attack by sentient gas-like creatures on a Euro Sea Gas plant. This left Victoria completely drained and she opted to settle down with the Harris family, despite efforts by the Doctor to persuade her to stay with him. During the course of this adventure, the Doctor used his sonic screwdriver for the first time.

When an explosion on the TARDIS meant the Doctor and Jamie had to abandon the ship, they were taken to a deep space station called the Wheel. The base, which was run by an international crew including logician Zoe Heriot, came under attack from the Cybermen, led by the Cyber-planner, who were looking to seize the base and use it to stage a full-scale invasion of Earth. When the threat was ended, Zoe joined the Doctor and Jamie. This also marked the first time we heard the Doctor use the pseudonym "John Smith," thought up by Jamie (although it was later revealed that he had a library card during his time on Earth with that name in his first incarnation).

When he helped to prevent the Dominators and their machine servants, the Quarks, from destroying the peaceful planet Dulkis, the Doctor ended up creating new active volcanoes that threatened the TARDIS itself. Removed from reality to save it from being destroyed, the TARDIS ended up in The Land of Fiction—a place where pure fiction became its own form of reality.

Back in our universe, the Doctor was reunited with the newly promoted Brigadier Lethbridge-Stewart, heading up a new international taskforce called UNIT—the United Nations Intelligence Taskforce. They were investigating International Electromatics, headed by Tobias Vaughn, who were in league with the Cybermen as they planned yet another invasion of Earth. On an unnamed planet, the Doctor freed the local people, the Gonds, from generations of slavery to the crystalline Krotons. By the end of the twenty-first century, Earth had become reliant on Transmat (T-Mat) technology, bringing a temporary end to manned space flight. However, the Doctor discovered that the Ice Warriors were hijacking the system, planning to infect the planet with deadly spores and then invade. He was able to lure the Martian fleet into the Sun.

After an encounter with deadly Space Pirates, the Doctor was pitted against another of his own kind, the War Chief, who was assisting the alien War Lord to kidnap numerous different armies from Earth's history, and forcing them into eternal, simulated battle to build a perfect army. Unable to return all the captured soldiers to their own times, the Doctor called for help from his own people, the Time Lords (the first time he used the name in front of his companions), at the risk of his own capture.

The Doctor was caught, and placed on trial by his peers for his crimes of interference across time and space. After he argued passionately that someone must fight the evils of the universe, the Time Lords agreed to enforce a regeneration and permanent

exile to Earth as a suitable punishment. Zoe and Jamie were returned to their own times with their memories erased, and the Second Doctor disappeared, seemingly, for the last time.

However the Second Doctor would appear, alone, twice more. Like his predecessor, he was pulled at some unspecified time out of his timestream to assist the Third Doctor during Omega's attack on Gallifrey, and then later, when visiting to celebrate Brigadier Lethbridge-Stewart's retirement from UNIT, he was captured by Borusa and transported, along with the Brigadier, to the Death Zone of Gallifrey, along with his First, Third, and Fifth incarnations.

The Second Doctor and Jamie also encountered his Sixth incarnation and his companion Peri in Seville, Spain. At some point, they were on a mission for the Time Lords without Victoria (who was studying graphology) and encountered the Sontarans and Androgums. Since Jamie was unaware of the Time Lords' existence prior to the Doctor's trial, it is impossible to accurately place this adventure in the Second Doctor's chronology.

The Second Doctor was often doubted by those around him, and occasionally gave the impression of foolishness, but he always proved himself to be the brave, reliable, moral guardian the universe needed.

THE THIRD DOCTOR

A more serious, dashing and aloof incarnation, the Third Doctor, exiled to Earth by the Time Lords for much of his life on Earth, was a more gadget-loving, paternal figure, with a general disregard for government bureaucrats. Working alongside UNIT as humanity faced one of its worst periods of alien aggression, not to mention the arrival of his arch-rival, the Master (see TIME LORDS), the Third Doctor was never short of action.

After arriving on Earth, the Doctor's weakened body was taken to Ashbridge Cottage Hospital, and quickly came to the attention of UNIT since he had arrived in the middle of a meteor shower. However, although the Doctor recognized the Brigadier, the UNIT commander did not initially believe that this was the same man who had previously helped him. In any case, he had already appointed Cambridge professor Liz Shaw (see COMPANIONS) as his Scientific Advisor. The Doctor proved his credentials by assisting them to foil the plans of the Nestene Consciousness to use Auton duplicates (see ALIENS) to conquer Earth. As he recovered, the Doctor showed a taste for velvet jackets and vintage cars, both of which he "acquired" at the hospital.

The Doctor agreed to stay with UNIT as a Scientific Advisor, in return for laboratory facilities to help repair the TARDIS. His first task was to broker a peace between humanity and the Silurians (see ALIENS), the original inhabitants of Earth.
Accidentally awakened, they sought to reclaim their world from the humans. However, when his attempts failed, the Doctor could only look on in horror when the Silurian base was blown up by UNIT.

The Doctor was more successful in arranging peaceful contact with another race of aliens, whose ambassadors to Earth had been kidnapped by a xenophobic general. During this, he traveled into space, displaying his superior physical and mental abilities over the human astronauts.

While investigating a secret drilling project codenamed Inferno, the Doctor was thrown into a parallel universe where Britain had fallen under fascist control. Witnessing the Inferno project destroy that world, the Doctor returned to our universe, just in time to prevent another Earth from suffering the same fate. Sometime after that, Liz Shaw decided to return to Cambridge to resume her studies.

The Brigadier assigned young trainee Jo Grant (see COMPANIONS) as the Doctor's new assistant, just in time for the arrival of his old sparring partner, the Master, as he led a second Auton invasion attempt on Earth. Although the Master escaped, the Doctor rendered his rival's TARDIS useless.

The Master attempted to use an alien mind parasite contained within the "Keller" machine, as well as his hypnotic powers and alien expertise to attack the first World Peace Conference, before escaping the Earth, only to be captured by the Axons and forced to aid their attempted invasion. The Doctor foiled both plans while continuing to work on the TARDIS, but his exile was temporarily lifted after Time Lord files were stolen. The Time Lords sent the Doctor and Jo to the desert planet of Uxarieus in the year 2472 where they found the Master plotting further schemes to rule the galaxy. Once he was defeated,

the Time Lords returned the Doctor immediately to Earth.

The excavation of the Devil's Hump burial mound unleashed a long-dormant alien life-form, a Daemon known as Azal. The Master hoped to use Azal's powers, but the Daemon threatened to destroy the Earth as a failed experiment. After Azal committed suicide, the Master was captured and imprisoned by UNIT.

Discovering an alternative future reality where the Daleks successfully ruled and occupied twenty-second century Earth, the Doctor broke a time paradox to give humanity a new chance for the future before attempting a test flight of the TARDIS. This was hijacked by the Time Lords who sent him to the planet Peladon, on the eve of the coronation of its new King. The Doctor helped an interspecies delegation, including the Ice Warriors, to allow Peladon to join the Galactic Federation.

Back on Earth, the Doctor visited the Master in captivity, initially not realizing that he was working with the Sea Devils, the oceanic-based cousins of the Silurians (see ALIENS), to try to retake the Earth. The Time Lords then sent the Doctor on a mission to deliver key documents to a scientist on thirtieth century Solos. On their return to the twentieth century, they discovered that the Master, who had escaped from his prison, was now carrying out time experiments. Both Time Lords traveled to the lost, and soon to be destroyed, continent of Atlantis before meeting one of the most powerful beings in the universe, a Chronovore.

The Time Lords themselves faced destruction when one of their own lost legends, Omega, began an assault on their home world from the anti-matter universe where he was trapped. When the Doctor also came under attack, he called for help, but all the Time Lords could do was break the First Law of Time and send his First and Second incarnations to assist. The combined intellect of the three Doctors defeated Omega, and as a reward, the Third Doctor's exile was lifted.

The Doctor returned to his life wandering the Universe, and his first test flight of the TARDIS brought him and Jo to a traveling peepshow of monsters and exhibits currently visiting the planet of Inter Minor. They then traveled on to the twenty-sixth century, at a time of heightened tensions between humanity and the Draconians. This was being fomented by the Master and the Daleks, and after helping to bring about peace, the Doctor and Jo helped a group of Thals to prevent the resurrection of a gigantic Dalek force on the planet Spiridon.

After they returned to Earth, Jo fell in love with biologist Dr. Clifford Jones during an environmental near-disaster caused by a corporate super-computer known as BOSS, and agreed to travel up the Amazon with him. With his hearts broken, the Doctor remained on Earth, continuing his work for UNIT, gifting Jo a blue crystal stolen from Metebelis Three.

Helping UNIT investigate the disappearance of several scientists saw the Doctor discover a Sontaran pilot marooned in Medieval England. He also met journalist Sarah Jane Smith (see COMPANIONS) who stowed away in the TARDIS. During this adventure, the Doctor revealed that Gallifrey was the name of his home planet for the first time. However, when he and Sarah returned to their own time, they found London evacuated, with dinosaurs roaming the streets. A group of conspirators within the government and military, including UNIT's Captain Mike Yates, were planning to use a Timescoop to turn back time, taking the "elite" of Britain back to a "Golden Age." The Doctor and Sarah then traveled in the TARDIS for a time, helping to defeat the Daleks on Exxilon, and the Ice Warriors on Peladon.

A final encounter with Mike Yates, now discharged from UNIT for his actions during the dinosaur invasion, set the Third Doctor on a fatal showdown with the deadly giant spiders of Metebelis Three. The Eight Legs (see ALIENS) sought the return of the crystal

the Doctor had stolen from the planet. Forced to enter the cave of the Great One, the largest and most deadly of the alien arachnids, the Doctor suffered a fatal dose of radiation, and returned to Earth. Dying in front of a distraught Sarah Jane Smith and a nonplussed Brigadier, the miracle of regeneration took place again.

In common with his predecessors, the Third Doctor was kidnapped by President Borusa and transported to Gallifrey. There he and Sarah Jane Smith encountered the Master as well as a party of Cybermen and a Raston Warrior Robot (see ROBOTS) as they traveled to the Dark Tower.

THE FOURTH DOCTOR

Suffering almost no signs of post-regenerative stress, the Fourth Doctor strode in the TARDIS bedecked in his almost bohemian, scattered outfit (that changed over time) with his brimmed hat and long, long scarf. His time was defined by his gregariousness and laughter in the face of danger, and also by some of the most horrifying and nasty aliens imaginable. However, by the time this incarnation came to its end, the Time Lord was much more somber, sensing his time had come.

Immediately after his regeneration, the Time Lord put on a display of fitness and alertness, although his initial choice of clothes was slightly odd and impractical. During the fight against the Scientific Reform Society and Professor J.P. Kettlewell's giant robot, K1 (see ROBOTS), he and Sarah bonded quickly again and, on being referred to as "childish" by the journalist, he responded, "Well, of course I am. There's no point in being grown up if you can't be childish sometimes."

Eager to see the universe, he took Sarah and UNIT doctor Harry Sullivan to Space Station Nerva, far in the future the population of mankind was in hibernation. Seeing this, the Doctor explained his admiration of humanity to his traveling companions, "Homo sapiens! What an inventive, invincible species. It's only a few million years since they've crawled up out of the mud and learned to walk. Puny, defenseless bipeds. They've survived flood, famine, and plague. They've survived cosmic wars and holocausts, and now here they are amongst the stars, waiting to begin a new life, ready to outsit eternity. They're indomitable!"

After hopping back to the future Earth, where they found Sontarans experimenting on human pilots, the Doctor and his friends were taken out of a transmat beam by the Time Lords. Taken to Skaro shortly before the creation of the Daleks, the Doctor was asked to avert their creation, alter their development, or learn about their weaknesses. The Doctor faced a moral challenge when he came within seconds of committing genocide of the Daleks. "Do I have the right?" he asked Sarah. He knew that if he wiped out a "whole intelligent life form, then I become like them. I'd be no better than the Daleks." His time on Skaro also saw his first meeting with the Daleks' creator, the crazed scientist Davros (see VILLAINS), and the two spent some time discussing the morals of power.

An encounter with another familiar foe, the Cy-bermen, followed before the Brigadier summoned the Doctor back to Earth. The Doctor was slightly antagonistic toward the Brigadier for interrupting his travels for what the Time Lord believed to be trifling matter—oil rigs being attacked in the North Sea—but he quickly changed his mind when he learned men were dying. When attacked by the Zygons, the shape-changing race responsible, the Gallifreyan revealed a trick he picked up from a Tibetan monk, hypnotizing Sarah Jane into holding her breath, and putting himself into a trance when they were trapped in a decompression chamber.

Harry left the pair after this adventure, and their travels took them into the far future on the planet Zeta Minor where the Doctor negotiated with creatures from an anti-matter universe. In 1911, the

Time Lord encountered the might of the malevolent Egyptian "god" Sutekh. Between these adventures, the Doctor explained a little about his alien nature to Sarah. "I'm a Time Lord. I'm not a human being. I walk in eternity," adding that he had been alive for around 750 years. He also showed his friend what the world would have been like under Sutekh, should they have chosen not to intervene.

After halting a planned invasion of Earth by the Kraals, where the Doctor and Sarah Jane met android duplicates of themselves and various members of UNIT, the Time Lord met another of his kind, the criminal Morbius. The two indulged in a battle of the minds which suggested that, perhaps, the Doctor had more personas than he was admitting to. After visits to contemporary Earth to fend off an attack by a Krynoid (see ALIENS), fifteenth century Italy where they prevented an invasion by the Mandragora Helix, and then back to 1970s England and the war-ravaged planet Kastria while dealing with the Kastrian criminal Eldrad, the Doctor and Sarah parted company. A recall from the Time Lords to his home world meant their adventures together were over, since he was not allowed to take a human to Gallifrey. (Later events would suggest that those rules were changed

at some point.) Upset at leaving, Sarah told the Doctor not to forget her. "Till we meet again, Sarah" were his final words to her as he mistakenly dropped off in Aberdeen (not South Croydon as promised). A somber Doctor made his way to Gallifrey, clearly dejected at the loss of his very good friend.

Another companion, however was not too far away. After a meeting with his old enemy the Master (now in an emaciated form) and a trip into the Matrix on Gallifrey, where the suggestion that Time Lords can only regenerate twelve times was first mentioned, the Doctor met the "savage" Leela (see COMPANIONS), a member of the Tribe of the Sevateem. On her planet, he discovered a carved replica of his own face on a cliff, indicating his previous presence on the planet. Although annoyed at his new companion's penchant for violence and knife-throwing, the Time Lord warmed to her swiftly, and began to educate her.

As they traveled away from her home planet, he teased her by letting her think a yo-yo controlled the "magic" of the TARDIS. The Time Lord also rather flippantly explained "transdimensional engineering" using two different sized boxes. He held one farther away from the other and asked which one was larger,

claiming, "If you could keep that exactly that distance away and have it here, the large one would fit inside the small one." The Doctor playfully referred to Leela as "mouse," when she gained a squeaky voice after inhaling some helium at the climax of their adventure on a sand miner where a robot revolution was taking place among the Dums and Vocs (see ROBOTS).

The Time Lord treated Leela to a pair of journeys to England near the turn of the twentieth century, then at the Bi-Al Foundation in the year 5000, the pair welcomed a new addition to the TARDIS, the canine-shaped computer K9 (see ROBOTS). After fighting the Fendahl on Earth, Usurians on Pluto, as well as a mad computer inside a forming planet, another visit to Gallifrey beckoned. Strangely, Leela was able to join the Doctor on this journey, unlike Sarah Jane Smith. Once he arrived, the Doctor immediately claimed the rightful role of President; this was part of a bid to destroy a Vardan invasion although he inadvertently opened up his home world to invasion by the Sontarans. Once they were repulsed, Leela, rather oddly, elected to stay on Gallifrey with a soldier she had just met, K9 choosing to remain at her side. Keen not to be alone, the Doctor built himself another K9, describing it as a "sensitive machine," but he was joined by another Gallifreyan at the bequest of the White Guardian (see FRIENDS). The Time Lady Romana (see TIME LORDS) was sent to help search for the six segments of the Key to Time. The couple had a frosty start, with her intelligence clearly outweighing his, her triple first besting his "fifty one percent at the second attempt" by some margin. During their quest the two became good friends. During the search for the final segment, the Doctor met an old classmate, Drax (see TIME LORDS), who addressed him as "Theta Sigma," and they discussed the tech course they took together in the "class of 92." Once the Key was assembled, the Doctor pretended the power of the universe belonged to him, menacingly stating, "As from this moment, there's no such thing as free will in the entire universe. There's only my will, because I possess the Key to Time!" Romana, however, saw through the Doctor's posturing.

After their epic search was over, Romana regenerated into a much softer, but still striking, female, apparently able to choose her body at will. The couple formed an even stronger bond (with Romana sometimes mimicking his clothes) as the Time Lord and Lady visited Skaro (encountering Davros, the Daleks and the Movellans), Paris, Chloris, and Skonnos. While visiting an old friend of the Doctor's in Cambridge the couple were taken out of space and time by Borusa in his quest for immortality. His other selves congregated in the Death Zone but the Fourth Doctor and Romana were stuck in a time eddy. Once the other Doctors had defeated the evil Time Lord, he and the Time Lady continued their travels.

Towards the end of their time together, the Fourth Doctor's clothing became more uniform, and less exotic, favoring a burgundy motif with no lapel badges of note or dazzlingly colorful scarf. HIs mood reflected this less gregarious state, as he approached his regeneration. Trying to return Romana to Gallifrey, they were pulled into E-Space, a universe which existed outside our own, where they met Alzarian math genius, Adric (see COMPANIONS). After some adventures there, Romana chose to stay in E-Space, with K9, to help the Tharils. Clearly moved to see her go, the Doctor bellowed, "I'll miss you. You were the noblest Romana of them all," adding to his new friend Adric, "She'll be superb."

The Time Lord and the Alzarian returned to our universe but the Doctor found himself up dealing with his old foe, the Master, who had been hiding out, still in an emaciated form, on the planet Traken, seemingly waiting for this moment to arrive. The Doctor foiled the Master's attempt to use the Source from the Traken Union to return to a normal state but the Master had enough power to take the form of Councilman Tremas, the father of Nyssa (see COMPANIONS), who would shortly become another companion in the TARDIS. But before the Master showed his hand, the Doctor was visited by the Watcher, an imprint of his future self. The mysterious being gave the Doctor knowledge of his impending regeneration.

Wanting to sort out the TARDIS' outer shell, the Doctor and Adric traveled to the planet of Logopolis, but there discovered the Master interfering with matters he didn't fully comprehend. In a desperate bid to save the universe from entropy, the two Time Lords returned to Earth, but the Master decided to use the opportunity to hold the universe to ransom. The Doctor stopped him, but fell from a radio telescope dish. Surrounded by Tegan (see COMPANIONS), Nyssa and Adric, the Doctor told his young friends that it was "the end, but the moment has been prepared for." The Watcher dissolved into the Fourth Doctor's body, starting the regeneration process.

THE FIFTH DOCTOR

The Fifth Doctor's regeneration initially appeared to be failing, before stabilizing into a more youthful, subtle individual than the Doctor had been before. Dressed in Edwardian cricket garb and sporting a piece of celery on his lapel, the Fifth Doctor became a quieter force of nature, often facing many adversaries whose paths he'd crossed before.

As he recovered from his regeneration, the Doctor faced an attempt on his weakened state by the Master, seeking revenge. Escaping the illusory world of Castrovalva with Nyssa, Tegan and Adric, the Doctor fully recovered and started his travels across the universe a renewed man.

After defeating an attempt by the Urbankans, led by their Monarch, to wipe out all life on Earth, a visit to the jungle planet Deva Loka brought the TARDIS crew into contact with the deadly Mara (see ALIENS) for the first time, as they formed a psychic link with Tegan. On seventeenth century Earth, they met the Terileptils, who planned to genetically enhance the plague carried by the rat population of London. This resulted in the TARDIS crew inadvertently starting the Great Fire of London. For the first time since his second incarnation, the Doctor was without the sonic screwdriver, after it was destroyed by the Terileptil leader. "I feel as though you've just killed an old friend," the Doctor opined ruefully, and it was many years before he decided to create a replacement.

The TARDIS crew visited 1920s England where they met Nyssa's double, Ann Talbot, before the Doctor faced off once more against the Cybermen, who

were planning to bomb twenty-sixth century Earth. Their defeat came at a high cost: Adric was killed as he attempted to unlock the controls on a freighter, as it spiraled back through time. The Doctor, Nyssa and Tegan could only watch as their young companiondied, in an explosion that also wiped out the dinosaurs.

Finally returning Tegan to her time and Heathrow Airport, the Doctor foiled a plot by the Master to use the supersonic aircraft Concorde, in a desperate bid to escape Earth after his TARDIS became badly damaged. Leaving Tegan behind, the Doctor and Nyssa set off once more. However, Tegan rejoined the crew when they all met in Amsterdam some time later. Omega was using the Doctor's DNA to try to take a permanent form in our universe, and the Doctor faced execution by his own people in their efforts to stop him. On Manussa, Tegan came back under the control of the deadly Mara before the Doctor encountered a retired Alastair Gordon Lethbridge-Stewart, now working as a teacher at Brendon Public School, as well as a mysterious student, Vislor Turlough (see COMPANIONS). Far from being an ordinary pupil, he was a stranded alien posing as a human who was contacted by the Black Guardian (see VILLIANS), offering him passage home if he agreed to kill the Doctor. Turlough joined the TARDIS crew, with the Doctor unaware of his intentions.

When Turlough sabotaged the TARDIS, an emergency landing brought the crew to Terminus, a time-ship at the center of the known universe whose inhabitants were ravaged by a deadly disease. Nyssa elected to remain behind to use her skills to help to develop a cure. Turlough's duplicity was eventually exposed, and he rejected the Black Guardian, who disappeared in flames.

Landing in England in 1215 A.D., the Doctor met the Master once more, who this time was using a shapeshifting android called Kamelion (see ROBOTS) to prevent the signing of the Magna Carta, and thus rewrite human history. After he suddenly collapsed while visiting the Eye of Orion, the Doctor set course for Gallifrey as his previous incarnations were pulled towards the Death Zone, captured by President Borusa, who was seeking the secret of immortality. Joining with the combined forces of his first three incarnations (the Fourth was trapped in a time eddy) the Fifth Doctor defeated Borusa, only to be offered the Presidency of the High Council. Choosing to flee the position, he took to the universe once more with Turlough and Tegan.

When the TARDIS was knocked out of orbit by a weapons satellite and materialized on the military Sea Base 4, the Doctor faced an alliance between the Silurians and the Sea Devils. They aimed to provoke the world's superpowers into a catastrophic war, allowing them to retake their planet. Forced to wipe out their army, the Doctor mourned their loss and wondered if the reptiles and humans could ever live together in peace.

A visit to Tegan's grandfather coincided with a Civil War re-enactment on Earth, which psychically

awakened the Malus in the year 1984, then the TARDIS made a dramatic visit to Frontios in the far future. There, a human colony was struggling against severe obstacles, including regular meteor strikes, orchestrated by the Gravis and his Tractators (see ALIENS), living deep below the ground.

Upon leaving Frontios, the TARDIS became trapped in a time corridor. It was the work of the Daleks, who had various plans running simultaneously: they needed Davros to save them from a Movellan (see ROBOTS) virus, and were creating duplicates of the Doctor and his friends to use to assassinate the High Council of the Time Lords. After some substantial bloodshed on all sides, Tegan decided to leave the Doctor in an emotional farewell which clearly gave him much to consider about the way in which he lived his life. Events on the island of Lanzarote led the Doctor and Turlough to the planet Sarn and another meeting with the Master. The Doctor gained a new companion, Perpeguiliam "Peri" Brown (see COMPANIONS) but lost Turlough, who was able to return home to Trion.

During a visit to Androzani Minor, the Doctor and Peri contracted the fatal infection spectrox toxemia as rival factions fought for control of the drug spectrox. The Doctor located the only cure (queen bat's milk) and fled the explosion-hit planet, with Peri in tow. However, with just enough cure for one person, he elected to save Peri, before collapsing on the floor of the TARDIS. The regeneration was not smooth, and even the Time Lord questioned, "Is this death?" as visions of his past friends and enemies appeared, including Adric whose appearance spurred the Doctor to fight on to achieve regeneration.

The Fifth Doctor made one further appearance, meeting his Tenth incarnation when their TARDISes collided in the Time-Space Vortex after the latter forgot to put his shields up. Initially disliking his later self, the two quickly became friends, helping one another save the universe.

* * *

THE SIXTH DOCTOR

Born out of the trauma of the violent regeneration on Androzani, the Sixth Doctor had, initially, a highly unstable personality, often openly resorting to force, and displaying an angry temperament and a lack of taste. However, in time, flashes of moral strength, humor and charm began to return to what was one of the Doctor's most troubled incarnations.

In the TARDIS after his regeneration, the Doctor chose a rather unusual and tasteless set of new clothes before unexpectedly attempting to strangle Peri during an uncontrollable mental breakdown. After realizing the trauma caused by his actions, he decided to become a hermit on the asteroid, Titan 3. When a nearby starship crashed close to the TARDIS, the Doctor quickly became embroiled in the kidnapping of the twins Romulus and Remus Sylveste, who had been taken at the behest of Menstor, a Gastropod who aimed to use their genius for his own nefarious ends. The Doctor's brash and somewhat rude attitude was called into question by Peri, but he reminded her that he was an alien, with different values and customs, and smugly commented that he was the Doctor, whether she liked it or not

An alien distress signal on Earth in 1985 brought the Doctor and Peri back to Totter's Lane and an encounter with the Cybermen, hiding in the sewer systems of London, along with Lytton (see VILLAINS).

The Cybermen were working from their tombs on Telos to redirect Halley's Comet to collide with the Earth, and prevent the destruction of Mondas the following year. The Doctor continued to display a more direct, violent streak but also a more whimsical determination to repair the TARDIS, including its chameleon circuit.

During an emergency visit to secure a vital power source, Zeiton-7, for the TARDIS, the Doctor met the nameless Governor of Varos, and the Thoran-Betan, Sil (see VILLAINS). Surviving a world of reality television executions, the Doctor and Peri prevented Sil from overthrowing the planet for his own ends. After that, the Doctor and Peri came face to face with not only the Master, but also the Rani (see TIME LORDS), another renegade Time Lord, who was using the residents of Killingworth in nineteenth century England for her experiments.

During a brief moment of peace on a fishing trip, the Sixth Doctor suddenly collapsed, his personal timeline altered by a possible death in his past. Seeking out the help of an old friend, Dastari, based at Space Station Chimera, he discovered his former companion Jamie McCrimmon in hiding, believing his Doctor (the Second incarnation) to be dead. Jamie joined the Sixth Doctor and Peri to mount a rescue mission, and they traveled to Seville in Spain. There it was revealed that Dastari, who was conducting genetic engineering on a race known as Androgums, was in league with the Sontarans and required a Time Lord to dissect for his plans. After witnessing the cannibalistic urges of Androgum chef Shockeye, the Sixth Doctor turned vegetarian.

After a meeting with H.G. Wells, and a journey to the planet Karfel (which the Third Doctor

and Jo had visited with another companion many years previously), the Doctor once again was embroiled in Davros' plans. On the planet Necros the Doctor met new Daleks, created by Davros from the genetic material of people held there in cryogenic suspension. Forces from Skaro (who unusually for the Daleks, didn't recognize the Doctor) arrived to capture Davros and to destroy his new creations, resulting in the beginning of a Dalek Civil War.

Some time later, the Doctor, traveling alone in the TARDIS, was forced to a Gallifreyan space station where he was put on trial by the High Council of Time Lords for his interference over the years (much as his Second incarnation had been). The prosecution was led by the Valeyard, and opened showing the events on Ravalox, taken from the records of the Matrix. On an Earth-like planet, recovering from a fireball, the Doctor and Peri encountered thief Sabalom Glitz (see FRIENDS) who was planning to

destroy a Black Light energy converter, and thus destroy the L3 Robot, so he could steal some secrets it was guarding. The Doctor's anger at the perceived lack of justice was demonstrated when it appeared that certain details had been redacted.

The Valeyard continued to present his case, next showing events on Thoros Beta, where the Doctor and Peri again encountered Sil, who was not only acting as an arms dealer, but also assisting with experiments in mind transference. As events descended into chaos, the Doctor attempted to rescue Peri from becoming the subject of a mind transfer, only to be recalled to the TARDIS in a hypnotic state—and to his trial. In the Doctor's absence, it appeared that King Ycranos had killed Peri, though this proved not to be the case.

Given the chance to defend himself, the Doctor chose an event from his future, aboard the Hyperion

III with new companion, Melanie Bush (see COMPANIONS). Human scientists had been genetically engineering a new plant-based race called the Vervoids (see ALIENS) for slave work. However, the Vervoids had an instinctive fear of humans and "animal-kind," and began a murderous spree throughout the ship. In saving all those aboard, the Doctor was forced to kill every Vervoid, and remorsefully admitted there was no other way. The Valeyard seized on this, instructing the court that the Doctor should face the charge of genocide.

Despite the Doctor's claims of false evidence and a hidden agenda, there was nothing he can do until, unexpectedly, both Mel and Glitz appeared at the trial, brought there by the Master. The Doctor's old foe revealed that the Matrix had been tampered with by the Valeyard, who was an alternative, evil incarnation of the Doctor, somewhere between his twelfth and final regeneration, seeking the remaining lives in the Doctor's life cycle. This information resulted in the Sixth Doctor using the court to morally denounce the High Council's corruption.

The Valeyard fled to the Matrix and engaged in a battle of psychic wills with the Doctor. Surviving the events—and declining the opportunity to rebuild the High Council as President—the Doctor set off with Mel, who promised to put him on a strict exercise regime with plenty of carrot juice.

The next we saw of the Sixth Doctor was when the TARDIS was attacked in flight over the planet Lakertya, knocking the Doctor and Mel unconscious. When it was brought down to the planet's surface, the Rani and her servant entered the ship, and reached down to the Doctor—whose face began to blur as, unexpectedly, he started to regenerate.

THE SEVENTH DOCTOR

Initially something of a lighter clown-like figure with a Panama hat, question-mark covered jumper and umbrella, the Seventh incarnation of the Doctor was destined to grow into a darker figure, an individual force that deliberately manipulated events and those around him, across the universe and throughout time itself.

Unusually, this regeneration was moderately smooth: the Seventh Doctor quickly healed and immediately recognized the threat posed by the Rani. However, his fellow Time Lord needed the Doctor for her latest scheme to build a Time Manipulator, so she rapidly induced amnesia in the Doctor. This resulted in her convincing him that she was really his companion Mel. In time, the Doctor's true memories returned, and reunited with Mel, he was able to thwart the Rani's plan to use a missile to harvest a Strange Matter asteroid. Some erratic traits developed as he recovered, including mixing his metaphors and an ability to play the spoons.

After travels to Paradise Towers and back to the 1950s, the Doctor and Mel visited Iceworld, a colony on the planet Svartos where they reunited with Sabalom Glitz. After defeating a centuries-old prisoner and his cryo-frozen mercenaries, Mel decided to remain with Glitz, while a waitress Ace (see COMPANIONS), who had been sent to Iceworld in a time storm, became the Doctor's new traveling companion.

It was now the Seventh Doctor began to show his darker side with a return visit to Totter's Lane in 1963 and an encounter with the Daleks, who had split into two factions. The Imperial

Daleks, led Davros, and the Renegade Daleks, under by a Supreme Dalek, were fighting a vicious civil war. Both sought a piece of Time Lord technology named the Hand Of Omega, which the First Doctor had hidden on Earth. It was during the course of these events that the burdens of the Doctor's actions began to weigh heavily on him, as he spent an evening in a café musing on the power of small choices to change people's destinies.

The Seventh Doctor's more aggressive and stronger nature was revealed further during a visit to Terra Alpha, ruled by the ruthless Helen A and her state-sponsored executioner, the Kandyman (see ROBOTS), who were determined to eliminate unhappiness and "killjoys." Once he discovered a resistance movement, the Doctor actively stirred up unrest and revolution, even daring Helen A's troops to look him in the eye and end his life, to gun him down in cold blood, if they dared. While there, the Doctor mentioned once more that his nickname at the Academy was Theta Sigma.

Returning to Earth in 1988 to enjoy a jazz concert, the Seventh Doctor had to protect another Time Lord weapon, a statue fashioned from a living Gallifreyan metal called validium. It was sought by a platoon of South American Nazis; an evil, sixteenth century time-traveler, Lady Peinforte; and a fleet of Cybermen. Despite Lady Peinforte's threats to reveal his true identity, the Doctor ruthlessly using the validium statue to bond with Lady Peinforte and destroy the Cyberfleet in orbit above Earth. However, he refused to answer Ace when she asked, "Who are you?" After a visit to a psychic circus, where he demonstrated the ability to do "real" magic tricks, the Doctor responded to a distress call echoing throughout time. It came from near Lake Vortigern, on the planet Earth late in the twentieth century. Here he teamed up with UNIT and the Brigadier once more and at one stage believed his old friend had been killed in action (though the Brigadier revealed he was very much still alive, much to the Doctor's relief—and annoyance).

The Doctor began to take an active interest in Ace's past life. He intentionally took her to Gabriel Chase in 1893, a building she had burned to the ground a few years before she started traveling with him after sensing evil there. Intensely curious about Ace's instinct about Gabriel Chase, he purposefully initiated events that caused its occupants to reveal their secrets.

Not long after, the TARDIS arrived at Maiden's Point, off the coast of Northumbria, England during World War II. Here the Doctor faced the Haemovores, the Ancient One and Fenric—a force of evil from the dawn of time itself who, after a game of chess with the Doctor, had been condemned to eternal imprisonment. Fenric had been manipulating the time-lines for eons, even causing the time storm that brought the Doctor and Ace to-gether. The Doctor claimed that he knew Ace was a trap set by Fenric all along, and that he had no interest in her beyond knowing she was part of a game; Ace was emotionally devastated by

this betrayal. However, this was just part of the Doctor's larger plan against Fenric, and he tried hard to rebuild her trust in him.

Perhaps in an effort to calm his companion, the Seventh Doctor returned Ace to her home in modern-day Perivale, where teenagers were going missing and an unusual black cat stalked the suburbs. The people of Perivale were being abducted, via a dimension jump, to another world for the indigenous Cheetah People to use for sport. The Doctor's old nemesis, the Master, was also affected. After first engaging the Master in a motor bike duel on Earth and then hand-to-hand combat on the planet in its last moments, the Doctor regained control of his mind in time to resist the lure of the Cheetah Planet, although the Master seemed to embrace it.

Many years later, when traveling alone (and back to eating Jelly Babies and using a sonic screwdriver), the Doctor collected the Master's remains from Skaro after he had been put on trial by the Daleks, with a view to returning them to Gallifrey. But the Master was still alive and caused the TARDIS to crash land in San Francisco on New Year's Eve, 1999. As the Doctor left his ship, he was accidentally gunned down in a street battle. Admitted to hospital for treatment, the resulting confusion over his physiology by Dr. Grace Holloway while in surgery resulted in a fatal error, killing him on the operating table. As a "John Doe," he was placed in the morgue...

THE EIGHTH DOCTOR

Younger than his previous regeneration, the Eighth Doctor was a romantic, trusting, wistful and lively incarnation, much younger and more handsome than his predecessor—but one about which we know very little.

The regeneration into the Eighth Doctor took place alone (a very rare occurrence for the Time Lord, since this process usually took place in the presence of others) after he had been placed in the hospital morgue. Demonstrating unusual strength (perhaps brought on by the regeneration), he broke down the huge, locked metallic door of his morgue locker and proceeded to explore the hospital in a confused state. When he caught a glimpse of his new self he was quite startled, bellowing, "Who am I?" Clearly, his mind was still unsettled despite his body forming quite nicely. To replace the surgical gown which he was still wearing, the Time Lord found a Wild Bill Hickok costume in a staff locker. His own belongings, including his sonic screwdriver, had been stolen by a young man, Chang Lee.

The Doctor instantly recognized Grace Holloway when he met her in an elevator and remembered the music she had been listening to during the disastrous operation. He tried to convince Grace that she was known to him. Various memories began to return: meeting Puccini and Leonardo da Vinci, and being near his home on Gallifrey with his father. When he remembered his identity, his relief was palpable, and he kissed Grace twice as the two shared a moonlit walk outside her home.

The Doctor realized that the Master had gained access to the TARDIS and knew he needed to find an atomic clock to stabilize his ship. The Master had stolen another body and was being assisted by Chang Lee, who believed the Master was the true owner of the TARDIS. The two Time Lords came face to face in the back of an ambulance, but the Doctor was able to escape. Despite Grace also coming under the Master's spell, the Doctor was able to prevent the destruction of the Earth, although he was unable to persuade Grace to accompany him on his journeys.

During his time in San Francisco, the Eighth Doctor displayed an uncanny knowledge of individuals' futures, and also claimed that he was "half-human" on his mother's side—a claim that seemed to be backed up by the Master discovering that the Eye of Harmony contained within the TARDIS only responded to a human eye. This aspect of the Doctor's nature, though, was not referred to directly again.

Somewhere between the Eighth Doctor's departure from San Francisco in 2000 and the arrival of the Ninth Doctor at Hendrick's department store in 2005, the Doctor became embroiled in a war that would rip the universe apart, and see the end of both the Time Lords and the Daleks. The story of the Time War has yet to be told, and no one knows for sure which incarnation of the Doctor was involved.

THE NINTH DOCTOR

Born out of hate and the vile bitterness of war, the Ninth Doctor was a very different man from his predecessors. After the difficult choices and terrible acts he had witnessed and participated in during the Time War, this version of the Time Lord was more somber, serious, intense, focused and reactive. Clad in leather with his usual style all but gone, and an accent like none of his forebears, this Doctor was obviously scarred by the loss of his people at his own hands.

The first time he saw his new face was in the residence of Jackie Tyler (see FRIENDS) and her teenage daughter Rose, where a mirror revealed his radically different look, in particular his ears. Initially, the Doctor did not encourage young Rose (see COMPANIONS) to travel with him, urging her to forget their meeting; he also refused the erotic advances of her mother. However, by the time their battle with the Nestene Consciousness and its Autons was over, the time-traveler was keen to have her aboard the TARDIS, asking Rose once and then tempting her further with the notion of time travel. However, he refused to offer a place aboard the TARDIS to Rose's boyfriend, Mickey Smith (see COMPANIONS).

The Doctor and Rose's earliest moments together could be quite tense, as they bickered occasionally with his alienness being a stumbling block, but they quickly grew to be very strong friends. The Doctor opened up to her, revealing that his people, the Time Lords, had all been destroyed in the Time War, and that he was the last of his kind. During adventures on Platform One in the year 5,000,000,000 and in Cardiff with Charles Dickens in 1869, Rose nearly died, but still admitted she was "so glad" to have met the mysterious traveler. The Doctor returned her to her own time back in London, but overshot by a year. Getting a slap from someone's mother was a first for the Time Lord, but that's precisely what he received from Jackie. This Doctor's disdain for humanity and "families" was displayed, claiming he didn't "do" them. After defeating the Slitheen attack on Downing Street with Mickey's help, the couple ended up in Utah in 2012 after answering a distress call. It was here, in the alien museum of Henry van Statten (see VILLAINS) that the Doctor came face-to-face with the enemy he thought was totally destroyed—a Dalek. His fear was palpable as it screamed "Exterminate!" but when he realized that it was unable to harm him, its impotence induced laughter and relief from the Time Lord as he taunted it, referring to the Dalek as a "great space dustbin" and reminding the Dalek that "Your race is dead! You all burned, all of you. Ten million ships on fire. The entire Dalek race wiped out in one second. I watched it happen. I made it happen." However, when he was asked about his own people, the Time Lords, he conceded that they burned too. "Everyone lost," he concluded sadly.

When the Dalek was restored to full strength and began exterminating the inhabitants of the base, the Doctor felt forced into brandishing a gun to defeat it, though he was prevented from destroying it by Rose. Though showing great contempt for Rose's new friend Adam (see COMPANIONS), the Time Lord let the young English boy join them in the TARDIS. However,

Adam failed the most basic of tests (taking future knowledge to the past) so the Doctor returned him to his home, stating that he only took "the best" with him on his travels. However, it was his beloved Rose who failed him in their next journey together, when she stopped the death of her father, Pete Tyler (see FRIENDS) when they went back to 1987. The Doctor's disappointment was clear as he left her, only to find the situation much more serious than he had imagined. Realizing that anyone can make a mistake, and after sacrificing himself to the Reapers (see ALIENS) in an effort to save the day, the Time Lord forgave her.

During the London Blitz in World War II, the Doctor tracked down Time Agent Captain Jack Harkness (see COMPANIONS). The two men had a spiky start to their friendship, since Jack had caused the spread of an alien disease in London. Their approaches were different: Jack preferred to use a blaster while the Doctor favored a banana. But the Time Lord saw the good in his fellow time-traveler, saving Jack's life when the omnisexual man was prepared to sacrifice his own life in recompense for his actions, and inviting Jack to join him and Rose.

When the trio stopped off in Cardiff to refuel the TARDIS, the Doctor had to face another villain he thought long dead, the Slitheen Margaret Blaine (see VILLAINS). At her request, the Doctor took her out for a meal before taking her back to face a court for her crimes. After she escaped, she was regressed back to an egg state by the TARDIS, and the Doctor returned her home, so that she might start her life anew. By the time the Ninth Doctor came to the end of his life, his outlook was lighter, joking with people he'd just met about reality television shows, and even flirting with strangers. But his levity was quashed when a Dalek fleet returned.

After realizing that the Daleks, led by their insane Emperor, were going to destroy the Earth, the Doctor prepared to make the ultimate sacrifice. The Time Lord made his greatest gesture toward his companion Rose, sending her back to safety in the TARDIS to her own time, leaving her a very touching holographic message inside the ship. However, Rose Tyler had other plans and with the help of her mother and Mickey, the former shop girl returned to save her friend.

After she looked into the heart of the TARDIS, something the Doctor had never done, she obliterated the Dalek fleet and restored a dead Jack to life. The Doctor, though, knew that the TARDIS energy and knowledge was too much for Rose's human brain, so to stop her from dying, in an act of selflessness, he kissed Rose, taking in the Time Vortex energy from her deliberately causing his own regeneration. Proud of his achievements and his time with his traveling companion, he let go of his life, telling her she was "Fantastic. Absolutely fantastic," and, in his very last words added that he had been too.

And in a first for the Doctor, he regenerated standing up, his arms open, head facing upwards...

* * *

THE TENTH DOCTOR

After the pensive and austere persona of his predecessor, the brighter and breezier Tenth incarnation had a joie de vivre unlike any former Doctors. His time in the TARDIS was marked by his love for words, specifically non-English phrases like "allons-y!" and "molto bene," as well as an unusual romantic predilection for Earth women (Madame de Pompadour, Joan Redfern (see FRIENDS) and, of course, his companion Rose Tyler). The Tenth Doctor lived life to the full, although this never dissuaded him from dishing out justice where required.

The new Doctor was initially perky, promising to take Rose to Barcelona but the regenerative process took its toll on the Time Lord. Once the TARDIS landed, somewhat bumpily, in London, he immediately collapsed and he was taken by Rose, Jackie and Mickey back to Jackie's flat. He slept for the most part as his body became accustomed to his new form, attracting Roboforms (see ROBOTS) in the process, but after some hot piping tea leaked in the TARDIS (thanks to Jackie) his senses awoke, bringing him back to full strength.

Facing the Sycorax (see ALIENS) leader, he cracked jokes about his hair color, the Disney film *The Lion King*, and compared himself with Hitchhiker Arthur Dent. It wasn't too long before he was battling the Sycorax leader in single combat, although he lost his hand during the fight (the hand fell to Earth but was to be reunited with its body some time later). Surprisingly, it grew back pretty swiftly, since the Doctor was still within the first fifteen hours of this regeneration, and he was able to defend the Earth successfully.

Disgusted by Prime Minister Harriet Jones' destruction of the Sycorax after they had already

surrendered and left, the Doctor arranged her removal her from office (muttering just six words to her aide: "Don't you think she looks tired?"). This rewriting of history led to the installation of Harold Saxon (the Master in disguise) as Prime Minister. Marking a different attitude to the "no families" rule set out by his previous incarnation, the Doctor enjoyed Christmas dinner happily with Rose, Mickey, and Jackie (after choosing a new, geek-chic-ier appearance).

Soon he took Rose to visit New Earth, where he found Cassandra (see VILLAINS) up to her old tricks, and indeed, in his body for a while, during which time "he" shared a kiss with Rose. In an

act of compassion, the Doctor gave the human trampoline a chance to see her younger body one more time before she died.

A trip to Scotland, though he was actually trying to get to see Ian Drury and the Blockheads in concert, saw the Time Lord break out a rather convincing Scottish accent. He claimed to be "Jamie McCrimmon" when he met, and was later knighted by, Queen Victoria—who then banished him from her land for his behavior during the fight against a lupine foe. The Doctor met his old friend, Sarah Jane Smith, accompanied by K9, at Deffry Vale High School during an attack by the Krillitane (see ALIENS). Although happy to see one another, the nature of their relationship was brought under the microscope with the time-traveler having to reveal some awkward truths. Saying goodbye, this time properly, the two parted on very good terms, with the Time Lord leaving a gift for his old friend, a new version of K9 to replace the one who had sacrificed himself to save the Doctor, Sarah, Rose and Mickey.

The Doctor's romantic side was further revealed when he, Rose, and Mickey traveled to eighteenth century France and met Reinette de Poisson, later to be known as Madame de Pompadour. The woman was being stalked by robots from the fifty-first century, who appeared at different points in her timeline, and she and the Doctor made a clear impression on the other. Once the robots were defeated, the Doctor returned to pick Reinette up to join him in the TARDIS, he had overshot by some years, and his new friend had died; his mournful reaction demonstrated clearly his love for the beautiful French woman.

No time for tears though, as the TARDIS broke down, leaving the Doctor and his friends in a parallel universe where the Time Lord had to face new versions of his old enemies, the Cybermen, and met an alternate version of Rose's father, Pete. In a bid to cheer Rose up (after Mickey decided to remain on the parallel Earth), the Doctor treated her to a trip to see Elvis in the late 1950s in New York. Resplendent with contemporary hair style, he actually ended up in London, 1953, facing the entity known as the Wire (see ALIENS).

A troubling encounter with the Beast (see ALIENS), a creature from before the universe began, truly rattled the Time Lord—although the prospect of having to settle down with Rose was also making him uncomfortable, when it seemed as if the TARDIS was lost. After a brief meeting with the Abzorbaloff (see ALIENS), the Doctor took Rose into her near future—London during the 2012 Olympics—where, in order to save the world, he carried the Olympic torch and lit the Olympic Flame.

His time with Rose came to an end in Torchwood One's headquarters at Canary Wharf in London where his incessant liveliness was at its height, singing the *Ghostbusters* theme tune and pretending Jackie was his companion. In saving Earth from being burned up by the Void (not to mention the invading Daleks and Cybermen), he lost his fellow time-traveler to the parallel Earth. Tearful and distressed he caressed the wall into which she had seemingly disappeared, but soon sought a way to contact her. Eventually, in orbit around a supernova burning up a sun, he was able to say an emotional final goodbye to her at Dårlig Ulv Stranden (also known as Bad Wolf Bay).

His tears had barely dried when he found Donna Noble, in full wedding dress, standing in front of him in the TARDIS. The two had a tense start but by the time they had vanquished the Racnoss (see ALIENS), Donna's advice not to travel alone, rang in the Time Lord's ears. It wasn't too long before he met bright medical student, Martha Jones (see COMPANIONS).

After she brought him back to life, in a hospital transferred to the moon by the Judoon (see ALIENS), the Doctor "rewarded" Martha by taking her on a trip back in Earth's past to meet William Shakespeare and then into her far future to New Earth. It was here that the Time Lord revealed the truth to her about his people in a touching moment of reminiscence.

But his mood quickly changed when he discovered the Dalek Cult of Skaro in 1930s New York, his disgust and bitterness clear at the Daleks' ability to survive. His own DNA was used in the creation of new Dalek/human hybrids though they were destroyed as almost as soon as they were born. During another trip back to Martha's time on Earth the Doctor cemented their relationship by giving her a key to the TARDIS, claiming she never really had been "just a passenger."

His huge faith in Martha was displayed when he entrusted her with his own safety as he used a Chameleon Arch to turn himself into a human to hide himself from the Family of Blood (see VILLAINS). In an English school just before the First World War, he became teacher John Smith and formed a strong emotional relationship with Joan Redfern. Sadly for Redfern, the Time Lord had to return to his normal self and any dreams of a future together, getting married with children, evaporated. Joan was not keen on the real man who had brought so much disaster to her home.

When the Weeping Angels sent the Doctor back to 1969 without his TARDIS, he was forced to coin the phrase, "timey-wimey wibbly-wobbly" to describe how time worked to Sally Sparrow (see FRIENDS), who was instrumental in reuniting the Doctor and Martha with the ship.

The Face of Boe once told the Doctor, "You are not alone," and on the planet Malcassairo, in one hundred trillion AD, the Time Lord discovered another of his race had also survived the Time War. Having picked Captain Jack up (literally) on the TARDIS after a pit stop in Cardiff, the Doctor had some harsh truths to face with his Time Agent friend, claiming Jack was "wrong" since he had been brought back to life by Rose using the TARDIS' energies. Jack also did the courtesy of returning the Doctor's hand, lost during his post-regeneration fight with the Sycorax leader.

However, the Doctor's problems with Jack paled into insignificance when his found his old enemy the Master posing as scientist Professor Yana. The Doctor pleaded with his nemesis, telling him they were the last of their kind but the Master stole his TARDIS, leaving Captain Jack to come to the rescue with his Vortex Manipulator to take them back to Earth. During the Master's rule, the Doctor faced more hardships when he was subjected to the Master's laser screwdriver, and turned into a shriveled old man. The Doctor was kept in a cage but managed to forgive him once he was freed. Martha spent a year traveling around the world spreading the word about the Doctor in preparation for the final showdown with the Master.

The Master died in the Doctor's arms after being shot by his wife Lucy Saxon (see VILLAINS), and despite the Doctor's pleas to him to regenerate, he refused. The Doctor then burned his body on a funeral pyre. To add to the Doctor's melancholy, Martha left the TARDIS, knowing he would never feel the same for her the way she did for him. As he left Earth, the starship *Titanic* crashed into the TARDIS, due to a mistake which was rectified with help from the Fifth Doctor. The Doctor then prevented the *Titanic* from crashing into Buckingham Palace, although his victory was marred by many deaths, including a young waitress, Astrid Peth, who sacrificed herself to save the Doctor. Before all hell let loose, though, the Doctor and Astrid had a brief meeting on Earth with a newspaper vendor, who he didn't realize at the time was Donna Noble's grandfather, Wilfred Mott.

It was not long before the Time Lord was reunited with the temp from Chiswick herself. Both were investigating strange activities at Adipose Industries in London. The Doctor was looking for someone to travel with, and welcomed Donna back into the TARDIS. The pair set off on an incredible journey which would be as fun and memorable as it was devastating and heart-breaking. They traveled back in time to Pompeii, where Donna managed to change the Doctor's mind and save a family who should have died in the eruption of Vesuvius, a feat not many companions could manage! They visited the planet of the Ood, the Oodsphere, where their entwined future was hinted at by the indigenous population, who referred to them as the DoctorDonna.

A call from Martha Jones brought them back to Earth where they countered a proposed hostile takeover by the Sontarans and bumped into Wilf once more. The Doctor also teamed up with UNIT again (bemoaning the lack of the Brigadier at one point), and displayed his slight contempt at their militaristic ways.

After saving the Earth once more, the Doctor,

Donna and Martha were quickly taken away by the TARDIS to Messaline in the year 6012 where the Time Lord's DNA was used to create Jenny, his daughter (see TIME LORDS). At first the Doctor was unreceptive to his offspring but grew to feel for her over their brief time together, grieving when she apparently sacrificed herself for him. A chastened Time Lord dropped Martha back in the twenty-first century and, as if in need of a jaunt, took Donna back in time to meet Agatha Christie, and then in to the future to show his friend the largest book repository in the universe, the Library. However, this was to provide more heartbreak for the Doctor when the mysterious River Song came into his life for the first time. The Doctor immediately knew there was a connection between them, noting her sonic screwdriver, which had been given to her by a future version of himself, and the fact she knew his real, secret name. River sacrificed herself to save her team, the Doctor, Donna, and other lives preserved in the Library, chaining the Doctor up to prevent him stopping her. Despite this, he managed to save her consciousness in the screwdriver and upload it into the Library computers.

After a frightening experience on the planet Midnight, where the Doctor found himself possessed, another treat for Donna on the planet Shan Shen went wrong when the Trickster's Brigade created an alternate universe around her. There, Donna met Rose who had been trying to contact the Doctor. Once her information was relayed to him, a horrified Time Lord sensed the end of the Universe was coming. He wasn't far wrong: it took a number of his friends to defeat Davros, the Daleks and their Reality Bomb after the planet Earth was transferred to the Medusa Cascade.

During the battle, a Dalek sparked a regeneration after blasting the Doctor, though the Time Lord was able to divert the energy to his severed hand, which was still in a jar in the TARDIS. However, this did result in another version of himself being created when the hand, bursting with regeneration energy, was touched by Donna Noble, creating a fusion of the two, a Meta-Crisis Doctor, as well as infusing Donna with portions of the Time Lord's consciousness: the DoctorDonna. The human Doctor triggered a cataclysm that exterminated the Daleks, something the Time Lord would not have done.

The Doctor had to leave his alter ego on the parallel Earth with Rose, and, sadly, he had to return Donna to her family with her memory wiped, since her brain was unable to handle the Time Lord consciousness. He traveled alone for some time, and made mistakes along the way, believing that, as the last Time Lord, he could make Time bend to his will. The death of Adelaide Brooke (see FRIENDS), as well as his guilt over the Time War and the treatment of his companions began to weigh heavy on the Doctor and during a conversation with Wilf in a London cafe, he broke down into tears, knowing his time was up.

The Master brought his old enemy to Earth and forced him to act against the Time Lords when they tried to bring Gallifrey back into Time in close proximity to the Earth. The Doctor refused to shoot either the Time Lord President Rassilon (see TIME LORDS) or the Master and, with the aid of the Master, sent them back into the Time War. His last selfless act was to save Wilf from certain death by absorbing a huge dose of radiation, which he knew would lead to his regeneration. Deeply upset as he realized what he happened, anger and bitterness spat out of him but then he rewarded himself for all the good he had done by saving old friends (Luke Smith, Mickey, and Martha) and visiting even older ones (Captain Jack and Rose).

Ever the giver, the Doctor handed a wedding present to Wilf to give to Donna, a lottery ticket that ensured their financial stability. But some of his more deeply held emotions came to the fore: a visit to Verity Newman, the great-granddaughter of Joan Redfern revealed that the Time Lord had obviously cared deeply for her.

His last words, "I don't want to go," displayed a man who believed that he still had much to give and was truly upset at his impending regeneration. Unusually, the Doctor regenerated by himself, the regeneration energy bursting out of him and causing the TARDIS itself to catch ablaze. But this was not the last of the Tenth Doctor's adventures. He was called into action to join his next self, the Eleventh Doctor, and the Doctor who broke their collective promise, to fight off the Zygons, Daleks, and more.

THE ELEVENTH DOCTOR

The Tenth's Doctor regeneration gave birth to an explosive start for his youthful sequel. His first moments saw him coming to terms with his new appearance (wondering if he was a girl and then being disappointed at not being ginger, again) as the TARDIS fell apart around him. But as the TARDIS careened toward Earth, he cried "Geronimo!," a word which sums up this incarnation—a man who would dive headfirst into any situation; brave, if a little silly; and his young looks belying great wisdom. This bow-tie loving, tweed-wearing, and odd-hat, aficionado caused such a stir throughout his travels, that he had to erase his name and reboot the universe.

His opening moments saw him fly high over London, clinging to the TARDIS, eventually crashing in the village of Leadworth on Earth in the mid 1990s. Popping out of his ship, the Doctor was immediately greeted by young Amelia Pond (see COMPANIONS), and the two enjoyed some fun in the kitchen where the Time Lord tried to decide on what food he liked, eventually plumping for fish fingers (fish sticks) and custard. His relationship with his new friend began on a slightly chilly note when the Doctor left her for what he thought would be minutes, but actually turned out to be twelve years.

When he returned to her house, Amelia was now a young woman (unrecognizable to him) dressed in one of her kissogram outfits, a policewoman. It took some time for the Doctor to realize what had happened but by the time the couple had dealt with Prisoner Zero (see ALIENS) and noticed the crack in her bedroom,

Amy (as she was now calling herself) and the Doctor were firm friends.

Keen to impress his attractive new friend, the Doctor took her into the future where the couple discovered a Space Whale and the future of humanity aboard Starship UK. A trip into the past quickly followed when Winston Churchill called for help from his old friend, the Doctor. The Time Lord was horrified to discover that Daleks had infiltrated the British army, and became an unwitting pawn in their plans for evolution, as they used his testimony to kick start a new Dalek Paradigm. Using a Jammie

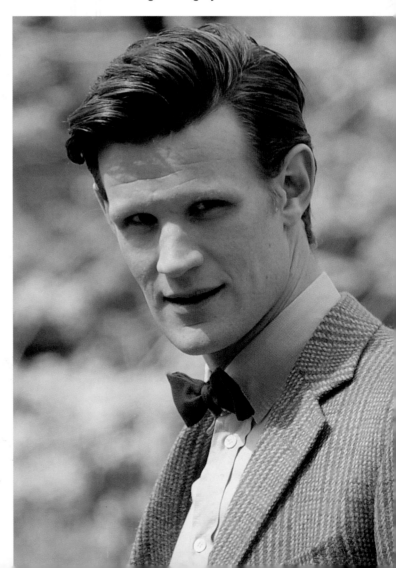

Dodgers cookie to keep them at bay, the Doctor's quirkiness turned to anger when his old enemies escaped once more.

A message from his future wife River Song dragged the Doctor and Amy into an encounter with a vicious army of Weeping Angels, where he learned a great deal about his stony foes but even more about the mysterious River. Importantly, he discovered the same crack in space and time that had been present in Amy's bedroom. However, he had to fend off the sexual advances of his new traveling companion before he could begin his investigation.

Her husband-to-be, Rory Williams (see COMPANIONS), found his stag party disrupted by the Doctor who whisked the couple off to Venice in 1580 for a romantic holiday, only to discover an invasion by the Saturnynes (see ALIENS). More trouble was to come when the trio was infected by psychic pollen, throwing them into a dream-like state where they could interact with one another.
The Doctor's dark side came out in the form of the Dream Lord who tried to kill the TARDIS crew. Although they won out against the shadowy reflection, the Dream Lord lingered, ready to return at any moment.

A jaunt into Amy's near future saw the Doctor try to broker negotiations with the Silurians, although like the efforts of his Third incarnation, these were to fail. Sadly, the Time Lord also lost his new companion Rory, who died taking a laser shot meant for the Doctor. Perhaps slightly cruelly, he left Amy's fiancé to the mercy of the crack, which began to erase him from space and

time. The Doctor then kept knowledge of his life from Amy, whose memory of him had been wiped out.

A trip to nineteenth century France saw the Doctor meet artist Vincent van Gogh, though the joy of his work was overshadowed by the fact that he was unable to help the painter through his depression. The Doctor then became separated from Amy and the TARDIS, and lodged with Craig Owens (see FRIENDS) in Colchester. A previously unseen Time Lord power was displayed when the Doctor head butted Craig, allowing him to access the knowledge of the Gallifreyan's life.

Another message from River Song prompted by the discovery of a disturbing painting of the TARDIS, sent the Doctor and Amy to Stonehenge, where an alliance of hundreds of alien species were awaiting to capture and imprison him in the Pandorica. Among them was an Auton replica of Rory. Despite his impassioned speech, a trait this Doctor was becoming adept at, he was placed in the prison, but he was able to escape by bouncing backward and forward in time. The Time Lord had to reboot the universe but by doing so, he removed himself from it.

However, he had thought ahead, implanting an idea in Amy's mind, and at her wedding to a properly reconstituted Rory, Amy Pond (now Williams, although that didn't really catch on) brought her raggedy man back into existence. While the newlyweds indulged in some cosplay on a crashing space cruise liner, the Doctor turned the malevolent Kazran Sardick (see FRIENDS) into a useful and kind human being by changing his past.

But the Doctor's fun was to end at Lake Silencio where an astronaut (later revealed to be River Song) killed an older version of him. After meeting President Richard Nixon, the Time Lord tracked down the Silence (see ALIENS) and with the help of River Song, Amy, Rory and former FBI agent Canton Delaware III (see FRIENDS), the Earth was rid of the parasites, although since he was not a violent man, the Doctor let his friends and the humans do all the killing.

Traveling with Rory and Amy, the Doctor's hopes that another Time Lord might still be alive were raised after he received some "mail," in the form of a Time Lord emergency messaging system, from his old friend, the Corsair (see TIME LORDS). In fact this was a trap to lead the Doctor out of his universe to be fed upon by House (see VILLAINS). His anger and sadness at the Corsair's confirmed death was briefly allayed when the TARDIS took over the body of a female humanoid, Idris. During their conversations she claimed she had chosen him, and not the other way around as the Doctor had always assumed. With the admission that he called her "sexy," the two became close after some initial physical bruising (and biting) but their time together was short, leading to a very tearful farewell.

Sensing there was something amiss with Amy Pond, he took the married couple to St. John's Monastery on Earth in the twenty-second century where human doppelgangers (known as "gangers") were being produced. After being replicated himself (where some of his previous selves came to the fore), he confronted and destroyed a "ganger" version of Amy which had been infiltrated into the TARDIS while the real Amy was being held captive, about to give birth. The Doctor and Rory formed an army to retrieve Amy and her baby, leading them to Madame Kovarian's headquarters at Demon's Run. Amy was rescued but her baby was kidnapped. River wasn't as concerned by this as her friends: she revealed that she was, in fact, Amy and Rory's daughter, indicating that the Doctor did succeed in his quest to find her.

He returned to his companions Amy and Rory some months later and, alongside their lifelong friend Mels, took a trip to Nazi Germany where a brief meeting with Hitler was on the cards. More shocks were in store when Mels regenerated into River Song, who then poisoned the Doctor. However, once convinced of her mistake, River, who had gained the power to regenerate because of her conception within the TARDIS, sacrificed her remaining lives to save him.

The Doctor shared more journeys with Amy and Rory but after nearly getting them killed by a Creature (see ALIENS) in a prison disguised as an 1980s hotel, the Time Lord took the couple back to Earth, buying them a house and a car. He believed leaving them behind was the decent, and safe, thing to do, since they were increasingly in danger.

However, it wasn't long before the trio were reunited in an alternative Earth time line where Amy and Rory didn't know each other and the Doctor was held captive by Winston Churchill. The world was stuck in a single moment, because River refused to obey her instructions and shoot the Doctor at Lake Silencio. The Doctor broke the anomaly by allowing his death to happen, although he tried to fool Time by using a Teselecta (a spaceship which could disguise itself as a physical being) in his place. He married his love River Song in a ceremony that also featured the Tesselecta Doctor (which suggested they perhaps weren't a married couple); their physical connection reset the timeline. Determined to wipe all trace of himself from history, the Doctor was chilled by a prophecy from his old friend Dorium Maldovar: "It's all still waiting for you. The fields of Trenzalore, the fall of the Eleventh, and the question—the first question. The question that must never be answered, hidden in plain sight. The question you've been running from all your life. Doctor who?"

The Doctor always repays his debts and after being helped by Madge Arwell (see FRIENDS) after falling out of a spaceship above Earth, he responded in kind by assisting her family with Christmas festivities. He then helped Rory and Amy reunite when they got into marital difficulties, and was delighted when Oswin Oswald, a young girl who had been transformed into

a Dalek, wiped all references to him from the Dalek databanks when he met her on the Dalek Asylum planet. With assistance from Egyptian Queen Nerfertiti, big game hunter John Riddell (see FRIENDS) and Rory's father Brian, the Doctor and the Ponds saved the Earth when a spaceship threatened the planet. The Doctor demonstrated uncharacteristic cruelty toward the trader Solomon (see VILLAINS), letting him die at the hands of a missile.

He then treated the Ponds to a jaunt to Mercy, USA in 1870, where he showed an unusual love for guns, before spending a great deal of time with them during the slow invasion of the cubes in their home on Earth, during which he met Kate Stewart, the daughter of Brigadier Alastair Lethbridge-Stewart. The trio then holidayed in New York, though this was to prove to be their last journey together after an attack by the Weeping Angels resulted in Amy choosing to be with her husband in the past, unable ever to see the Doctor again. River stayed with the Doctor to console him.

His mood stayed somewhat downbeat as he

squirrelled himself away in nineteenth century London, though his friends Silurian Madame Vastra, her maid Jenny, and the Sontaran Strax kept in touch with him. The Doctor met governess Clara Oswald who helped in a battle against his old enemy the Great Intelligence (see ALIENS). Clara died helping the Doctor and her dying words repeated the last words that Oswin Oswald had said to the Time Lord, "Run, you clever boy, and remember." This prompted the Time Lord into searching for an answer to the mystery that surrounded her double existence.

After spending some time considering the problem in a medieval monastery, the trail led the Doctor to modern day London (after a brief stint as a flat-haired monk) where he met Clara Oswald. This was the third time that they had met, although Clara had no knowledge or memory of the other two versions of her. Initially suspicious of the Doctor, the nanny eventually joined him in the TARDIS, visiting the Rings of Akhaten and ending up aboard a Russian nuclear submarine in 1983, where they faced the Ice Warrior Skaldak (see VILLAINS).

Continuing his quest to discover who exactly Clara was, the Doctor visited Caliburn House

in 1974 in the hope that empathic psychic Emma Grayling (see FRIENDS) might be able to reveal her true identity. But it was the Doctor who discovered that she was simply Clara during what he believed to be their final moments in the TARDIS as it was about to be destroyed. He expressed great relief toward a baffled Clara as any thoughts that she was sent to destroy him faded. (Clara didn't remember this conversation, since Time was reset by the Doctor.)

Still hoping to jog her memory, he took Clara to Yorkshire, 1893 where the Doctor was struck down by the Crimson Horror, only to be saved by Jenny, Vastra, and Strax, and he then treated Clara's charges, Angie and Artie, to a trip to Hedgewick's World of Wonders. During this visit, the Doctor's mind became infected by Cyber technology, resulting in a deadly fight of chess against himself, a fight which saw him once again evoke his older selves.

After Clara received a mysterious message from Madame Vastra, the Doctor had to go to the one place he should never visit: his own tomb within the TARDIS on Trenzalore. The Great Intelligence had set a trap for the

Doctor, and it gained access to the Doctor's timestream, the relic of the Doctor's lives, that lay within the tomb, killing him in multiple times and places. Dying and crippled on the TARDIS floor, the Doctor could only look on as Clara explained her mystery by also entering into the timestream and appearing throughout all the Doctor's lives—including on the Dalek Asylum planet, and in Victorian London. When a ghostly image of River Song pointed out that she could only still exist if Clara were alive, the Doctor entered his own timestream. He guided Clara to safety but was then presented with the vision of his former selves running around, and the even more shocking sight of a version of himself, one that had never been seen before. A Doctor who acted in a way that broke the promise of the name, the Doctor…

This was not the last that we see of this older-looking (and abandoned) version of the Time Lord. The Eleventh Doctor teamed up with the Tenth Doctor in an adventure that saw him dangling from the TARDIS above London, reunited with Kate Stewart, and fighting off Zygons, Daleks, and more in the lead up to his own regeneration into the Twelfth Doctor.

THE ONE WHO BROKE THE PROMISE

This dark, mysterious man stood alone with his back turned while the Eleventh Doctor saved Clara (as the Gallifreyan's previous selves ran around his own time stream after an attack by The Great Intelligence). Upon discovering the man, the Doctor was rattled

to see him—a man he was all too aware of; a man he described as a "secret" to Clara.

The Eleventh Doctor explained to his companion that this version of the Doctor broke the "promise" of his name, chosen so many hundreds of years ago. The older-looking Time Lord could see the disappointment in the Eleventh Doctor's youthful face, from the future, and answered for his actions—claiming they were done "in the name of peace and sanity." "But not in the name of the Doctor," came the stern reply from The Eleventh Doctor. The pair teamed up with The Tenth Doctor in an adventure that saw the mysterious man bemused by the antics of the younger-looking Time Lords.

THE TWELFTH DOCTOR

Older in appearance than his youthful-looking predecessor, this Twelfth incarnation of the Doctor had a tumultuous beginning which put him in the thick of it after the Eleventh Doctor's time in the TARDIS. With a slightly more austere face and piercing gaze, the Gallifreyan's experienced demeanor was a shock for Clara (not to mention the Doctor himself), but the odd couple soon got on with the business of saving the universe once more.

Curiously, the Twelfth Doctor bears a striking resemblance to Caecilius, whom the Tenth Doctor and Donna met in Pompeii shortly before Vesuvius erupted in 79 A.D. Luckily for old Caecilius, he was saved along with his family by the kind stranger from the volcano's devastation.

THE COMPANIONS

Over his years wandering the universe in the TARDIS, the Doctor has accumulated a number of traveling companions; young and old, male and female— and sometimes the odd alien too (though most them were still quite human-looking). Over the next few pages, you'll meet the chosen few who got to be that special someone in the Time Lord's life.

ACE

Meeting the Seventh Doctor in the colony Iceworld on the planet Svartos, Ace was a feisty friend for the Time Lord. Dubbing him "the Professor," the former resident of London's Perivale had a penchant for bombs containing Nitro-9—an explosive of her own concoction. Ace was the nickname she had chosen for herself, since she disliked her given name, Dorothy, intensely.

During her travels with the Doctor, she encountered both the Daleks (facing off against a number of them in a London school, armed only with a baseball bat) and the Cybermen (using a simple catapult and gold coins). She also came face-to-face with the renegade Time Lord, the Master (see TIME LORDS) on Cheetah Planet. The teenager also met the Doctor's trusted ally, Brigadier Lethbridge-Stewart, when fighting the sorceress Morgaine and the Destroyer in Carbury in the late 1990s. She spent time with her own grandmother, Kathleen Dudman, during World War II. It was at this point that Ace learned that she had been part of an evil plan by Fenric, an enemy of the Doctor, and her meeting with the Time Lord had not been an accident.

Ace's last adventure with the Doctor has not been recorded, but they were no longer traveling together when the Time Lord went to collect the Master's remains from Skaro at the end of his seventh life.

The Doctor's earlier companion Sarah Jane Smith discovered in 2010 that "Dorothy something" was now running a charity "A Charitable Earth," suggesting that Ace had returned home at some point.

ADAM MITCHELL

Not everyone can deal with the responsibilities of traveling in time. Adam caught the eye of Rose Tyler when she and the Ninth Doctor visited a secret base in Utah, where the young genius was one of those assisting millionaire Henry van Statten. Adam's first trip in the TARDIS took him to Satellite Five where he disappointed the Doctor and Rose by indulging himself in some tech and then sending future secrets back in time to himself. Unimpressed, the Doctor quickly took him back to his native time.

ADELAIDE BROOKE

Captain of the Bowie Base One on Mars in 2059, Adelaide was part of a doomed exhibition to the red planet. She was destined to die under mysterious circumstances along with her team, after their water supply became infected with an alien life form. Initially cold toward the Tenth Doctor, she warmed to him, telling him about her unusual meeting with a Dalek as a child. When she realized that by saving her, the Doctor had changed the future, Adelaide made the decision to take her own life to keep history on course.

ADRIC

This math wizard from the planet Alzarius, in a pocket universe called E-Space, stowed away in the TARDIS after an adventure with the Fourth Doctor, Romana, and K9. He remained with the Doctor through his regeneration but did not get on as well with the new, apparently younger, Fifth Doctor.

He left the TARDIS in heartbreaking circumstances. Stuck aboard a freighter that had been set to crash into the Earth by the Cybermen, Adric had a last minute brainwave which might allow him to free the controls. Sadly, for the badge-wearing boy genius, one last Cyberman thwarted his actions thus dooming the pair to certain death in an explosion that was responsible for the extinction of the dinosaurs. Some time later, during the Fifth Doctor's traumatic regeneration, the significance of his former companion's death became apparent as the Time Lord hallucinated seeing Adric encouraging him not to give up. His last word was the young boy's name. The guilt of losing a close friend clearly weighed heavy on his mind for some time.

ALISTAIR GORDON LETHBRIDGE-STEWART

See FRIENDS

Fan Fact Note:
"Adric" was the last word uttered by the Fifth Doctor before he regenerated.

AMY POND (WILLIAMS)

Just after the Tenth Doctor regenerated into the Eleventh, the TARDIS crash-landed in the beautiful sleepy English village of Leadworth. Discovering the time machine was a seven-year-old Scottish girl named Amelia Pond who instantly befriended the Time Lord, sharing her kitchen's supply of food with him—finally settling on fish fingers and custard.

The ginger Scot would meet up with him twelve years (and numerous therapist appointments) later—revealing that the Doctor's five minutes was in fact much longer. Her anger eventually subsided as her "raggedy man" (her childhood name for the Doctor) saved the world from Prisoner Zero and flying eye-ball, the Atraxi (see ALIENS).

Although engaged to local boy Rory Williams, Amy kept this quiet from the Time Lord for some time. She even chose to leave the night before her wedding, and flew off to meet the Space Whale on the Starship UK, battle the Daleks with Winston Churchill (see FRIENDS), and become a victim of the Weeping Angels.

After her admission to the Doctor that she was soon to be married, Rory joined the pair as they ventured back in time to Venice, became involved with the mysterious Dream Lord (see VILLAINS), and met the Silurians. It was at this point that Rory was taken out of time completely and Amy's memory of him disappeared—temporarily.

Shortly after, Pond would become the inspiration for artist Vincent van Gogh and meet River Song (dressed as Cleopatra) a the Doctor discovered the Pandorica. It was here that she reunited with Rory, but she still could not remember him.

It took being stuck in the Pandorica for 2,000 years, the restart of the universe, and the Doctor to blink out of existence, but Amy's memory finally returned (as did her parents—Augustus and Tabetha). Her wedding to Mr. Williams could finally continue, and the couple spent a little time away from the TARDIS. The Doctor invited them back to witness his death at Lake Silencio. It was here that Amy would encounter the Silence and reveal her pregnancy to the Doctor and finds pictures of herself in an orphanage with a new-born baby.

After an adventure on pirate ship, the *Fancy*, and then a journey to a bubble universe where a being called House took over the TARDIS, the Amy traveling would be revealed to be a "ganger"—a carbon copy of her body. She had been taken by

Madame Kovarian to Demon's Run where her child, Melody Pond (see RIVER SONG) was born, only to be taken by Kovarian and the Silence in their war against the Doctor.

The Doctor would search in vain for the child, but it was Melody who would reveal herself to the Ponds (as their friend Mels, who would regenerate into River Song). With the mystery of their missing child revealed, Amy would get turned into a Peg Doll (see MONSTERS), meet an older version of herself and then be left by the Doctor on Earth after being possessed by a Nimon-like creature. But this was not to be the end, as she returned to the Doctor's side once more to fight off the Silence and Ma-

dame Kovarian (in an alternate version of Earth). The Doctor then made a festive visit at Christmas, but her marriage with Rory had broken down. It would take a battle with the Daleks in their Asylum to bring them back together again.

Amy and Rory stayed at home until the Dotcor visited to take them on adventures. On a spaceship full of dinosaurs, into the past in the western US, and to face the slow invasion of cubes in modern day.

In the end, Amy chose to follow her husband back in time and let the Weeping Angel zap her to the 1930s (where she did indeed meet up with Rory), leaving her raggedy man for good.

Alternate Universe Note:
In a parallel time-line, Amy would be left on Apalapucia where she would grow old and alone (save for her Robot Rory) until the return of her younger self with her husband and the Doctor. Ultimately, this version of Amy would die.

ASTRID PETH

Though she didn't receive a trip in the TARDIS, this diminutive resident of Sto caught the Tenth Doctor's eye when he took a trip on the starship *Titanic* above the planet Earth. The young waitress was treated to a brief jaunt down to London, where the smell fascinated her, shortly before the ship was hit by meteoroids. Their time together was cut short when Astrid sacrificed herself driving a forklift to save the Doctor from ship's owner, Max Capricorn (see VILLAINS).

Fan Fact Note:
Astrid is an anagram of TARDIS

BARBARA WRIGHT

Coal Hill School history teacher Barbara joined the First Doctor on his travels after she and colleague Ian Chesterton became suspicious about the home life of a mysterious pupil, Susan Foreman—the Doctor's granddaughter. When they met the old man in the junkyard that was apparently Susan's home, Barbara was less skeptical than Ian when the Doctor and Susan explained who they really were. When the Doctor decided that he couldn't risk Barbara or Ian talking about what they had learned, he operated the TARDIS controls and the teachers were taken back to 100,000 B.C. and then to the planet Skaro. Here Barbara and her new traveling companions encountered the Daleks for the first time.
Over the next few months, the teacher was able to experience periods of Earth's history she had simply

read about before. The TARDIS took them to China in 1289, meeting Marco Polo and Kublai Khan; the Aztec period in fifteenth century Mexico, as she was mistaken for a high priestess; Revolutionary France in 1794, where the guillotine awaited her and Susan; the Roman Empire in 64 A.D. where she had to evade Emperor Nero, and Ian was sent to a slave galley; and twelfth century Palestine, when she pretended to be King Richard the Lionheart's sister, Joanna, and Ian had to come to her rescue.

She also traveled into her own future, meeting the Daleks on twenty-second century Earth, and encountered alien races including the Voord on Marinus; the Sensorites from the Sense Sphere; the Menoptra and the Zarbi on Vortis; and the Moroks on Xeros. In her final adventure with the Doctor, Barbara battled the Daleks for a third time as she and her friends were chased through time by the intergalactic pepper pots (landing aboard the *Mary Celeste*, amongst other places, along the way). She and Ian left the Doctor when they used a Dalek time machine to return to London, two years after they left Coal Hill School—and discovered that bus fares had increased dramatically during their absence, Sarah Jane Smith's investigations revealed that Barbara married Ian Chesterton and was a professor at Cambridge University. Rumor had it that they had not aged since the 1960s.

* * *

BEN JACKSON

Young able seaman Ben was one of a number of companions who traveled with more than one regeneration of the Doctor. Ben helped the First incarnation in 1966 London, after meeting Dodo Chaplet, who was currently traveling with the Doctor, and 1960s-chic secretary Polly in cool London nightclub, the Inferno. When he and Polly returned Dodo's TARDIS key to the Doctor, they ended up traveling with him.

Shortly after that, during his first encounter with the Cybermen, the Doctor regenerated for the first time. Initially Ben did not take to his new persona at all, simply refusing to believe that anyone could change that drastically. During an encounter with the Daleks, though, he realized this was still the Doctor.

Ben met Jamie McCrimmon in eighteenth century Scotland, and after adventures fighting the Cybermen on the moon, and the Macra, the TARDIS took them to contemporary Gatwick Airport. After defeating the Chameleons' plans, Ben realized that it was the exact same day that he and Polly had left with the Doctor, so he could still be in time to report for duty on his ship. The pair therefore left the Doctor and Jamie. Sarah Jane Smith learned that by 2010, Ben and Polly were working in India, running an orphanage.

CAPTAIN JACK HARKNESS

The pansexual Time Agent arrived in the Ninth Doctor's life in London during World War II. At first, their relationship was slightly tense as the Time Lord, was suspicious of the Captain's motives, with good cause. Jack was a Time Agent and was in the middle of a confidence trick when Rose fell into his arms—or, rather, his spaceship. Jack had engineered a Chula ambulance to land on Earth, but this had caused many people to become infected with a plague that made them look like "gas mask zombies."

After Jack helped the Doctor to rectify the situation, the Time Lord invited him aboard the TARDIS. Jack traveled with the Doctor and Rose, stopping by clothing store Topshop in Cardiff, while the TARDIS was refueling at the Time Rift there. He met Rose's boyfriend Mickey Smith, although initially their relationship was frosty.

After various other adventures with the Doctor, Jack found himself on the Game Station at the hands of two robots, Trine-E and Zu-Zana—although, in typical Jack-fashion, he managed to escape after pulling a small weapon he had concealed in his backside. During the defense of the station, Jack was exterminated by the Daleks, although his death was short-lived since Rose brought him back to life after she had looked into the heart of the TARDIS.

Jack found himself on Earth unable to die, and became a key member of alien investigation unit Torchwood, eventually becoming head of Torchwood Cardiff early in the twenty-first century. He had rescued the Tenth Doctor's hand which the Time Lord had lost in a battle with the Sycorax leader shortly after his regeneration, and this indicated when the Doctor was nearby. When the Time Lord stopped in Cardiff to refuel the TARDIS with Martha Jones,

Jack jumped on to the ship, and clung on as it sped through the Time Vortex to the planet Malcassairo far into the future.

During this adventure he discovered why he couldn't die: Rose had brought him back to life "forever," which meant that the Doctor and the TARDIS were both slightly scared of the captain. After the newly regenerated Master stole the Doctor's TARDIS, Jack, Martha and the Doctor were able to use Jack's Vortex Manipulator to return to twenty-first century London.

Jack's next encounter with the Doctor came when the Daleks sought to use Earth as part of their Reality Bomb. His last sight of the Tenth Doctor was in an alien bar where the Doctor helped Jack meet midshipman Alonso Frame (see FRIENDS), although the Time Lord and Jack never spoke directly.

CLARA OSWALD

A tricky entry this one. The Eleventh Doctor met Clara, after a fashion, firstly in the far future—or at least he met a version of her, known as Oswin Oswald. She was a human who had been mutated into a Dalek and placed on the Daleks' Asylum planet. Sadly, their meeting was short-lived, as was the Dalek Oswin who sacrificed herself to help the Doctor (after erasing him from the Daleks' databanks).

The Time Lord then met another iteration of Clara, this time a young governess, on Earth during an attack by the Great Intelligence in 1892. Again, Oswald died helping the Doctor. However, after Clara echoed Oswin's earlier words, "Run, you clever boy, and remember", the Doctor realized that there was a connection between the two and set out to discover her secret.

In the present day, Clara Oswin Oswald was looking after some children in London when the Doctor rang her doorbell and discovered there was something lurking in the wifi controlling certain humans, also the work of the Great Intelligence. Although she didn't hop aboard the TARDIS immediately, Clara became a time and space traveler the following day.

Her request to visit somewhere "awesome" was granted by the Doctor and the pair flew to the Rings of Akhaten where Clara helped the Queen of Years (see FRIENDS). Clara used the memory of the leaf which had led to her father meeting her mother, but then also remembered the Doctor's presence in her life as a child. During their travels, Clara discovered the TARDIS was not exactly her friend and, after an encounter with an Ice Warrior on a Russian submarine, she found the time

machine was acting hostilely towards her. This hostility continued when the couple visited Caliburn House on Earth in 1974, with the ship proving to be quite the "cow" (Clara's words) when she needed its help. Clara soon experienced the full power of the Doctor's ship when she discovered a calcified-like version of herself (from the future) roaming the corridors. During these wanderings, the young nanny learned much about the Doctor, including his real name, from the book The History of the Time War. She and the Doctor argued about her previous presence in his life, which she could genuinely not re-

call, but her memories of these hours in the TARDIS were temporarily erased when the Doctor managed to divert Time onto a different course.

After a journey to Yorkshire in 1893 where she faced the Crimson Horror and was trapped in suspended animation for a while, Clara returned home to find that the children in her care, Artie and Angie, had discovered her time-traveling secrets through a series of photographs. To placate them, they were taken to Hedgewick's World of Wonders. However, this jaunt turned into a nightmare as it saw the return of the Cybermen. Clara was placed in charge of the resident soldiers by the Doctor as he faced a battle of his own, a promotion the young girl took to very well. So well, Emperor Ludens Nimrod Kendrick Cord Longstaff XLI, also known as Porridge (see FRIENDS), was impressed enough for him to ask her to marry him. Sadly, for him, Clara declined his offer.

While attending to the Maitland children, Clara was drugged by a soporific candle, which allowed Madame Vastra, Jenny, Strax and River Song (whom she was surprised to learn was a woman) to make telepathic contact with her. It was this meeting that led the Doctor and Clara to the Doctor's tomb on Trenzalore, where she found River was still able to contact her, despite being dead. When the Great Intelligence entered the Doctor's timestream to destroy him in all his lives, Clara realized that it was her destiny to save the Doctor, and stepped into the timestream herself. She was scattered into fragments throughout space and time, across the Doctor's lives, meeting him time and again, and saving his life on numerous occasions in numerous regenerations.

Clara even took time to speak to the First Doctor, accompanied by his granddaughter Susan, encouraging the Time Lord, who was fleeing Gallifrey at the time, to choose a different TARDIS. To save her from death once she had completed her task, the Eleventh Doctor also stepped into his own timestream, where they then both met a previously unknown incarnation of the Time Lord. This much older Doctor was described as the "one who broke the promise" of their name…

DONNA NOBLE

Like a number of companions of the later Doctors, when Donna met the Time Lord, she did not immediately feel the need to bounce off into the universe for adventures with him. And, also like many companions, their relationship got off to a tense start.

On her wedding day, Donna suddenly found herself aboard the TARDIS, much to her and the Doctor's amazement and annoyance. Donna believed her "spaceman" had kidnapped her, and was not shy about making demands of him. When the truth of the Racnoss' plans was revealed, it was the "Chiswick temp" who convinced the Doctor to be lenient with the Empress of the Racnoss and her children. Although she chose to stay in London, Donna encouraged the Doctor not to travel alone.

It wasn't too long, however, before their paths crossed again after both were investigating the odd goings-on at Adipose Industries, a company producing "diet pills," fronted by Miss Foster (see VILLAINS). Knowing this was the sort of thing that would intrigue the Doctor, Donna had pursued enquiries hoping to run into him, and this time Donna definitely wanted to go traveling with him.

This Donna had moved on from her days blinkered by drink and scuba-diving, and now embraced the world, and the universe. Taken back in time to the cataclysm at Pompeii, Donna again engaged the Doctor's compassion to save the lives of Lucius Caecilius Iucundus and his family. It was this empathy that hurt her so much when she met the Ood slaves, many years in the future.

The Doctor encouraged her to learn how to fly the TARDIS, but her lesson was interrupted when they had to return to Earth, and her family (grandfather Wilf and widowed mother Sylvia). There, Donna endured a Sontaran attack and met the Doctor's former companion Martha Jones, now working for UNIT. Shortly after, the ship unexpectedly whisked all three off to the planet Messaline, where Donna was present at the creation of the Doctor's daughter. Donna named her Jenny and formed a close relationship with her. Donna met British crime writer Agatha Christie and visited the Library where she met the Doctor's future wife, Professor River Song, who was aware of who Donna was. When the Vashta Nerada attacked, Donna was saved by the Library's computer and turned into a Node. In the virtual reality within the computer, Donna experienced a new life, marrying and having children.

After returning to the real universe, Donna relaxed at the Leisure Palace on Midnight and then visited a fortune teller on Shan Shen. There, a Time Beetle created an alternate universe where Donna did not meet the Doctor, thus causing him to die during his fight with the Empress of the Racnoss. She met Rose Tyler, who convinced her to help as the world was coming to an end. Donna was sent back in time to the moment which started these alternative events— choosing to turn left rather than right in her car. The alternate Donna died after being hit by a vehicle allowing Time to reflow on its correct path, although Rose was able to give her a message to pass on to the Doctor. As a result, the Doctor took Donna to the Shadow Proclamation and she was then trapped in the TARDIS by the Daleks when they reached the

Dalek Crucible. It was here that her human DNA caused an instantaneous biological Meta-Crisis, after she touched the Doctor's spare hand which had been infused with regeneration energy by the Time Lord earlier. This resulted in another version of the Tenth Doctor being created, although he only had one heart, but it also meant that Donna became part Time Lord. When she was blasted by Davros, her brain fired up to Time Lord level. Sadly, for Donna, this situation wasn't tenable and the Doctor had to erase all her memories of him and their adventures, otherwise her mind would burn up. The Doctor returned Donna to Wilf and Sylvia's care. During the Tenth Doctor's final battle with the Master, he discovered that Donna was in a relationship with Shaun Temple and they were due to be married. Donna became a target for the Master but the Doctor had installed a defense mechanism in her head to ensure she couldn't remember the past. Donna remained oblivious to all her adventures with The Doctor. At her wedding to Shaun, she was given a winning lottery ticket purchased by the Doctor with a pound coin given to him by her late father. The TARDIS used a holographic image of Donna Noble to talk to the Eleventh Doctor as he was dying after being poisoned by River Song in World War II Germany.

DOROTHEA "DODO" CHAPLET

Mistaking the TARDIS for an actual Police Box, Dodo entered the ship on Wimbledon Common in 1966. She was almost instantly taken away by the First Doctor and Steven Taylor, who noted her similarity to Anne Chaplet, a young serving girl whom they had just left to her fate in 1572. During Dodo's brief time in the TARDIS, she traveled to the far future where she met the last remnants of mankind and the Monoids, giving them a dose of the common cold to endure. She contested with the Celestial Toymaker and, when the Doctor was urgently seeking a good dentist, she visited Tombstone in the Wild West of the USA. Following a trip to a savage world in the far future, she chose to stay in contemporary England after being hypnotized during the Doctor's battle against the War Machines. She didn't get to say goodbye to the Doctor in person, instead sending a message via new companion, Polly.

DR. GRACE HOLLOWAY

Few companions spent less time with the Doctor than this surgeon from San Francisco, who had only a few hours in his company during the last days of the twentieth century. Grace met the Time Lord in both his Seventh and Eighth regenerations and was instrumental in causing his regeneration.

Faced with the Seventh Doctor's alien physiology on the operating table when she was treating him for gunshot wounds, she inadvertently injured him fatally, and was upset that the "John Doe" had died, even after she saw an X-ray showing the Time Lord's two hearts. She found it impossible to believe that the younger man who approached her for help bearing no resemblance to John Doe was the same person, but slowly she started to trust him. She was quite happy to kiss him, and helped him in his battle against the Master.

Unfortunately she was possessed by the evil Time Lord, who killed her when he had no further use for her. The Doctor was able to reverse Time, and the TARDIS revived Grace. When the Doctor asked her to join him in her travels, she refused—but asked him if he would consider staying on Earth with her.

HARRY SULLIVAN

Former Naval surgeon Harry was working for UNIT as medical officer when he first met the Time Lord, straight after his regeneration into the Fourth Doctor. After helping the Doctor to defeat the K1 robot, he agreed to humor the Doctor's delusions by going aboard the TARDIS. His first trip with the Doctor and Sarah Jane Smith saw him help the occupants of Space Station Nerva battle the threat of the alien Wirrn.

Harry then helped deal with the Sontaran Styre on an almost uninhabited post-solar, flare-ridden Earth, and then was taken to the planet Skaro, home of the Daleks, where he was present at the genesis of the creatures. Returning to Nerva, Harry came face-to-face with the Cybermen. Back on Earth, Harry encountered the Zygons and the Loch Ness Monster, or Skarasen, in Scotland. After this adventure, Harry left the Doctor and Sarah to rejoin UNIT, although their paths crossed again when the Kraals attempted an invasion a few months later In later years, Harry Sullivan went to work for NATO and Sarah Jane Smith discovered that Harry died some point before 2010 after developing vaccines and saving thousands of lives,

IAN CHESTERTON

Ian, a science teacher at Coal Hill School, London, had a very chilly start to his relationship with the Doctor when they first met in the early 1960s on Earth. Suspicious of the behavior of one of his pupils, Susan Foreman, Ian followed the schoolgirl home, accompanied by fellow teacher Barbara Wright, to find Susan's grandfather in a somewhat irascible mood.

After entering the TARDIS, Ian did not believe the Doctor's claims that the Police Box was, in fact, a spaceship that could travel in space and time. But after landing thousands of years in his own planet's history, the skeptic became a believer, although he remained still slightly distrustful of the old man. Alongside Barbara he visited various times and places in Earth's past and future, as well as many other civilizations across the universe. During this time, Ian demonstrated considerable resourcefulness, helping to locate an English spy in Revolutionary France, and embarking on a mission to rescue Barbara from Saracen hands in twelfth century Palestine—for which he was knighted as Sir Ian of Jaffa by King Richard.

In time, he and the Doctor became good friends and their final goodbye, after meeting the Daleks for a third time, was an emotional one for both as Ian and Barbara returned to Earth, roughly to their own time.

JAMIE McCRIMMON

Hailing from the Scottish highlands in the eighteenth century, Jamie was one of the Doctor's longest serving companions. He journeyed alongside the Doctor for almost the entirety of one of his lives, a feat that few others have achieved.

Jamie joined the Second Doctor, Ben, and Polly after the Battle of Culloden and the young Scotsman easily adapted to his surroundings and the threats they posed. During his time in the TARDIS, he also traveled with Victoria Waterfield and Zoe Heriot. He became close to Victoria and despite his own personal protestations, she left him and the Doctor, upsetting Jamie greatly.

Jamie faced some of the Doctor's greatest foes too, encountering Cybermen (on four occasions), Daleks, the Ice Warriors (twice), as well as the Great Intelligence and its Yeti (also twice). At some point, he also faced the Sontarans when he and the Doctor met Peri and the Sixth Doctor in mid-1980s Spain. His travels were cut short when the Time Lords erased Jamie's memory of his TARDIS adventures and set him back to his own time after the Doctor had been put on trial. An illusion of Jamie appeared to the Second Doctor in the Tower of Rassillon, and the Tenth Doctor adopted his name to introduce himself to Queen Victoria.

JO GRANT

A fun-loving and vivacious employee of UNIT, Jo Grant was a cheeky contrast to the more austere presence of Liz Shaw when she joined the Third Doctor during his exile on Earth. While not the most academically gifted (she eventually admitted to the Doctor that she never said she'd passed the A Level science that she claimed she studied for), Jo certainly was a quick thinker.

Although their friendship got off to a bad start when Jo ruined one of the Doctor's experiments, they became firm friends. Though it would be a short time before she left Earth in the TARDIS or faced some of the Doctor's more familiar foes, Jo regularly came face-to-face on Earth with the renegade Time Lord known as the Master.

Jo met the Daleks, both on Earth and on the planet Spiridon; the Ice Warriors on Peladon; and the Sea Devils, after her baptism of fire against the Nestene Consciousness and the Autons. She also encountered the Axons, the Daemon Azal, Drashigs, Ogrons and Draconians, and traveled to planets such as Solos in the thirtieth century, Inter Minor, and Draconia, as well as visiting Atlantis in the distant past. Jo Grant also met the Second Doctor when they faced a threat against the whole universe from the ancient Gallifreyan, Omega. She eventually left the Doctor after falling in love with Welsh biological activist Professor Clifford Jones, who, she admitted to the Doctor, reminded her of a younger version of the Time Lord. Clearly hurt, the Doctor left her engagement party early to drive alone back to London. She married Cliff and took off on an expedition down the Amazon River, returning the wedding gift the Doctor had given her of a Metebelis Three blue crystal by mail because it seemed to be bringing them bad luck.

Jo felt slighted over the years that the Time Lord never came to visit her. They were, however, reunited when Jo attended the "funeral" of the Doctor, now in his Eleventh incarnation, at UNIT Base 5, where she met another of the Third Doctor's companions, Sarah Jane Smith. The Doctor, of course, was not dead, but had been kidnapped by the Shansheeth who wanted his TARDIS. Jo was upset that the Doctor now traveled with a married couple, but he told her that he had, in fact, kept up to date with her life, and had not forgotten her.

Still married and engaged in political activism (she once handcuffed herself to dictator Robert Mugabe, according to her grandson), Jo Grant had a happy and fulfilled family life.

K9

See ROBOTS

KAMELION

See ROBOTS

KATARINA

A very short-lived companion in more than one sense, this handmaid was serving Cassandra, Princess of Troy, when she was sent to spy on the First Doctor, Vicki, and Steven. After helping the latter out with his wounds she joined the TARDIS crew as Vicki left. Never quite fully understanding her surroundings (sometimes referring to the Doctor as a god, Zeus), Katarina committed suicide aboard a spaceship by opening an airlock after a mad prisoner took her hostage and was trying to force the Doctor to change course.

LIZ SHAW

Doctor Elizabeth Shaw had just been brought into the employ of UNIT when she first met the Doctor, just regenerated into his Third incarnation. Liz had several degrees and was at Cambridge University when Brigadier Lethbridge-Stewart asked her to be UNIT's new Scientific Advisor. Highly intelligent by human standards, but by no means the equal of the Time Lord, she and the Doctor sparked off each other, sometimes to the bemusement of the Brigadier.

During her short time with the Doctor, she battled the Nestene Consciousness and the Autons, tried to help the Silurians and some alien ambassadors, and participated in the Inferno project. The Doctor encountered an alternate version of her during this time on a parallel Earth, where she was a sadistic Section Leader in the military, However she became frustrated by the Doctor's attitude to her and decided to return to Cambridge. However by 2010, Liz was working on the UNIT Moonbase.

LADY CHRISTINA DE SOUZA

Jewel thief Christina got more than she bargained for when she bumped into the Tenth Doctor aboard a London bus. After a wormhole transported the bus from Earth to the planet San Helios, they worked together on a plan to get all the travelers back home safely. She and the Time Lord befriended two Tritovore (see ALIENS) and became a formidable team as they successfully returned the bus and its occupants safely. The Doctor didn't want a new travel companion so resisted her pleas to join him on his journey, although he did help Christina evade arrest by releasing her handcuffs so she could escape in the now flight-capable bus.

LEELA

Hailing from warrior tribe the Sevateem, Leela was exiled from her people, after profaning their god. When she met the Fourth Doctor, traveling alone, she accused him of being the "Evil One" from the myths of her tribe (who would turn out to be descendants of humans far in the future). With a tendency to resort to violence—janis thorns were her weapon of choice—the Doctor was initially unwilling to let her join him but she ran aboard the TARDIS regardless and started her adventures. After visiting a sandminer and encountering robots who had been programmed to kill humans, Leela changed out of her savage leathers into Victorian garb as she and the Doctor teamed up with Professor George Litefoot and Henry Gordon Jago in Victorian London on the trail of Li H'sen Chang, servant of Weng Chiang.

Leela visited Earth again at the start of the twentieth century at Fang Rock, where a Rutan (see ALIENS) was picking off the inhabitants of a lighthouse, and then again in the late 1970s where the Fendahl was being summoned. The one-time savage also traveled far into the future, where she met K9 (who began traveling with them), and visited Pluto.

Her last adventure with the Doctor was on the Time Lord's home planet of Gallifrey. Knowing Leela could fend for herself in a hostile environment, he apparently turned his back on her, and she worked with the Outsiders—non Time Lord Gallifreyans—to help defeat the invading Vardans and Sontarans. She decided to stay behind with Andred of the Chancellory Guard, with whom she had formed a relationship with, apparently. K9 felt obliged to stay with his mistress.

Fan Fact Note:
Leela's weapon of choice?
Lethal janis thorns.

MARTHA JONES

This doctor-in-training first met the Tenth Doctor on her way to work at the Royal Hope Hospital, when he indulged in some time-traveling tie antics. She met him properly hours later at the hospital as he investigated odd events. They became firm friends when Martha proved her mettle on the moon, when a platoon of Judoon were searching for Florence Finnegan (see VILLAINS).

During her time with the Doctor, Martha met Shakespeare, faced the Dalek Cult of Skaro and found herself floating off into space without the Doctor. But of most significance was her role in helping protect her traveling companion when he turned himself into a human, using a Chameleon Arch disguised as a fob watch, to evade the Family of Blood.

Not long after, Martha met another man with a similar fob watch, Professor Yana, who turned out to be the Master. When they all returned to the twenty-first century, Martha's family became the Master's prisoners, as did the Doctor. Martha herself evaded capture and spent a year walking the Earth, preparing the people for revolt against their new ruler. Thanks to the Paradox Machine turning time back, this year never actually happened, although Martha retained her memory of it. This affected her deeply and she chose to stay with her family.

However, Martha wasn't gone from the Doctor's life for good. After joining UNIT, she contacted the Doctor for help to deal with what turned out to be a Sontaran invasion and then briefly traveled once more in the TARDIS alongside Donna Noble, and met Jenny, the Doctor's daughter on Messaline.

They were reunited again, when the Daleks' invasion of Earth forced Martha, now based in New York, to implement the use of the Osterhagen Key in order to threaten the Dalek fleet. She, along with many of the Doctor's other companions, helped him fly the TARDIS and the Earth back into its correct position at the end of this adventure.

Although she was once engaged to Thomas Milligan (whom she originally met in the "year that never was"), Martha ultimately married Rose Tyler's former boyfriend, Mickey Smith. At the end of his Tenth life, the Doctor saved them both from a Sontaran attack.

Alternate Universe Note:
In the alternate universe, caused by the Trickster's Brigade, Martha died in the Royal Hope Hospital, along with Sarah Jane Smith, since the Doctor wasn't present to save the day.

MELANIE BUSH

Due to the rather unusual way the Doctor's time line transpired, it is not possible to accurately pinpoint how Melanie Bush, or Mel as she was better known, came aboard the TARDIS. Their relationship began both during and after his trial by the Time Lords. In his defense, the Doctor presented footage from his own future, which included a companion he was yet to meet, Mel Bush. A perpetual optimist, Mel was keen on a healthy lifestyle and encouraged the Doctor to lose some weight (as he was beginning to look slightly heftier in this regeneration) through carrot juice and an exercise bike. However, at the end of the trial, the Doctor and Mel departed together—despite the fact that the Doctor had not yet met her. Mel was present at the Sixth Doctor's regeneration although she had been knocked unconscious, and met—and was impersonated by—renegade Time Lord, the Rani. Mel didn't stay with the Seventh Doctor for long, choosing to leave with Sabalom Glitz after an adventure on Iceworld, where she introduced the Doctor to his new companion, Ace.

MICKEY SMITH

Rose Tyler's boyfriend Mickey did not trust the Ninth Doctor for a considerable time. He was left behind by Rose after an encounter with the Autons and the Nestene Consciousness in London and during her absence for over a year, he was suspected of her murder. He spent some time investigating the Doctor online, becoming something of a computer expert.

Mickey's inner heroism came out when he battled a Slitheen with a baseball bat to save Rose's mother's life. His resentful feelings towards the Doctor, whom he realized was the object of Rose's affections, mellowed, and he helped Rose return to Satellite Five in the year 200,100 in the TARDIS to rescue the Doctor.

When Rose returned with the Tenth Doctor, the new version of the Time Lord instantly took a shine to the mechanic. Mickey alerted the Doctor to unusual goings on at Deffry Vale High School, where it emerged that a species known as the Krillitane were utlilizing the children as part of their quest to unravel the Skasis Paradigm. After some encouragement

from Sarah Jane Smith, Mickey was taken aboard the TARDIS and he then encountered Clockwork Droids on a spaceship in the fifty-first century and Madame de Pompadour in the eighteenth. In a parallel universe Mickey met a version of himself, known as "Ricky" (coincidentally the name that the Ninth Doctor had deliberately misused for him). Mickey chose to stay on the parallel Earth but crossed back into our universe to help out the Doctor at Torchwood in the Battle of Canary Wharf.

Mickey stayed with Rose and her family after returning to the parallel Earth but found a way back across the dimensions to battle the Daleks when Davros threatened the universe with his Reality Bomb. Conscious of Rose's feelings for the Doctor, Mickey moved on, and ended up marrying Martha Jones.

NYSSA

Daughter of Consul Tremas on the planet Traken, the noble-born Nyssa met the Fourth Doctor and Adric during an attack by the Master on her home world. Her father's body was taken over by the renegade Time Lord, though she didn't learn this until she was taken to Logopolis by the Watcher (see TIME LORDS).

As a result of the Master's meddling, Traken was destroyed, and Nyssa joined Adric, Tegan and the Doctor as they battled to save the universe from a premature end from entropy. She and her two new friends witnessed the Doctor regenerate into his more youthful Fifth incarnation.

Nyssa helped the Doctor to undergo post-regenerative healing and again faced the Master, this time in the virtual world of Castrovalva, and then later in Earth's distant past. During her time in the TARDIS, she was a sympathetic ear for the more disgruntled Tegan and homesick Adric and her scientific skills were useful during the battle with the Terileptils in seventeenth century England. She came face-to-face with her own double, Anne Talbot, at Cranleigh Hall in 1925, and was kidnapped by Anne's fiancé who couldn't tell them apart, and then was devastated when Adric was killed in an explosion caused by the Cybermen.

Nyssa's caring nature finally led to her departure from the TARDIS crew. Not long after Turlough began his travels with the Doctor, Nyssa stayed behind on the Terminus spaceship to help find a cure for those affected by Lazar's disease.

PERI

Perpugilliam Brown, to give her full name, met the Fifth Doctor while she was vacationing in Lanzarote on Earth in 1984. When she got into trouble in the ocean while swimming, the Doctor's companion Turlough came to her rescue. Brought aboard the TARDIS to recover, she became embroiled in the Doctor's encounter with shape-shifting robot Kamelion (who took the form of her stepfather) and then the Master on the planet Sarn, where Turlough left the TARDIS crew. The Doctor saved Peri from death by spectrox toxemia on Androzani Minor, tracking down an antidote and then feeding it to her, although since there wasn't sufficient for them both, he had to regenerate to survive.

However, the Sixth Doctor suffered from trauma after his regeneration and in his madness tried to kill Peri. It took some time for her to trust him again. During their travels she met assorted Time Lords, including Azmael on Titan III, the Rani in Victorian England, and the Doctor's own Second incarnation. Peri also came up against the Cybermen, the Sontarans, and the Daleks, and even met science-fiction writer H.G. Wells.

Sadly, though, she didn't get a chance to share a proper goodbye with the Doctor. During their adventure on Thoros-Beta, the Doctor was taken out of space and time shortly before Peri was due to receive the mind of Mentor Lord Kiv.

According to the Valeyard, Peri was killled by King Yrcanos after the transfer. However, this turned out to be a fabrication and the Doctor was relieved to hear that she had in fact married Yrcanos.

POLLY

This trendy Sixties girl-about-town joined the First Doctor while she was working as a secretary for the creator of the artificial intelligence computer WOTAN in the Post Office Tower in London. At the conclusion of that adventure, she and able seaman Ben Jackson (who teased her about her "posh" accent and nicknamed her "Duchess") were whisked away in the TARDIS to seventeenth century Cornwall and then the South Pole. After the Doctor's first traumatic regeneration, Polly was quicker than Ben to accept that this new younger figure was the same man.

After fighting the Daleks on Vulcan, a trip to Scotland in 1746 (where Jamie McCrimmon joined them), an encounter with the Cybermen on the moon, and a visit to Atlantis where she was nearly converted into a "Fish Person," Polly and Ben arrived in the TARDIS at Gatwick Airport in 1966. Polly was hypnotized by the Chameleons, and once she was restored to herself, decided to stay in England. Sarah Jane Smith discovered in 2010 that the couple were working in India, running an orphanage.

RIVER SONG

Where to start with the Professor? Well, from River's point of view, she was conceived by the Ponds just after their wedding (which, it should be noted, River attended) following the Eleventh Doctor's reboot of the universe. She was delivered at the asteroid named Demon's Run into the hands of Madame Kovarian who planned to use the baby as a weapon against the Doctor. The Time Lord recovered both mother and child, only to discover the newly born Melody Pond was, in fact, a ganger baby!

The real Melody was raised in the Graystark Hall Orphanage on Earth and, after being shot at in 1969 by her own mother, she escaped in a spacesuit and wandered the streets of America until she found herself regenerating in front of a hobo in a New York alleyway. She traveled to the UK where she became friends with her future parents Amy Pond and Rory Williams, while they were all at school. By 2011, calling herself Mels, the precocious young lady met the Eleventh Doctor and, at gunpoint, forced him to take them all to meet Hitler in Berlin, 1938.

More surprises were in store, however, for Team TARDIS, after Mels took a bullet, fired by Hitler himself at a Nazi officer-disguised Teselecta, causing another regeneration—where she transformed in the more recognizable (to the Doctor, Amy, and Rory, at any rate) River Song. However it was immediately apparent to the Time Lord that his would-be wife was in no mood for pleasantries as the former "time baby" tried to kill the Gallifreyan. Sent by the Silence, she was now a "bespoke psychopath" created by Kovarian and her chums. Melody did succeed in fatally poisoning her future hubby, though, with her treacherous lips (a trick he really should have been aware of), thus sending him towards his own death, since he was unable to regenerate. But when the Ponds' offspring was presented with testimony of the Doctor's compassion as she was tortured by the Teselecta, she gave the Time Lord his life back by using her remaining regenerations to save his life (through a nice big kiss on the lips). This ordeal left Melody in hospital, where the Gallifreyan left her a rather large blue diary as a gift.

As she was left to ponder exactly who it was who saved her life, Melody changed her name to River Song and, in the year 5123, began to study archaeology at Luna University in order to find this "good man." It was here that Madame Kovarian and the Silence returned to enact their murderous plan against the Doctor. River's tampered memory resulted in her attempt to kill the Eleventh Doctor at Lake Silencio.

But River couldn't bring herself to kill her lover, and all of time collapsed. A new time line was born, a time line stuck in one particular moment. Upon their marriage, and the physical contact of the couple's kiss, the Doctor returned them to the moment at Lake Silencio—where River did her duty for space and time and "killed" the Time Lord (or rather a Teselecta duplicate of him). River was sentenced to a considerable term of imprisonment for killing the Time Lord, and was held in the Stormcage Containment Facility, in the fifty-second century.

But this prison was nothing to River who chose to escape when she pleased, usually to spend time with the Doctor. She turned up at Demon's Run to reveal her true identity to the Doctor, Amy, and Rory.

A letter from the Eleventh Doctor then invited her to watch his own death (which she caused) but helped as his past self appeared and the gang fought off the Silence in 1969; the pair used their diaries to coordinate where/when in their relationship they were. Heartbreakingly, for River, she realized that their two time lines were becoming more disparate and as she got to know him more, he knew her less. What for the Doctor was their first kiss, as he returned her to the Stormcage, was to prove particularly poignant for the archaeologist, since she knew it was their last as far as she was concerned.

But she still called upon him when needed, leaving him messages throughout space and time to catch his attention. A warning from van Gogh's painting of the TARDIS led River to disguise herself as Cleopatra and bring the Eleventh Doctor to the Pandorica, where she found a petrified Dalek terrified of her. Upon the universe being rebooted, River visited her parents' wedding briefly (though they had no knowledge of their familial link as of yet). Another escape (and another timey-wimey message) brought the two together at the Crash of the Byzantium on Alfava

Metraxis and a ghastly meeting with the Weeping Angels. For the Doctor, this was only the second time the couple had met and he discovered that River had been imprisoned for killing a "good man" but also that she carried pictures of all his faces she had encountered.

Before returning to the Stormcage, River stopped off to share a glass of wine with her parents, sharing with them the news that Doctor was still out in the universe somewhere (since they thought he'd gone from their lives forever). Some time later, River lured him back to New York during the 1930s (after placing various clues for him in her Melody Malone novel) where the Weeping Angels were in abundance. Their relationship proved to be as stormy as ever with barely a polite word spoken between the two. It was during this adventure that her mother and father, Amy and Rory Williams, left the TARDIS for good and River offered to travel with her "husband" to console him after their departure.

Her last physical meeting with the Time Lord was while he was in his Tenth incarnation and was the moment River had feared for many years: the moment when the love of her life no longer knew her. Professor Song met this version of the Doctor in the Library, when he was traveling with Donna Noble. Much confusion was caused (and would continue to be so for the couple) as the Gallifreyan began to unravel the mystery of their relationship. Armed with a sonic screwdriver of her own, River's diary was forbidden for the Doctor to look at, for fear of "spoilers" regarding his future. Her own future was short-lived as the archaeologist sacrificed herself to save her team and the Doctor, although the Time Lord had other plans. He was able to download her consciousness into the Library, thereby "saving" her.

After her death at the Library, River psychically linked with Madame Vastra, Jenny, Strax, and Clara, when an attack by the Great Intelligence and its Whispermen took Team Vastra to Trenazalore. River continued to communicate with Clara once she and the Eleventh Doctor arrived on the planet (although he, apparently, could not see her). River allowed the Intelligence to gain access to the TARDIS tomb, by speaking the Doctor's name, and to her surprise was then able to speak "face-to-face" with the Doctor revealing she was always there with him—something which he admitted to her that he knew already. Her mental link showed the Time Lord that Clara had not died after stepping into his timestream, allowing him to look for her.

With her trademark "Spoilers!" and a "Goodbye, sweetie," (an reversal of her first words to him as the Tenth Doctor, "Hello, sweetie") River faded from the Doctor's life once more. But was this really their final farewell?

RORY WILLIAMS

The future husband of Amy Pond met the Eleventh Doctor, while working as a nurse in Leadworth. The Time Lord noticed Rory because he was taking pictures of normal people in a park, rather than the huge spaceship in the sky.

Rory played second fiddle to the Doctor for some time, despite being engaged to Miss Pond, and was slightly agitated over Amy's interest in the Time Lord.

After the Doctor popped out of a cake at his stag party, Rory ended up traveling with Amy and the Doctor to Venice in 1580, where they met "fish from space," the Saturnynes. After this, the Dream Lord created an alternative universe in their minds where he and Amy were already married and expecting a child. Amy's love for Rory was amply demonstrated when she decided that a world without him could not be the real one.

Rory died, for the first time in 2020, at Cwmtaff, Wales after an encounter with Silurians. He took a shot meant for the Doctor, and was then swallowed up by a crack in space and time. This meant that Amy lost all her memories of him.

However, he reappeared as an Auton duplicate, one of the fake Roman army created as part of the giant trap to ensnare the Doctor into the Pandorica. Despite his best efforts, he was responsible for the near-death of his fiancée, and then guarded her for two thousand years after the Doctor placed her in side the Pandorica to heal, ensuring his love was safe. When the Doctor rebooted the universe, he was brought properly back into existence and married Amy.

Their daughter, Melody Pond (later known as River Song) was conceived during their wedding night aboard the TARDIS, though they spent most their honeymoon away from the Doctor. Some time later they received an invitation from him to travel to Lake Silencio, where they saw the Eleventh Doctor apparently die at the hands of an astronaut. During the battle against the Silence, Rory faked his own death and was brought in by Canton Delaware III and the FBI. During this time he met American President, Richard Nixon.

Rory nearly drowned after a meeting with a Siren on board the pirate ship, the *Fancy*, and faced death at the hands of House when it took control of the TARDIS, and fooled Amy into thinking Rory had died. During this adventure, the TARDIS communicated psychically with Rory (or "the pretty one" as she called him), with a message to pass on to Amy.

Rory's naturally trusting nature meant that on twenty-second century Earth, he was tricked by the ganger of Jennifer Lucas, who he had befriended. Worse was to come when he discovered that the Amy traveling with him and the Doctor was, in fact, also a ganger and that the real Amy was about to give birth to their child elsewhere.

He and the Doctor went to war in order to find Amy and his child, and came up against Madame Kovarian, who managed to escape with the baby. Things became more complicated when the Doctor's wife, River Song, revealed that she was their daughter, now grown up, and Rory learned that his and Amy's childhood friend, Mels, was in fact an earlier version of River.

During his subsequent travels Rory met Adolf Hitler (hitting him and locking him in a cupboard) as well as a Peg Doll version of his wife, and a future, older version of Amy who he had to leave behind to die to save the Amy he loved. After further adventures, the Doctor decided to take Rory and Amy home, and they enjoyed a new home and car supplied by the Time Lord.

Rory faced marital troubles with Amy (due to the fact she was unable to have more children) but, with a bit of help from the Doctor, the pair worked through them during a battle with the Daleks in their Asylum. After more escapades, featuring dinosaurs, a gunslinging cyborg in the American Wild West, and the Doctor spending some time living with them, Rory's final trips through Time came in New York where he was sent back to the 1930s by a Weeping Angel and saw an older version of himself die. At the end of this adventure, a Weeping Angel sent Rory back in time. Amy chose to join him, and they lived out their days in New York until both died naturally. They adopted a son, Anthony, in 1946.

ROSE TYLER

In her own timeline, Rose actually met the Tenth Doctor before she began her travels with the Ninth. She was approached very early on New Year's Day 2005 by a stranger who predicted, "I bet you're going to have a really great year"—this was the Tenth Doctor during his last visit to Earth before he regenerated.

A few months later she was working at Henrik's in London when she encountered some Autons in the basement. Thankfully the Ninth Doctor was on hand to grab her hand and tell her to run. He left her almost immediately, only to return to her flat the next day, where she lived with her mother Jackie Tyler. After helping the Doctor fight off the Nestene Consciousness, Rose turned down his offer to leave with him in the TARDIS. It was only when he revealed that the ship could also travel in time that she agreed.

Initially, their relationship was slightly sparky, with Rose a little annoyed that Time Lord technology was used on her brain to help her understand alien languages without her knowing, but she quickly came to trust the Doctor.

On returning home to pick up some clothes, Rose discovered that she had been away from Earth for a year instead of the few days the Doctor had promised. This caused no end of disharmony

with her boyfriend Mickey, who had been accused of her murder, She had other things on her mind when London became the focal point of an alien ship crash-landing in the Thames. The Doctor had come to admire Rose's bravery as they waited in 10 Downing Street, unsure whether they would live or die, but he couldn't promise Jackie that Rose would be safe. Even knowing this, Rose wanted to continue her travels with the Time Lord.

Shortly after, Rose met a solitary Dalek in Utah, 2012 which played on her trusting nature. The Dalek used her background time radiation to restore itself to full power, but disgusted at the impurity, begged Rose to order it to destroy itself. The Doctor sardonically referred to Adam Mitchell—whom Rose met in Utah—as her "boyfriend," but neither she nor the Time Lord were impressed with his behavior on Satellite Five.

The Doctor took Rose back to see her parents' wedding, but when they went to the day in 1987 that her father died in a road accident, Rose ("a selfish stupid ape," according to the Doctor) intervened to save him. This caused a wound in Time, and eventually the Doctor's disappearance. Rose told her father who she was, and he chose to sacrifice his life to set Time straight again. She then traveled further back in time to World War II where she met Captain Jack Harkness and subsequently reunited with Mickey.

After rescuing Rose from a Dalek saucer, the Doctor knew he was going to be captured by the mutated misfits on Satellite Five, so he sent

Rose home in the TARDIS. However, she refused to accept his loss, and found a way to look into the heart of the TARDIS. With these newfound powers, she destroyed the Dalek fleet and Emperor, and also resuscitated Captain Jack who had been exterminated. Knowing she could not cope with the energies involved, the Time Lord gave up his life in order to save her and regenerated into the Tenth Doctor in front of her in the TARDIS.

At first, Rose was confused and dubious about the new man but she returned home to look after the Doctor in his post-regenerative state. Within days, the two were firm friends again and, indeed, a new spark seemed to exist between them that wasn't present before.

The Doctor treated Rose to adventures in the future on New Earth, where she met Lady Cassandra again, the past where she encountered Queen Victoria, and then back to present day London. Also there were the Doctor's former companions Sarah Jane Smith and K9. Rose's relationship with Sarah was difficult at first as they tried to out-do one another, but they became good friends while defeating the Krillitane.

After briefly returning home, Rose and the Doctor traveled back in time to London 1953 where her face was removed by the Wire. From there, the pair traveled into space and into the future where a dark force lived deep within a planet orbiting a black hole. Here Rose received a warning from the Beast in the planet that she would "die in battle." The prophecy was to come true, in a fashion, as she would be counted among the dead after the Battle of Canary Wharf. That battle, caused by Cybermen from the parallel universe encountering Daleks who had existed in the Void between the worlds, saw the Doctor and Rose separated. Rose was trapped in the parallel world, with the Time Lord only able to send a message through the last of the breaches between the two worlds. The pair said their goodbyes at Bad Wolf Bay.

However, Rose was to prove that her love for the Doctor could break the boundaries of universes and, after near misses in London and on monitors, she finally connected with the Time Lord after breaking through to the correct universe (after meeting Donna Noble in a universe created by the Trickster's Brigade) to warn him about an impending disaster. Their reunion was short-lived but when she returned to her own time and space, after teaming up with friends to help the Doctor, she was accompanied by an alternate, human, version of the Doctor, who was able to express himself where his true Gallifreyan version could not.

Rose briefly teamed up with the Tenth Doctor again in an adventure which saw her Doctor meet more than one version of himself in the 50th anniversary special.

Alternate Universe Note:
After a trip to pre-revolutionary France, Rose, Mickey, and the Doctor ended up in a parallel Earth where she met alternative versions of her parents and Mickey. Rose revealed her true identity to her alternate father, though he was not receptive to the notion. Mickey decided to stay in the parallel world.

ROMANA

See TIME LORDS

SARA KINGDOM

See FRIENDS

SARAH JANE SMITH

Sarah Jane Smith stands proud in the bastion of companions as one of the few to enjoy ongoing adventures with multiple Doctors, and have a few of her very own! Known to the Doctor as Sarah— but insisting on both names to others in later years—Miss Smith's adventures spanned nearly forty years with the Time Lord.

As a journalist, working for Metropolitan magazine, Sarah Jane Smith met the Third Doctor while infiltrating UNIT. Her intrepid nature made her stow away aboard the TARDIS as it traveled to thirteenth century England where she met a Sontaran named Linx. This was not the only time Sarah came into contact with the aggressive inhabitants of Sontar.

As the Third Doctor was still loosely associated with UNIT, she came in close contact with the Brigadier, who insisted on addressing her formally as "Miss Smith," Mike Yates, and Sergeant Benton. She helped to solve a dinosaur invasion, then met the Daleks on Exxilon, visited Peladon where her feminist nature caused a stir, and was possessed during an attack by the Giant Spiders from Metebelis III. It was at the close of this adventure that Sarah said goodbye to the Doctor she knew, as he regenerated in

front of her and the Brigadier. It didn't take long for Sarah to become close to the Fourth Doctor and their relationship was stronger than ever. Her first trip with him, accompanied by UNIT doctor Harry Sullivan (who often referred to Sarah as "old girl"), was to Space Station Nerva where almost immediately she was put into a cryogenic sleep. Before they returned to Earth, she met another Sontaran, then was present when scientist Davros unveiled his new creations, the Daleks on the planet Skaro, and, finally, encountered the Cybermen.

During the rest of her time with the Fourth Doctor, she met an assortment of monsters, including Zygons, anti-matter creatures, the ancient Egyptian god Sutekh the Destroyer, the Kraals, and the Krynoids. She also coped with blindness on the planet Karn, and possession both in sixteenth century Italy and by

the crystalline, silicon-based criminal, Eldrad. When the Doctor received a summons from Gallifrey, he had to return home, but without Sarah, since aliens were not allowed there at this point. After an emotional goodbye, the journalist was dropped off with her things near her home in Croydon, or so she thought—as it transpired, she was actually left in the Scottish city of Aberdeen.

The Doctor hadn't forgotten her—when she went to her aunt's house five years later, she found a box containing K9 Mark III left for her by the Doctor. A few years after that, Sarah was picked up by the Timescoop and dropped into the Death Zone on Gallifrey where she was reunited with the Third Doctor and the Brigadier and also met the First, Second and Fifth Doctors, Turlough, Susan, Tegan, and the Master, and had a fresh encounter with the Cybermen.

Her adventures with the Doctor were still not over. Many years later, when investigating unusual activity at Deffry Vale High School in 2007, Sarah Jane met the Tenth Doctor. During this meeting, her true feelings for him were revealed as she explained that she had waited for his return for many years. The journalist also got to know Rose Tyler, and after a tense start, they soon warmed to one another.

Much to Doctor's amusement, Sarah had kept K9 although the tin dog needed some repair. The Doctor upgraded K9 Mark III and after the canine computer sacrificed himself to save their lives, he left Sarah a replacement. Once the Doctor had gone on his way, Sarah continued her own investigations from her house in Bannerman Road in Ealing, adopting an alien boy, Luke, as her son, and working with local teen-agers to save the world. During this time, she kept in touch with the Brigadier.

Her paths crossed with the Doctor again during a Dalek invasion and she came face-to-face with Davros once more, as well as all of the Doctor's recent traveling companions. Some time later, Sarah Jane (as she now referred to herself) was tricked into falling in love with barrister Peter Dalton by the Trickster and was only prevented from marrying him by the arrival of the Tenth Doctor, traveling alone toward the end of his life. The Doctor helped Luke and his friends to dispatch the time meddler.

During his "farewell tour" of old companions shortly before he regenerated, the Tenth Doctor saved Luke from involvement in a car accident. When he turned sadly away into the TARDIS, she realized this would be the last time she would see the Doctor in this guise. In his Eleventh incarnation, the Time Lord was captured by the Shansheeth who faked a UNIT funeral for him. Sarah Jane was invited to the funeral, and met her predecessor in the TARDIS, Jo Grant. The two women were convinced the Doctor wasn't truly dead, and were delighted when he reappeared.

Alternate Universe Note:
In the alternative time-line, caused by the Trickster, Sarah Jane died when investigating at the Royal Hope Hospital while it was transported by the Judoon to the moon.

STEVEN TAYLOR

Steven was one of the few companions who wasn't chosen by the Doctor, but instead stowed away aboard the TARDIS. Imprisoned on the planet Mechanus, the Earthborn pilot had spent two years alone as a prisoner. He helped the First Doctor, Ian, Barbara, and Vicki to escape from the Mechonoid (see ROBOTS), but was injured himself. While Ian and Barbara were saying goodbye to the Doctor, he stumbled into the Ship, and awoke once the TARDIS was in flight.

In 1066 he met the Monk, another Time Lord, and went on to have adventures in Ancient Troy, Paris in 1572, the American Wild West, and on various un-named planets where he faced enemies such as the Drahvins, the Daleks and the Celestial Toymaker. He left the Doctor to help two opposing factions rebuild a far-off civilization.

SUSAN FOREMAN

See TIME LORDS

Fan Fact Note:
Steven Taylor does look a lot like an American tourist named Morton Dill that the Doctor met just before his path crossed with Steven Taylor. In fact, they were both played by the same actor, Peter Purves.

TEGAN JOVANKA

Tegan unwittingly joined the TARDIS towards the end of the Fourth Doctor's time. Training to be an air stewardess, she was on her way to her first job when she mistook the Doctor's ship for a Police Box. The independently-minded Australian found herself navigating her way through the TARDIS until she came across the Time Lord and companion Adric.

Her Aunt Vanessa, with whom she had been traveling, was a victim of the Master's Tissue Compression Eliminator and was found shrunk in their car. Tegan witnessed the Doctor's regeneration but her headstrong attitude continued as she repeatedly requested to be returned to her own time and place. The Doctor tried to oblige, but instead he landed on a spaceship occupied by the Urbankans while on a second attempt they arrived in the right place but the wrong time, in plague-ridden seventeenth century England. In-between these attempts, Tegan was subjected to the Mara, an entity which possessed her mind and attempted to influence others. After the Doctor apparently defeated it, Tegan was unsure whether she was free from its grasp, and, indeed, it did return some time later forcing Tegan to pilot the TARDIS to Manussa where it tried to control her again.

During her initial travels with the Fifth Doctor, their friendship was markedly spiky, with numerous disagreements between them about her desire to go home. However, shortly after the death of Adric and another encounter with the Master, she was left behind when the Doctor and Nyssa left her at Heathrow Airport. They were reunited some time later in Amsterdam.

This time, Tegan chose to travel with the Doctor, and remained for most of the rest of his Fifth incarnation. During that time Nyssa left, and new companions

Turlough and Kamelion came aboard. She met numerous foes including the Black Guardian, the Silurians and Sea Devils, and the Tractators, and had fresh encounters with the Cybermen and the Master on the Death Zone on Gallifrey, where she spent time with the First Doctor and his granddaughter, Susan.

After a particularly bloody encounter with the Daleks in London, Tegan made it clear to the Doctor that she was unhappy with his lifestyle, and left, leaving the Time Lord to rethink his ways. Moments after the TARDIS had dematerialized, she returned only to find him gone, revealing that perhaps, she wasn't quite ready to end her time with him just yet.

Sarah Jane Smith revealed in 2010 that Tegan had been campaigning for Aboriginal rights.

VICKI

Born on Earth in the twenty-fifth century, Vicki met the First Doctor on the planet Dido where she was one of two survivors of a space expedition. The young orphan took to the Doctor straightaway and as it was not long since he had said goodbye to Susan, it would seem the Doctor was looking for a granddaughter figure in his life.

Not scared and slightly precocious, Vicki fitted in well with Ian and Barbara (and later Steven Taylor) and shared adventures with them in Earth's history in first century Rome and then the Crusades. She wasn't frightened of asserting herself, helping to run a rebellion on the planet Xeros, and standing up to the foes she encountered. She elected to leave the Doctor in Ancient Troy, after falling in love with the Trojan prince Troilus, and walked into history under the name of Cressida.

VICTORIA WATERFIELD

Victoria joined the Time Lord and Jamie with little other choice, after the death of her mother, and her father's extermination by the Daleks. Her time in the TARDIS was packed full of adventures, as she met the Cybermen, the Ice Warriors, and the Yeti on two separate occasions. Although she did change from her Victorian-era clothing for something more practical, she still missed her old time and her family.

After her amplified screams were used to destroy a deadly weed that had been invading gas pipes, Victoria left the TARDIS in the late 1960s on Earth, choosing to live with manager Frank Harris and his wife Maggie at the Euro Sea Gas refinery. Jamie, in particular, was very saddened to see her leave, knowing he would miss the prim and proper Victoria who he had enjoyed teasing so much.

VISLOR TURLOUGH

A native of the planet Trion, Turlough was exiled to Earth and was posing as a schoolboy in England when he entered the TARDIS uninvited. He was on a mission from the Black Guardian who was seeking revenge on the Doctor (now in his Fifth incarnation). As a pupil at Brendon Public School he was under the tutelage of former UNIT Brigadier Alistair Gordon Lethbridge-Stewart. At first, Turlough was happy to follow his orders so the Black Guardian would keep his promise to send him back home, and almost hit the Doctor with a rock at one point, but mainly he kept his insubordination to sneakily skulking round corridors and looking over his shoulder every five minutes. After some time in the Time Lord's company, Turlough decided to side openly with the Doctor and go back on his deal with the Black Guardian. Once he was a free agent, Turlough joined Tegan and the Doctor in England in 1215 where the Master was hoping to avert the signing of Magna Carta, and then remained in the TARDIS in the Death Zone on Gallifrey as the Doctor met up with earlier versions of himself and former companions.

Before he left the TARDIS, Turlough faced Sea Devils and Silurians, the Malus, Daleks, Tractators (whom his race had encountered before) and then the Master again. While on Sarn, he discovered that his brother was still alive and that an amnesty had been granted against political prisoners and his exile is at an end. Turlough left the Doctor, amicably, leaving the Time Lord to travel on with new companion Peri.

ZOE HERIOT

Born on Earth in the twenty-first century, Zoe's outlook was overly hidebound by logic, to the detriment of her emotions. The young scientist stowed away on the TARDIS after she helped the Second Doctor and Jamie defeat the Cybermen on Space Station W3 (also known as "The Wheel") where she was based. During her time with the Doctor, she sometimes underestimated the threat before her, such as with the Quarks (see ROBOTS) although her computer-programming skills came in handy when the Cybermen attempted an Earth invasion in the late 1970s. Zoe also encountered Krotons, Ice Warriors, Space Pirates and the War Chief before her memory of her time with the Doctor was wiped by his own people, and she was sent back to her own time.

The Second Doctor saw an illusion of Zoe alongside Jamie in the Tower of Rassilon, when he was brought there by Time Lord President Borusa.

FRIENDS & ALLIES

Over his one thousand years or so of traveling through space and time,
the Doctor has met many, many people—some good, some bad. Here you'll find
some of those special characters who found a special place in the Doctor's hearts—
and those who could be regarded as his friends and allies...

ADA GILLYFLOWER

Ada unwittingly met the Eleventh Doctor, calling him her "monster" after he was rejected from her mother's preservation process. Blinded by her mother's experiments in attaining the process, which left some with the affliction known as "the Crimson Horror."

Ada cared for her monster secretly after being instructed to dump the body in a river. Her mother, Winifred (see VILLAINS), had told Ada her blindness was caused by her father but when the Doctor told Ada the truth after he had been restored back to normal, she attacked her mother.

Winifred died not long after holding a gun to her own daughter's head, leaving Ada somewhat bitter though resilient. As a final act against her mother, she squashed the prehistoric red leech, Mr. Sweet, before the Doctor could return it to its own time. Undeterred by her experience, Ada looked forward positively in life.

ALEC PALMER

This humble professor met the Eleventh Doctor in late 1974 while investigating ghost-like activity at Caliburn House with his assistant, psychic Emma Grayling. Though Alec was now a scientist, the Doctor was aware of his background in World War II as a specialist in "espionage, sabotage and reconnaissance behind enemy lines," as well as his talent for painting watercolors. Alec's guilt over the deaths he believed he was responsible for during the war lived with him for many years, driving him into ghost-hunting, thinking he could help those who died.

Believing the Time Lord and Clara were from "the Ministry," Palmer let them have access to i nvestigate the Witch of the Wells, only to discover that no ghosts were present. The apparition was that of Hila Tacorien, a time-traveler stuck in a pocket universe, who was, in fact, a descendant of Palmer and Grayling.

ALEX & GEORGE

Father and son met the Eleventh Doctor, Amy, and Rory after the TARDIS received a distress call and tracked it to young boy George, living with his parents, Claire and Alex. The boy was a fearful soul believing there to be monsters in his cupboard, and, after some investigation, the Doctor realized that George was, in fact, an alien, since Claire and Alex could not conceive. As a Tenza, his telepathic powers granted him extraordinary powers, and through his fear of rejection he placed his father, along with the TARDIS crew, in a doll's house where they were confronted by Peg Dolls (versions of other people George had put in there). When Alex revealed his fatherly love for George, their safety was ensured and sanity restored. The Doctor left the family stating that everything would be fine in the future, although he noted that puberty was "always a funny time" with the Tenza.

ADELAIDE BROOKE

Captain Brooke was in charge of Bowie Base One, the first manned human habitat on Mars. In November 2059, the Tenth Doctor, traveling alone, was taken in for questioning by the base's robot, Gadget (see ROBOTS). He quickly realized who the team were and showed great admiration for them all, knowing they were all fated to die shortly in a catastrophe that was a fixed point in time. But he became embroiled in an attack on the base by a water-based alien, the Flood. Adelaide told the Doctor of an incident during her childhood when a Dalek approached her bedroom window but didn't kill her. The Time Lord ventured that even the Daleks recognized the fixed point in time, hence why it couldn't exterminate her.

Sadly, the Doctor didn't follow the Dalek's lead and he decided to save Adelaide from death. Claiming to be the "Time Lord Victorious" he changed the course of Time. However, Adelaide recognized something wrong in the Doctor and ended her own life minutes after he brought her back to Earth. Her death inspired her granddaughter Susie Fontana Brooke to travel into space, piloting the first lightspeed ship. Her descendants engaged relations with aliens and started a new species.

ALISTAIR GORDON LETHBRIDGE-STEWART

Or, the Brigadier, as he was better known. Alistair was one of the Doctor's oldest friends, meeting him in a number of different regenerations and over many decades.

He first crossed paths with the Time Lord when he was a colonel in the British armed forces as they battled an attack by the Great Intelligence using Robot Yeti in the London Underground, at some point in the mid-1970s. The Doctor was in his second incarnation and traveling with Jamie and Victoria.

Just a few years later, promoted to Brigadier, Lethbridge-Stewart encountered the Second Doctor again, now traveling with Jamie and Zoe. He was in charge of the British section of the newly formed UNIT (United Nations Intelligence Taskforce, later renamed Unified Intelligence Taskforce) dealing with an attack by the Cybermen in London.

Realizing that the Doctor's help had been invaluable, the Brigadier tried to find him to offer a position as Scientific Advisor to UNIT, but without success. He therefore offered the post to Cambridge scientist Dr. Elizabeth Shaw, but shortly afterwards met the Doctor once more, shortly after his forced regeneration by the Time Lords and his exile to Earth. The Doctor, much to his chagrin, became UNIT's scientific advisor working alongside Liz Shaw. This sometimes caused a little friction between the Time Lord and the Brigadier, as they disagreed over UNIT's methods.

It was during this time on Earth that the Doctor spent the most time with the Brigadier. During these years they combatted an invasion by the Nestene Consciousness and their Autons, a skirmish with Silurians (an event which saw the Doctor horrified at the Brigadier apparently committing genocide), dinosaurs running amok in London, and a meeting with the Daleks. The Brigadier assigned Jo Grant as the Doctor's assistant, welcomed journalist Sarah Jane Smith as his companion after Jo's departure, and on many occasions faced the threat of another Time Lord, the Master. He was present at the Third Doctor's regeneration, raising a laconic eyebrow and muttering, "Here we go again," as the Time Lord's appearance began to change.

His relationship with the Fourth Doctor was not as strong, mainly because the Time Lord left Earth, with Sarah and Harry Sullivan, as soon as he could. Calling him back to Earth, the Brigadier sought the Doctor's help in Scotland where they discovered that the Zygons were planning a hostile takeover of the planet.

It would be many years until the two men met again but when they did, they did so in the most timey-wimey fashion imaginable. The Fifth Doctor met Alistair at a boys' school in 1983, although his memory of the Time Lord was non-existent until jogged. At the same school, six years earlier, companions Tegan and Nyssa also met Alastair, after being separated from the Doctor. He had just started teaching mathematics there after his retirement. Eventually, the "two" Alistair Gordon Lethbridge-Stewarts met and touched, causing the memory loss in his younger self. He emerged otherwise unscathed from the trauma.

The Brigadier was one of the Doctor's few friends who were present when two of his regenerations were in the same place at the same time. He met the

Second Doctor again during the attack by Omega (and saw an image of the First Doctor on a scanner). That incarnation also visited a UNIT reunion from where he and Alastair were kidnapped and sent to the Death Zone on Gallifrey, where the Brigadier came face-to-face with the Third and Fifth Doctors again and met the First properly.

Some years later, in the mid-to-late 1990s, he came out of retirement to help UNIT deal with the sorceress Morgaine and met the Seventh Doctor, who was traveling with Ace at the time. Ever the hero, the Brigadier took on the Destroyer by himself.

Over the years, the Doctor had a great deal of affection for his old friend and hoped for his presence during the Sontaran ATMOS incident only to be told the now knighted Sir Alistair was in Peru. Sadly, the Eleventh Doctor learned of the Brigadier's death over the telephone. Sir Alastair's nurse told him that a glass of brandy had often been poured in case of the Doctor's return.

The Eleventh Doctor formed a close relationship with Sir Alistair's daughter, Kate Stewart, who succeeded him in charge of UNIT, who told the Time Lord that her father spoke of him and their adventures together right up to his peaceful death in a nursing home.

ALONSO FRAME

Newly promoted to Midshipman aboard the starship *Titanic*, Alonso was a timid character, though brave enough to stand his ground. His professionalism was to prove a sore point, literally: when he questioned Captain Hardaker, he was answered with a gunshot. Luckily for Alonso, it did not prove fatal and he managed to help the Tenth Doctor rescue the remains of the ship and some of its passengers. Excited by the sailor's name, the Time Lord finally got to proclaim "Allons-y, Alonso!"

Some time later, Alonso met Captain Jack Harkness in a space bar, after the Doctor had slipped Jack a note to introduce the two.

ANGIE & ARTIE MAITLAND

Clara had been looking after this pair of youngsters after their mother had died. They discovered some pictures of Clara in Victorian London, in a Russian submarine in the 1980s, and in Caliburn House in the 1970s, which proved to them that she had been traveling in time with her "boyfriend," the Doctor. To appease them, the Time Lord treated them to a journey to Hedgewick's World of Wonders, the biggest amusement park in the universe. Here they faced the return of the Cybermen and were partly converted, although the Doctor eventually returned them to their original state. This didn't deter the pair, who appeared to enjoy the day thoroughly. Angie and Artie met the Doctor again, although they tricked him so they could illicitly pop out to the cinema.

BANNAKAFFALATTA

A feisty and prickly character, but ultimately brave and helpful, Bannakaffalatta met the Tenth Doctor during a Christmas journey on the starship *Titanic* when it was hit by meteors, as planned by the ship's owner, Max Capricorn. The Zocci hid his cyborg side, still ashamed of the stigma it had in some societies, though it would prove useful when he used his implant to create an electromagnetic pulse that destroyed some nearby Heavenly Hosts (see ROBOTS). Bannakaffalatta used up too much power and died, but he made his feelings known to Astrid Peth whom he liked very much, before his lights switched off for good. Some time later, the Tenth Doctor described the little guy as "brilliant" to two members of a similar race, the Vinvocci, whom he met on Earth.

BILLY SHIPTON

Billy was a police investigator who had the misfortune of stumbling across the Weeping Angels. DI Shipton was in charge of the "Wester Drumlins Collection:" a number of cars found abandoned outside the Wester Drumlins estate. Sally Sparrow was investigating the disappearance of her friend Kathy Nightingale at the same venue, and when she met Billy, the two hit it off instantly, with Sparrow giving him her phone number.

Sadly, straight after this, the policeman was touched by a Weeping Angel and sent back to 1969, where he met the Tenth Doctor and Martha Jones. It was here he learned his fate and helped the Doctor and Martha get back to the twenty-first century by inserting "Easter eggs" into a series of DVDs. The day after she first met Billy, Sally Sparrow visited the now elderly man in hospital. She stayed with him until he died.

DR. BLACK

The curator of an exhibition of van Gogh paintings, Dr. Black met the Eleventh Doctor and Amy when they took a trip to the Musée d'Orsay in Paris, France. Both men shared a distinct love for bowties. When the Doctor and Amy discovered a painting which apparently contained an alien–a Krafayis (see ALIENS). They made a swift exit. They returned with Vincent van Gogh himself who learned of his fame, long after his death, from Dr. Black, who was a huge fan of the painter's work.

BRIAN WILLIAMS

Lovely Brian, father to Rory, found himself surrounded, literally, by the TARDIS while attending to a light bulb in the Ponds' home. Quickly he, Amy, and Rory were whisked off by the Eleventh Doctor to 2367 where they met Queen Nefertiti of Egypt and John Riddell. On the Silurian Ark, he came face-to-face with some dinosaurs and used one of his golf balls to befriend a Triceratops; however, he also found himself on the receiving end of a blast from one of Solomon's robots (see ROBOTS). He and Rory were able to pilot the ark, to safety, thanks to their genetic link. After this first meeting with the Eleventh Doctor, Mr. Williams traveled with him in the TARDIS for some time, sending postcards of his destinations back to Amy and Rory.

During an attack on Earth by Shakri (see VILLAINS), using mysterious cubes, Brian helped out by studying the unknown objects, recording their activities on his camera. He was captured by Shakri's orderlies in the hospital and transferred to the alien's ship. The Doctor returned Brian home, after defeating Shakri, where Mr. Williams encouraged his son and daughter-in-law to continue traveling with the Time Lord.

CANTON DELAWARE III

Canton Delaware III was an ex-FBI agent called in to help President Richard Nixon with some unusual telephone calls when the Eleventh Doctor was investigating the White House in 1969 with Amy, Rory, and River Song. Recognizing the Time Lord's vast intelligence immediately, Delaware trusted that the stranger, obviously the most intelligent man in the room, could help with the President's dilemma. Their journey together saw the uncovering of the Silence. Canton filmed a Silent in a dwarf star alloy prison saying, "You should kill us all on sight!" and used this to help humanity attack the Silence.

Once their task was completed the Doctor suggested to Nixon that he let Delaware get married (since he had been forced out the FBI for having a relationship with an African-American), but Canton's revelation that it was a man he wished to marry gave the President much to think about.

Many years later, in 2012, Canton Delaware III was present after the Eleventh Doctor was "killed" beside Lake Silencio. Receiving an invitation by mail, the elderly former agent met River, Amy, and Rory once more as they put the "dead" Doctor on to a boat for a Viking funeral.

CAPTAIN ERISA MAGAMBO

Tough to call Erisa Magambo a "friend," as such, but this UNIT Captain had the best interests of the world when she commanded scientific Malcolm Taylor to close the wormhole through which the Tenth Doctor was about to come from San Helios. She exchanged pleasantries with the Doctor on his arrival, but the Time Lord remained unaware how close he had come to being eaten alive by flying stingray-like creatures, on a bus in the desert.

In the parallel time line caused by the Trickster's Brigade, the captain assisted Rose Tyler to send Donna Noble back in time and into her own universe to restore the proper timeline. This version of Magambo blinked out of existence when Donna succeeded.

CAPTAIN HENRY AVERY

Captain Avery and his crew encountered the Eleventh Doctor with Amy and Rory after the TARDIS landed on the pirate ship the *Fancy* in 1699. Henry was suspicious of the trio at first but came to trust the Time Lord when they all found themselves battling the Siren, a mysterious entity who seemed to be taking the lives of the ship's crew. After learning that the Siren was an automated doctor on an alien ship, Henry was reunited with his son, who had stowed away on the *Fancy*, and the rest of his crew.

Avery returned with his son and crew to help the Doctor at the Battle of Demon's Run.

CAPTAIN ZHUKOV

When the Doctor mistakenly materialized the TARDIS in a Russian submarine under the North Pole in 1983, the captain and his crew were suspicious of the ship's new visitors. After the appearance of Ice Warrior Skaldak, Zhukov still did not trust the Doctor fully, disallowing him access to the captured alien. But once the Ice Warrior escaped, the captain knew he was out of his depth, and sided with theDoctor to contain the rowdy rampaging alien. By the time Skaldak had left, the two men were on much better terms, with the Doctor asking for a lift to the South Pole.

CHANTHO

The last of the Malmooth, Chantho was the female assistant to Professor Yana on the planet Malcassairo. The two were working together in his laboratory to help the last of mankind travel to Utopia. The alien started every sentence with "Chan" and end it with "tho"; if she didn't, it would be rude, the equivalent of swearing for humans.

The Tenth Doctor, aided by Martha Jones and Captain Jack Harkness, helped Yana fulfill his dream and the two men became good friends instantly, recognizing genius in each other. Chantho, in turn, became good friends with Martha, and they shared their feelings of longing for the men they were with. When Professor Yana revealed himself to be the renegade Time Lord, the Master, Chantho was fatally injured by him. Though greatly saddened, her last action was to shoot him, causing the Time Lord to regenerate.

DR. CONSTANTINE

MR. COPPER

The physician's meeting with the Time Lord at Albion Hospital, London, during the Second World War proved short-lived. Constantine was caring for a number of patients who were all infected by a kind of plague which turned people into "gas mask zombies," caused by nanogenes from an alien ship. Constantine told the Doctor what he had noticed before he himself was affected, uttering, "Are you my mummy?" as he transformed into one of the zombies. When the Doctor used the nanogenes to revert everyone back to normal, Constantine was cured.

The delightful, if ever so slightly wrong, Mr. Copper claimed to have a first-class degree in "Earthonomics" from the planet Sto and was employed on the starship Titanic. In fact, Copper had been a student at Mrs. Golightly's Happy Traveling University and Dry Cleaners. The Tenth Doctor met the retired traveling salesman when a group of passengers, including the Time Lord and his new friend Astrid Peth, took a trip down to London, one Christmas Eve.

After surviving Max Capricorn's attempts to destroy the ship, Mr. Copper refused the Doctor's offer to travel with him in the TARDIS, and elected to stay on Earth. As a parting gift, the Time Lord would leave him some money on his credit card—money which he would use to start the Copper Foundation, which created the subwave communications network later used by Harriet Jones.

CRAIG OWENS

Stuck on Earth, after the TARDIS dematerialized with Amy on board, the Eleventh Doctor approached Craig Owens in order to rent a room from him; his previous flat mate had just moved out after coming in to some money, rather mysteriously.

Though slightly taken aback by this unusual lodger, Craig warmed to the Time Lord after he prepared an omelet for them both to enjoy. This friendliness wasn't to last as Craig became jealous of his new chum's football skills and became suspicious of the Doctor's intentions towards Sophie, the love of Craig's life.

After being confronted about his strange behavior, the Doctor telepathically told Craig who he was—headbutting him to impart the information! Owens learned of a spaceship above him and discovered Sophie was about to die, but then saved the day through his love for her. The ship vanished as did the upper story of the

building. Craig and Sophie became a couple and gave a set of house keys to the Doctor, so that he could visit at any point, although they hardly expected him to. Some time later, the Doctor found Craig at his new house where he met Craig and Sophie's baby, Alfie (who preferred to be known as "Stormageddon"). The Time Lord was able to "speak baby," and helped Craig bond with his new son.

They were reunited again in a local toy shop where the Eleventh Doctor was now employed. Craig was captured in a Cybermen ship and almost converted into a Cyberman himself. However, thanks to some coaxing from the Doctor, Craig was able to break free of his Cyber-shell through the power of love for his son.

The two men had a close friendship, and were sometimes mistaken for a couple. They parted on good terms, with the Doctor borrowing some blue envelopes and a Stetson hat before he left.

DORIUM MALDOVAR

Before the Eleventh Doctor was trapped in the Pandorica, River Song paid him a visit at his Maldovarium bar in 5145, looking for a Vortex Manipulator. He was all too happy to oblige, having attained one "fresh off the wrist of a handsome Time Agent." River drove a hard bargain, almost killing Dorium in the process with micro-explosives placed in his drink.

It's not entirely clear when the big blue one first met the Doctor (or, indeed, in which regeneration) but when the Eleventh Doctor went looking for favors to recall, Dorium was on that list of those who owed the Time Lord. The Doctor was assembling an army to find Amy at Demon's Run and he used his old acquaintance to hack into Madame Kovarian's battleship's computer. Sadly, for Dorium, he was beheaded by the Headless Monks, though his head lived on, and the Doctor was taken to him in the Seventh Transept.

Here Dorium revealed that the "fall of the Eleventh" would take place on the fields of Trenzalore, where a question that must never be answered would be asked. The Doctor took Dorium's cased head with him in the TARDIS on his "farewell tour" but returned it, disguised as a Monk. Dorium reminded the Doctor about the first question in the universe, "Doctor Who?"

EDWIN BRACEWELL

The Eleventh Doctor met scientist Edwin Bracewell when he was invited to help out his old friend, Prime Minister Winston Churchill during the Second World War. Thinking he was helping Britain against the Nazis, the Paisley-born man invented the "Ironsides," although in fact they were part of a Dalek trap to lure the Doctor. The Daleks revealed that Edwin was really a Dalek construct containing an Oblivion Continuum, a very powerful bomb. Amy Pond reminded Bracewell of his humanity and ultimately defused the threat. Some time later, Bracewell passed on a Vincent van Gogh painting depicting the TARDIS to Churchill, believing it to be a message for the Doctor.

ELTON POPE

As one of the original members of L.I.N.D.A. (London Investigative 'N' Detective Agency) Elton met the Tenth Doctor twice. The first time was when he was a small boy, on the night he discovered his mother had been killed by an Elemental Shade. This meeting started a life-long search for the mysterious stranger and his blue box that resulted in meeting fellow Doctor-hunters Ursula Blake, Colin Skinner, Bridget Sinclair, Bliss, and Victor Kennedy.

During his journey to find the Time Lord he met Jackie Tyler, though she quickly became suspicious of his motives. The ELO-loving musician was saved by the Tenth Doctor and Rose just before the Abzorbaloff consumed him, as it had already done to the rest of L.I.N.D.A. As a parting gift, the Doctor left Elton with the still-living head of his girlfriend Ursula, encased within a paving slab (and they did enjoy a "love life", apparently). Pope documented all his adventures on camera.

EMMA GRAYLING

This psychic and empath met Clara and the Eleventh Doctor in 1974 when they were ghost-hunting in Caliburn House. Emma was Professor Alec Palmer's assistant and used to capture images of the apparition thought to be haunting the building. After the Doctor's discovery that the apparition was, in fact, a real human from the future, Hila Tacorien, trapped in a pocket universe, the Time Lord used the strong psychic link to create a wormhole to the universe (with a little help from a Metebelis III crystal) and save Hila. A brave woman, Emma risked her life in doing so and then did so again when she helped the Doctor go back in to the pocket universe to reunite two alien creatures. Before departing, the Time Lord revealed that Hila was a descendant of both Emma and Alec, hence the link between them.

FRANK

This young Tennessee boy was living in Hooverville, New York, when he met the Tenth Doctor and Martha Jones in 1930. He worked for Mr. Diagoras on the construction of the Empire State Building. Frank was caught by Pig Slaves (gruesome experiments serving the Daleks) in the Manhattan sewers and made to serve the Cult of Skaro in their final experiment. Once the Doctor had defeated their plan, Frank returned to Hooverville with Pig Slave Laszlo, pleading with its residents to give him a home there.

GIBBIS

Difficult to call such a sniveling coward a "friend" but the Eleventh Doctor met this inhabitant of Tivoli (a planet whose population enjoyed being invaded and subjugated by alien forces) in a computer-generated hotel, which was actually a prison cell for the Nimon-like Minotaur beast. At every turn, the mole-like Gibbis upset and annoyed his fellow captives with his cowardice. Though not outwardly nasty or offensive, he did sacrifice Howie Spragg to the beast, and he managed to remain a survivor throughout, along with the Time Lord, Amy, and Rory. The hotel room displaying his biggest fear contained the Weeping Angels. The Doctor dropped Gibbis off after the Minotaur died.

GWEN COOPER

Part of Captain Jack Harkness' Torchwood team, Gwen Cooper learned much about the Doctor from her boss before actually meeting him. She was introduced to the Time Lord via the subwave communications network when he was aboard the TARDIS with Harkness and she was in the Torchwood Hub in Cardiff after just fending off an attack by a Dalek. Gwen and fellow Torchwood member Ianto Jones helped return the Earth to its rightful place after it was moved to the Medusa Cascade by Davros and his allies.

Gwen's family had been established for many years in the Welsh city; the Ninth Doctor and Rose had previously met a young maid, Gwyneth, during an aborted invasion by the Gelth, who bore a strong resemblance to Gwen. The Time Lord suggested this was due to "spatial genetic multiplicity." Gwen continued to serve alongside Captain Jack in Torchwood until it was disbanded.

HARRIET JONES

The UK MP for Flydale North met the Ninth Doctor in 10 Downing Street, where she had been hoping to see the Prime Minister. An attack by the Slitheen meant that her meeting would not happen and Jones was pitted against some inhabitants of Raxacorico-fallapatorius. She bravely helped the Time Lord and Rose Tyler as the trio survived a missile attack on the building. The Doctor was sure that he knew her, and remembered that she was responsible for a "Golden Age."

Not long after, Harriet became Prime Minister, and she had to deal with the Sycorax the next Christmas when their alien ship flew over London. She was transferred to their ship where she came face-to-face with the newly regenerated Tenth Doctor. At first skeptical of the new man, she quickly knew it was him after he reminded her of experiences together.

Harriet displeased the Time Lord by arranging for the ship's destruction, and he caused her downfall by simply murmuring the phrase, "Doesn't she look tired?" to her assistant. She was deposed and re-placed by Harold Saxon, an alias for the Master.

They did not meet in person again but Harriet developed the subwave network in order to help the Doctor battle the Daleks' invasion of Earth. She con-tacted Captain Jack Harness at Torchwood, Martha Jones, and Sarah Jane Smith but, for her, it was too late. She was exterminated by the Daleks.

IANTO JONES

Like the rest of Captain Jack's Torchwood crew, Ianto had already heard many stories about the Doctor before being introduced to him. After an attack on the Torchwood Hub by a Dalek (which had been frozen in a time lock), Harkness' lover came face-to-face with the Tenth Doctor over the subwave communications network, and took quite a shine to him.

JACKIE TYLER

Rose Tyler's mother proved to a formidable match for the Ninth Doctor when he met her not long after his regeneration at her flat in London. Jackie had been a widow and a single mum to Rose for many years, and took an instant shine to the mysterious stranger, who was investigating an Auton invasion at the time, when he appeared in her bedroom. Sadly, for her, the Doctor was immune to her flirting and charms and this saw the start of a rather rocky relationship between the two.

After the Time Lord returned Rose to London, the travelers discovered they had been away for a year— causing much unhappiness for Jackie. Rose's mum smacked the Doctor in the face, much to Rose's amusement. When a member of the Slitheen family attacked Jackie and Rose's boyfriend Mickey Smith, the pair fought it off successfully. Despite returning

Rose unharmed after an explosion at 10 Downing Street, Jackie was still suspicious of the Doctor, though grateful. When Rose was sent back from the far future, she helped her daughter gain entry to the TARDIS with the aid of a pick-up truck whose owner owed her a favor, but it wasn't until that Christmas when she actually saw the Time Lord again, now regenerated.

His new, more youthful appearance seemed to have warmed her heart as she looked after him . From here on the two would be closer, sharing kisses (sometimes a little uncomfortably for him) and pleasantries.

When Rose was off traveling with the Doctor, Jackie missed Rose hugely and worried tremendously, although she never let her daughter know. She was

also extremely protective of Rose, and when Elton Pope came snooping around, Jackie was all too wise to his escapades.

Jackie was reunited with a version of her dead husband Pete Tyler when the parallel version of him broke through in to her world. (The parallel version of her had been converted into a Cyberman some years earlier.) Although understandably surprised, the pair picked up from where they left off, as much as possible. It wasn't long, however, before the couple returned to the other world and started a new life. Jackie became pregnant within months, and she and Pete helped Rose, stuck in the parallel universe, to contact the Tenth Doctor for an emotional farewell on Bad Wolf Bay.

But this was not the last of the Doctor and Jackie's relationship. Jackie returned to our world to help defeat the Daleks in their invasion and creation of the Reality Bomb. She was taken to the Dalek Crucible along with a number of the Doctor's friends, and she helped in the destruction of the Dalek fleet. After a trip home in the TARDIS, which she was not allowed to pilot, she joked with the Doctor that she had named her son after him (he was actually called Tony).

* * *

JACKSON LAKE

It's not often the Doctor meets somebody who thinks he's the Doctor, but that's exactly what happened in London in 1851. Jackson believed that he was the Time Lord, complete with companion Rosita, TARDIS (really a hot air balloon), and sonic screwdriver (which was just a plain old screwdriver), when the Tenth Doctor, traveling alone, bumped into him. The two faced a Cybershade and the Cybermen before the Doctor revealed the truth about Jackson's identity.

Jackson carried a fob watch, not unlike Time Lords wishing to hide their true persona, but the Doctor noticed the initials "J.L" on it and deduced the truth. Lake had been affected by a Cyberman info stamp, which included information about the Doctor's history. His own memories had been replaced by the Time Lord's. Jackson was reunited with his son, whom he had lost on the same night his memories were altered. The Cybermen had been using child slave labor to build a Cyber King. The Doctor joined Jackson, Rosita, and his son for a Christmas meal before departing in the TARDIS.

JAKE SIMMONDS

The Tenth Doctor met Jake in a parallel version of Earth in London, where the youngster was part of a gang known as the Preachers, led by Ricky Smith (the parallel version of Mickey Smith). Jake helped out in the fight against John Lumic and his new Cybermen, ensuring that the UK was safe from the metal creatures. When Mickey decided to stay in the parallel world, he traveled with Jake to Paris.

During the Cybermen's invasion of the "normal" universe, Jake followed with Mickey and assisted in the battle against Cybermen and Daleks at Canary Wharf, London. Jake then returned to his own world.

JENNY FLINT

The Doctor's first meeting with Jenny is as yet unrecorded, although he prevented Jenny's death during that encounter. Jenny became maid (and lover) to Silurian Madame Vastra, and met the Eleventh Doctor when he gathered his own personal army to launch an attack on Kovarian and the Headless Monks at Demon's Run. When the Doctor retreated into depression after the loss of Amy Pond and Rory Williams, Jenny helped to look after the Time Lord. She teamed up with the Doctor, Vastra, and Sontaran Strax in Victorian London to combat an attack by the Great Intelligence and his Snowmen.

Jenny met the Doctor again in the Sweetville factory where she rescued him from captivity. Pleased to be restored to his former self (he was struck down with the "Crimson Horror"), the Time Lord planted a kiss on Flint, to which the lesbian maid responded with a slap! Jenny helped defeat the threat of Winifred Gillyflower and her minions with her considerable leather-clad physical prowess.

Soon after, Jenny was murdered by the Whispermen servants of the Great Intelligence during a psychic "conference call" with Vastra, Strax, River Song, and Clara Oswald. She was transported to Trenzalore where she was brought back to life quickly by her Sontaran friend and where she met the Doctor once more. The Great Intelligence's movement through the Doctor's timestream erased Jenny from existence, only for her to be brought back when Clara set things straight.

JOAN REDFERN

Just before World War I, this nurse met the Tenth Doctor when he taught at Farringham School for Boys. The Gallifreyan had used a Chameleon Arch to hide his Time Lord physiology from the Family of Blood and hid on Earth, posing as a teacher called John Smith, with his companion Martha Jones, who was working as a maid at the same school. "Smith" was oblivious to his former life as a time-traveler (though he sketched some of his memories in his journal), and fell in love with Joan.

Joan cared very much for the boys in her school; violence was abhorrent to her, since she had lost her husband in the Boer War.

She and Smith were very happy together for a short time until the Family of Blood tracked the Doctor down. To save the school, its pupils and staff, the Doctor had to regain his memories. Once he was in his normal form, Joan became distant towards him and even cold, now the possibilities of their future together had vanished. The Time Lord asked her to accompany him in the TARDIS, but she refused.

Almost one hundred years later, Joan's great-granddaughter Verity Newman wrote a book called *A Journal of Impossible Things*, based on the history of John Smith and Joan, using his journal. The Tenth Doctor visited Verity at a book signing where she revealed that her great-grandmother died happy.

JOHN RIDDELL

Game hunter Riddell joined the Eleventh Doctor, Amy, Rory, Brian, and Queen Nefertiti on board the Silurian Ark in 2367. Despite his rather outdated and misogynistic outlook on his female companions (not to mention Amy's dislike of his love for hunting animals), his charm won them over as he hunted down dinosaurs and battled against Solomon and his robots. He was joined by the Egyptian Queen on Earth back in his own twentieth century after their clear chemistry brought them together.

KATE STEWART

During the Year of the Slow Invasion, as alien being the Shakri used his mysterious cubes to infiltrate the Earth, Kate was Head of Scientific Research at UNIT and called upon the help of the Doctor. Although she tried to keep the information from the Time Lord, he knew her father was his old friend the Brigadier; Kate had dropped "Lethbridge" from her surname as she didn't want any favorable treatment from UNIT because of her parentage. She and the Doctor shared a tender moment together before he departed, safe in the knowledge that UNIT was in good hands.

But this was not to be the last time Kate would face the Doctor. She would summon her father's old friend to London and pass on an envelope with instructions from Queen Elizabeth I. Kate would also face the threat of The Zygons, along with the Doctors.

KAZRAN SARDICK

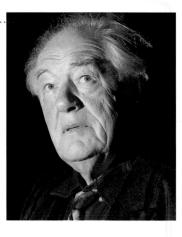

This cantankerous bully was both a villain and a friend to the Doctor. The Eleventh Doctor asked him to allow a space liner carrying the newly married Amy and Rory to land in Sardicktown on Ember since Kazran controlled access to the clouds. He point blank refused. This caused the Doctor to go back in time to change the man's ways.

Visiting Kazran as a boy, they encountered a flying shark, indigenous to the planet; as a result, they became firm friends. During this encounter the pair uncovered Abigail Pettigrew, "sleeping" in cryogenic suspension in one of Kazran's father's chambers. The young Sardick took an instant liking to the beautiful singer, who was in fact incurably ill and was in suspension until a cure could be found. He and the Doctor visited her every Christmas Eve, and over a number of years the pair fell in love.

However, when he learned that she only could survive for a very short time outside suspension, Kazran had to stop these meetings, which made the young man deeply unhappy. However when this younger Kazran saw his unhappy older self, he was reminded of the cruelness of his own father, and the older Kazran then helped the Doctor rescue his friends and the space liner. Kazran was reunited with his love Abigail, and the shark he met as a youngster for one last time.

LARRY NIGHTINGALE

Video store worker Larry was a huge fan of the Tenth Doctor before they physically met. Nightingale had found a number of DVDs that all featured the same Easter Egg showing the Time Lord having a one-sided conversation to camera, with the odd interjection from Martha Jones. "The angels have the phone box" was his favorite quote.

Larry did not realize for some time that his sister Kathy had been sent back in time by a Weeping Angel but then found himself under attack by a group of the stone aliens. He survived thanks to the Angels being tricked into looking at one another.

The following year, Larry finally saw the Doctor and Martha in person, as they ran by his store. He was too shocked to speak to them, but all was well in his life, having finally made a special connection with his sister's friend, Sally Sparrow.

LIZ TEN

Liz Ten—or to provide her proper title, Queen Elizabeth X—knew all about the Doctor and his past long before the Eleventh Doctor and Amy Pond visited her aboard Starship UK. Although she thought she was only aged fifty, Liz was actually centuries old and had been continuously ruling the Starship, although the government wiped her mind whenever she came close to learning the truth about the Star Whale which piloted the ship. Acting like a superhero, the Queen patrolled among her citizens, looking for the truth, which the Doctor helped her find.

In 5145, some time after she had set matters straight on the starship, Liz X caught River Song in the Royal Collection trying to steal a van Gogh painting. After a brief tete-a-tete at gunpoint, she let the professor go free, believing she would help the Doctor.

LORNA BUCKET

Brave Lorna had waited all her life to see the Doctor again, and became a Cleric of the Church in order to do so. As a youngster, she had met him in the Gamma Forests where he told her to "run!" In her native language, "Doctor" translated as "mighty warrior," and Lorna wanted to be a part of his life. She presented Amy Pond with a prayer leaf at Demon's Run shortly before she tried to help the Eleventh Doctor in the battle; sadly, she was killed in the conflict. The Doctor was not sure if he had met her at all, or if he was yet to, but she had won his admiration.

LUKE SMITH

Adopted son of journalist Sarah Jane Smith, Luke learned of an impending Dalek attack with his mother but remained at home in Ealing, London. Using the subwave communications network, Luke contacted the Doctor, and together with his own computer Mr. Smith and K9 helped bring the TARDIS back to Earth. Luke met the Tenth Doctor again at his mother's wedding, and finally, very briefly, when the Time Lord prevented him from being the victim of a road accident.

LYNDA MOSS

A contestant on the Games Station in the year 200,100, Lynda met the Ninth Doctor when he was transported to the Big Brother house. He instantly took a shine to the girl, and when she clarified the spelling of her name he took immense pleasure in calling her, "Lynda with a Y!" Their relationship was flirtatious from the start, sharing a love for reality television.

The couple escaped the Big Brother compound, met up with Captain Jack Harkness, and discovered Rose Tyler in The Weakest Link studio, where the Doctor's companion was disintegrated in front of their eyes. Lynda helped the Doctor against the Daleks who had invaded the satellite although she died doing so.

MADAME VASTRA

When the Eleventh Doctor was gathering his army to attack Demon's Run, he called upon the help of Vastra. along with her maid, Jenny, in his fight against Madame Kovarian. Some years earlier, the Time Lord had found her in the London Underground where she was taking revenge on workers for the deaths of her sisters. During the battle, the Silurian wielded two swords against the Headless Monks, displaying much skill and prowess.

While living in London, during what the Doctor referred to as his "dark times" following the loss of Amy and Rory, Vastra looked out for the Doctor and assisted him, alongside Jenny, Strax and Clara Oswald, against the might of Dr. Simeon, and the Great Intelligence. During this struggle, Vastra watched Clara die. The Doctor and Vastra were reunited at the Sweetville Factory shortly after. Vastra had discovered the image of the Time Lord on the eyes of a dead man, leading her and her gang to investigate, rescue the Doctor, and defeat Winifred Gillyflower.

Shortly after this, when interrogating serial killer Clarence de Marco, the Doctor's name came up, as did the word "Trenzalore." Using a special mental "conference call," Vastra linked up with Jenny, Strax, River Song, and the twenty-first century version of Clara Oswald to share her news. Sadly, for her, the Whispermen attacked, killing her wife, Jenny.

Vastra, Strax, and Jenny's corpse (which was resuscitated by Strax) were taken to Trenzalore where they met the Doctor, Clara, and the Great Intelligence, who had taken to mimicking Dr. Simeon's appearance. The Intelligence stepped into the Time Lord's timestream and reversed many moments from the Doctor's life, including Jenny being saved by Strax, and Vastra's friendship with the Sontaran. They fought and she disintegrated him. Luckily, for them and the universe, Clara was on hand to reverse the Great Intelligence's actions, bringing Jenny and Strax back to life. Vastra then looked on as the Doctor stepped into his own timestream.

MALCOLM TAYLOR

A huge fan of the Time Lord, knowing all about his past adventures on Earth, Malcolm worked for UNIT as a scientific advisor, the role the Doctor had taken for some time years earlier. Before he met his "greatest hero" in person, the quirky Welshman was in contact with the Doctor by phone after a bus the Time Lord had been traveling in was transported via a wormhole to the planet of San Helios. Though slightly irked by his new fan's enthusiasm, the Doctor came to be very fond of the scientist and his unique units of measurements such as "Malcolms" and "Bernards." When the two men finally met, after Taylor had helped save the day, Malcolm told the Doctor, "I love you!" to which the time-traveler responded with a smile and a point.

OSGOOD

As a scientific advisor at UNIT, this young lady was most definitely a fan of the Doctor (particularly his fourth incarnation). Osgood worked alongside Kate Stewart and met the Eleventh Doctor and Clara when the TARDIS was picked up and transferred to London. Thrilled to meet the Time Lord, she wore her scarf which was not unlike a certain scarf worn by the Fourth Doctor. Osgood is a descendant of Sgt. Osgood, a UNIT technical officer who served under Brigadier Lethbridge-Stewart and helped out the Third Doctor at Devil's End, fighting against the Master and Azal.

MADGE ARWELL

Three years before he came to work for Madge Arwell and her family at Christmas 1941 as their Caretaker, the Eleventh Doctor was helped back to the TARDIS by Mrs. Arwell when he fell to Earth after falling from a spaceship, although, because he had put his spacesuit on in a hurry back to front, she never saw his face.

The Time Lord helped Madge come to terms with loss of her husband Reg by looking after her children, Lily and Cyril. Following the Doctor and her children through a dimensional gate, Mrs. Arwell proved to be quite a formidable force as she saved the Time Lord, and her children, by piloting a vehicle, vacated by three Harvest Rangers, toward them. She also piloted the mother ship of the Wooden King and Queen through the Time Vortex and, in the process, ensured her husband's death was averted. The couple were then reunited back on Earth.

PETE TYLER

Our world's Pete Tyler, Rose's father, was a rather disorganized and unreliable man who died when Rose was tiny, leaving her to be brought up by her mother Jackie. When Rose asked to see how her father died, the Ninth Doctor took her back to 1987. However, Rose caused major problems by insisting on going back again, and then saving him from being killed in a car accident. As a result, the Reapers came through the wounds in time and slowly began to devour everything. When Pete realized who Rose was and what was happening, he sacrificed himself, which reasserted the time line. His daughter was with him when he died.

In a parallel universe, Tyler was much more successful and had built up his own empire as an entrepreneur with his many inventions. As in our world, Pete was married to Jackie, though there, their marriage was rocky, and they did not have a daughter. Tyler met the Tenth Doctor and Rose and helped defeat John Lumic and the Cybermen, although his Jackie Tyler was converted into a Cyberman and killed. When he was presented with the evidence as to who Rose was, Pete denied that she was his daughter, and ran off, leaving her to return to her own world with the Time Lord.

It wasn't too long before he traveled into her world, alongside Mickey Smith and Jake Simmonds, following the Cybermen and the Daleks through the Void. Pete assisted during the Battle of Canary Wharf and ultimately saved Rose from being sucked into the Void at the very last moment, taking her back to his world. By now, he had accepted Rose as his own daughter and met our world's version of Jackie, with whom he fell in love; Pete helped Rose find a connection with the Doctor in Bad Wolf Bay. Pete and Jackie later had a son called Tony.

Alternate Universe Note:
In an alternative timeline, Pete and Jackie had a rocky marriage and did not have a daughter.

PORRIDGE

This little guy was helping out Mr. Webley in his World of Wonders (formerly Hedgewick's World of Wonders) by controlling a deactivated Cyberman in a chess game. The ruse was uncovered by Artie and Angie Maitland, who were visiting the abandoned theme park with the Eleventh Doctor and Clara. After an attack by Cybermites, Porridge fought alongside Clara and the troops based there against the newly upgraded Cybermen. After being confronted by Angie, he admitted that he was the Emperor, ruler of a thousand galaxies, who had activated the desolator to destroy three million Cybermen. Porridge contacted the Imperial Flag Ship and he and the survivors were transferred there before the Cyberiad exploded. Describing the position of Emperor as the "loneliest job in the universe," the diminutive ruler asked Clara to marry him and keep him company. Sadly, for him, she refused.

PROFESSOR GRISENKO

Working on Russian submarine the Firebird, the Professor thought he had discovered a mammoth in the ice at the North Pole in 1983. But, in fact, it was an Ice Warrior, who escaped from its armor and wreaked havoc. A brave man, Grisenko saved Clara from the clutches of Skaldak and, in turn, put his own life on the line. As a fellow scientist, he and the Doctor became friends quickly while the Russian demonstrated his love for British music by constantly singing out loud to Ultravox and Duran Duran on his Walkman.

QUEEN NEFERTITI

Dubbed "Neffy" by the Eleventh Doctor, the young queen fell for the Time Lord in a big way after he saved her people in Egypt from giant locusts. He took her to the Silurian Ark in 2367 where they faced Solomon, his robots, and some dinosaurs. She offered herself as a sacrifice to Solomon to save the lives of the Doctor, Amy, Rory, Riddell, and Brian Williams. Solomon took her with him, but the Doctor rescued her. During their enforced time together, Nefertiti and Riddell had a combative and flirtatious relationship, which continued when they settled down together on Earth in the early twentieth century.

THE QUEEN OF YEARS

Clara befriended this young girl, whose real name was Merry, when visiting the Rings of Ahkaten with the Eleventh Doctor. The Queen of Years was required to sing in front of thousands of residents of the planet, including representatives of numerous different species, but was scared of getting the song wrong. Clara managed to convince her into performing, only to find that Merry was taken by the very god she singing to. The Doctor and Clara saved her and, in the process, defeated the god (actually a parasitic planet that fed on memories) through song and their own valuable memories.

RITA

Poor lovely Rita, one of the inhabitants of the computer-generated hotel, on a prison ship containing the Minotaur, a Nimon-like being. A devout Muslim, Rita was incredibly smart and displayed her intelligence with ease and a liveliness, so much so that the Eleventh Doctor briefly considered replacing Amy with her. The two quickly became friends as they discussed the threat at hand, so her death came as a great shock and upset the Time Lord. Rita kept talking to him while waiting for the Minotaur to come for her, but bravely wanted to face death alone. The cameras monitoring her were switched off before she was killed. In the room that displayed her greatest fears was her own father, angry at her exam results.

SABALOM GLITZ

A rather sneaky and shady fellow although he would probably have preferred being thought of as a loveable rogue, Glitz met the Doctor on three occasions.

Their first encounter was on the planet Ravolox during the Doctor's Sixth incarnation when he was traveling with Peri. Glitz, accompanied by his buddy Dibber, was trying to destroy the black light system so he could steal secrets from Drathro (see ROBOTS).

This incident formed part of the evidence at the Doctor's trial, and the Master brought Glitz to the space station where the trial was

taking place. Glitz's testimony was key in helping the Doctor reveal the machinations of the Time Lords and the Valeyard, and Glitz assisted the Doctor when he was caught in the illusions within the Matrix. The Doctor asked the Time Lords to set Glitz free, believing him, essentially, to be a good man.

Their paths crossed again on Iceworld, when the Seventh Doctor was traveling with Melanie Bush. Glitz was in debt to the cruel ruler of Iceworld, and the Doctor helped him to extricate himself. Mel decided to travel with Glitz in a stolen spaceship he christened the Nosferatu II.

SALLY SPARROW

In 2007, amateur photographer Sally Sparrow found an unusual message addressed to her beneath wallpaper in a disused house. It was from the Doctor who was trapped back in 1969 and needed Sally's help to retrieve the TARDIS. Returning to the house, her friend Kathy Nightingale was touched by a Weeping Angel and sent back in time to 1920. Through a series of DVD Easter Eggs, Sally realized the bespectacled stranger had advice for her. Their conversation through time was recorded by her friend's brother, Larry, but the Weeping Angels, about whom the Doctor had warned them, attacked. They followed the Time Lord's advice and found the TARDIS which dematerialized around them, causing the Weeping Angels to become harmless once more.

Sally gave the notes Larry had made to the Doctor the following year, although he was slightly confused, since the events referred to had not yet happened for him. He took her advice and notes, and went on his way. Sally and Larry never looked back. Or blinked.

STRAX

When the Eleventh Doctor was gathering his personal army for an attack against Madame Kovarian, the Sontaran Strax, working as field nurse, was approached in 4037 at the Battle of Zaruthstra. Owing the Time Lord a debt, he abandoned his post and joined the Doctor's crusade. Strax died at Demon's Run but was brought back to life by Madame Vastra and her lover Jenny Flint, to whom he then owed his life.

Strax returned with them to Victorian London, and helped the Doctor against the Great Intelligence. He became accustomed to his new time period, using his weekends off to travel to Glasgow where he partook in fights with the locals. After an incident at the Sweetville factory, where Strax had a chance to flex his gun-loving muscles, he was transported to Trenzalore by the Whispermen where he met the Doctor once more.

After the Doctor's timeline was changed by the Great Intelligence, Strax's memory of his friendship with Vastra was wiped, and after a fight, she reluctantly took his life. When Clara restored the "normal" timeline, Strax returned to life again.

SYLVIA NOBLE

Donna Noble's mother was a rather difficult woman who didn't suffer fools gladly, and showed little respect for her family. When her daughter's wedding failed to happen, Sylvia dismissed Donna's reason for disappearing from the event out of hand.

During the Sontaran attack, Sylvia met the Tenth Doctor, and was not impressed at his failure to save her father, Wilf, from an ATMOS device (Sylvia smashed the car window to free him). She and her father were rescued from a Dalek attack by Rose Tyler, at which point Wilf told her that Donna had been traveling with the Doctor. When the Doctor was forced to wipe Donna's memories of him, he returned her daughter to Sylvia, who asked the Doctor to leave and not return.

When the Master attacked, Sylvia did not want anything to do with the Doctor, worried about what his presence might do to Donna. However she finally realized that the Doctor was humanity's best hope when Gallifrey appeared in the skies, and she was almost welcoming when he brought Wilf home. They met one last time, at Donna's wedding; the Doctor had bought a winning lottery ticket with a pound he had borrowed from Sylvia's late husband, Geoff. In the parallel world, created by the Trickster's Brigade, Sylvia was equally unsympathetic, criticizing Donna at every turn. Along with her father Wilf, the three of them were evacuated to Leeds, where Sylvia succumbed to depression and admitted that Donna had always been a disappointment to her. This time-line was closed off by Donna's self-sacrifice.

THOMAS KINCADE BRANNIGAN

Cat person Brannigan encountered the Tenth Doctor in New New York City in the year 5,000,000,053 when the Time Lord slipped into his flying car during a very long traffic jam. He, his wife, and their kittens had been traveling for twelve years, moving only six miles, but thanks to the Gallifreyan, with a little help from the Face of Boe, they were free to rise to the surface when the motorway was opened upwards.

TIM LATIMER

The Tenth Doctor met pupil Tim Latimer at Farringham School for Boys in 1913 when he was hiding from the Family of Blood. The Doctor had used a Chameleon Arch to store his Time Lord DNA inside a fob watch, and as far as Tim and the other pupils were concerned, he was teacher John Smith. The schoolboy telepathically felt the resonance of the Time Lord through the fob watch and foresaw his future on the battle fields in World War I, giving him knowledge that would save his life. When Scarecrows brought to life by the Family of Blood attacked his school he refused to fight, and was called a "coward" by his peers.

Many years later on Remembrance Day, the Doctor and Martha Jones visited elderly Tim Latimer, now wheelchair-bound. The old man recognized his former friends, thankful they saved his life; he still retained the fob watch.

TRINITY WELLS

American newscaster Trinity never met the
Doctor, in any of his bodies, but she reported on
many alien threats to Earth for the news channel
AMNN, including the Slitheen attack on Downing
Street, the Sycorax ship hovering above Earth, UK
Prime Minster Harold Saxon's first contact with the
Toclafane, and the Sonataran's
ATMOS attack. She also covered
US President Barack Obama's ad-
dress to the world shortly before
the Master used the Immortality
Gate to imprint his own body on
Obama, Wells and everyone else in
the world.

She was returned to her normal
self after Rassilon reversed the
renegade's actions.

TOSHIKO SATO

Standing in for a colleague, as a favor, Toshiko was the
doctor on hand to investigate a Space Pig, the pilot
of a ship which had crash-landed in London's River
Thames, after smacking into Big Ben. She briefly met
the Ninth Doctor, though she was completely out of
her depth as this was not her field of expertise.

Toshiko was in fact a member of
Torchwood Cardiff, and died in the
course of duty some time later. However, her legacy lived on through her
invention of a "time lock" which saved
both Ianto Jones and Gwen Cooper
from a Dalek attack in the Torchwood
Hub during their Earth invasion and
the subsequent transference of the
planet to the Medusa Cascade.

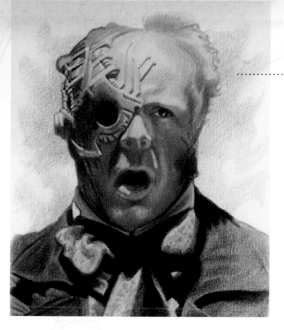

THE WHITE GUARDIAN

This eternal being chose the Fourth Doctor to seek out the pieces of the Key to Time, a device which allowed its holder to put the universe on hold and reset the balance. He had the power to pull the TARDIS out of time, and the Doctor treated him with great respect when they met. Apparently a harmless elderly man, dressed in white, sipping sherry from a glass, the White Guardian asked the Doctor to collect all six pieces of the Key so that order could be restored to the galaxy, and he warned the Time Lord that his counterpart, the Black Guardian, was also seeking the Key.

The Doctor, Romana, and K9 succeeded in their quest and brought the Key to Time together, presumably allowing the Guardian to achieve his aims (although he was never seen doing so). Some years later, when the Fifth Doctor was traveling with Tegan Jovanka and Turlough, the White Guardian appeared again at the end of a race by beings known as the Eternals seeking "Enlightenment." The Time Lord was offered a diamond crystal, containing huge powers, not unlike the Key to Time, but he refused to take it.

MR. WEBLEY

Hiding in Hedgewick's World of Wonders, Mr. Webley was looking for a way to leave the amusement park for six months before the Eleventh Doctor, Clara, Artie, and Angie landed for a day out. Introducing himself as "Impresario Webley," he had been unaware the park had closed down when he landed there some time earlier but was happy to show the TARDIS crew around his world of wonders while he hid from the soldiers stationed there. Webley let Artie play a game of chess against a deactivated Cyberman, happy to take a sandwich as payment. Soon after, the Cybermen returned and partly upgraded Webley along with Artie and Angie. Once the children were restored, Webley, under Cyber control, attacked the pair, only to be stopped by his partner, Porridge. Webley was not returned to his former self and died in the explosion of the Cyberiad.

Turlough threw the prize at the Black Guardian, thus temporarily removing him. Before he vanished, the White Guardian warned the Doctor that the Black Guardian would seek revenge and would always be present as long as the White Guardian lived.

WILFRED MOTT

Newspaper vendor Wilf had a fleeting meeting with the Tenth Doctor when the time-traveler popped down to Earth with Astrid Peth from the spaceship cruise liner, the Titanic, one Christmas Eve. Wilf was proud to stay in London, despite the likelihood of an alien attack, but was left perplexed when the couple vanished in front of his eyes.

The Doctor didn't realize that Wilf was, in fact, the grandfather of Donna Noble, whom he had met the previous Christmas. After the incident with the Adipose, Wilf saw his beloved granddaughter fly off into the sky in the TARDIS. He then came face-to-face with the Doctor during the Sontarans' attempted takeover of the world.

During the Daleks' invasion of Earth, Wilf fought against the intergalactic menace using a paintball gun, but was saved from extermination by Rose Tyler. He was confined to his own home as the Earth was transported to and from the Medusa Cascade. Donna was returned to him by the Doctor after he erased her memory of all their journeys together, something which saddened Wilf immensely.

Also caring deeply for the Doctor, Wilf set up the Silver Cloak, a group of older people looking out for the Time Lord. When the two men met again, they sat in a cafe and discussed their woes, with the Time Lord breaking down into tears with his old friend. More horror was to come, however, with the return of the Master, who Wilf had visions of in his sleep. The pair confronted the renegade when he transformed the human race into versions of himself (the Doctor protected Wilf by sealing him in a protective cubicle with Vinvocci glass) and eventually escaped his clutches.

During this time Wilf was also having visions of a mysterious woman. She came to him to provide help, advising Wilf what to do in order to help the Doctor. No one else could see her but Wilf met her both in a church and on a Vinvocci spaceship, and saw her on television.

Ultimately, Wilf inadvertently was responsible for the Tenth Doctor's regeneration. The solemn knocks on the glass he gave the Doctor to indicate that he was still trapped inside a cubicle fitted the prophecy of "knock four times" that the Doctor knew heralded his end. In order to release the lock on Wilf's cubicle, the Doctor had to go into another cubicle into which the full force of the radiation would be transferred. Wilf was saved but the radiation initiated the beginning of the Doctor's regenerative process. The Doctor managed to stave off the regeneration for some time, traveling to visit old friends, and on Donna's wedding day, gave Wilf and his daughter Sylvia a winning lottery ticket.

Ever the gentleman, Wilf was easily identifiable by his unique whistle and skip as well as his respectful salutes, and his love for the Queen and telescopes.

In the parallel world, created by the Trickster's Brigade, Wilf found himself living in cramped conditions in a house in Leeds after London was destroyed by the spaceship Titanic. He befriended Rocco Colasanto (though their friendship was to be short-lived when the Italian was taken away to a death camp) and told Donna that the stars were going out, which led to her contacting UNIT. This version of Wilf disappeared when the time line was restored.

YVONNE HARTMAN

"People person" Yvonne was in charge of Torchwood in Canary Wharf, London, when their long-sought target the Doctor turned up on their doorstep Hartman was delighted when the Tenth Doctor and his TARDIS were located and welcomed him warmly to the facility. Hartman was proud of what she had achieved with Torchwood and proud to be a part of the British Empire as she showed off the items they had retrieved. Yvonne was currently investigating what the Doctor later identified as a "Void Ship," which the Torchwood building was built round.

Yvonne eventually agreed to stop the "ghost shifts" after the Doctor advised that more cracks in time and space could burn up the planet. But it was too late: the Cybermen had already planned their route through, and they were swiftly followed by the Daleks. Yvonne was captured by the Cybermen and converted. Her personality though managed to survive the process, and she died as a Cyberman proclaiming, "I did my duty," blasting other Cybermen with a gun.

ROBOTS

Well, not just robots. Here is a selection of some of the
finest (and some admittedly not so fine) robots and androids that
the Doctor has had to face over the years.

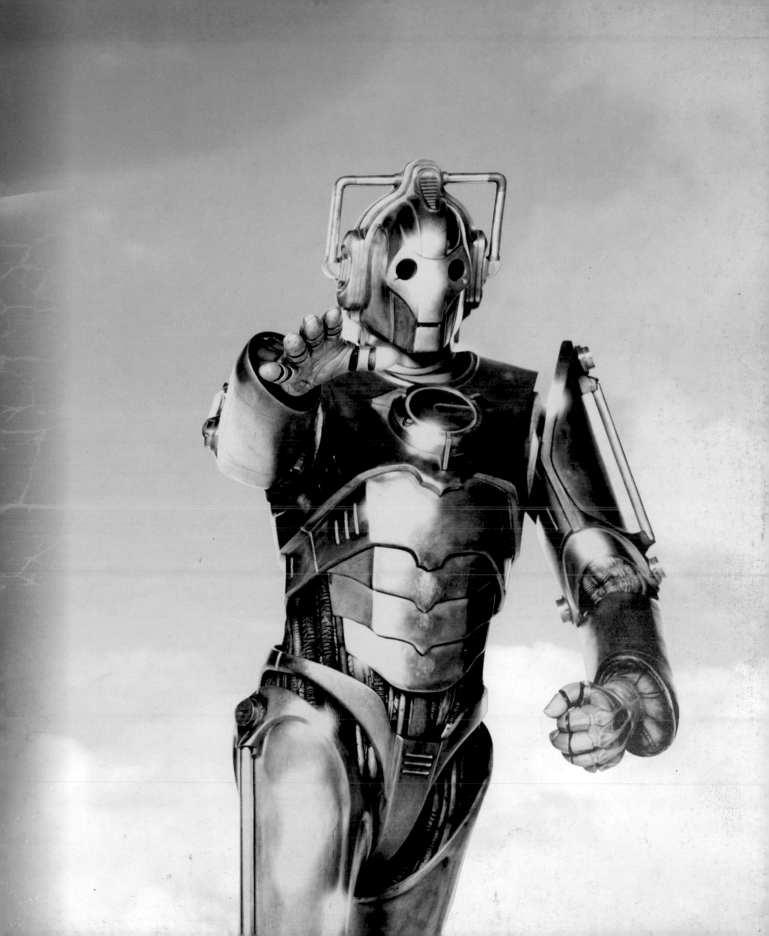

ADHERENTS OF THE REPEATED MEME

The Ninth Doctor and Rose came into contact with these tall, cloaked mysteries on Platform One in the year 5.5/apple/26 (five billion A.D.). Initially they were introduced as hailing from Financial Family Seven, but they were later revealed to be mechanical pawns of the last human, Cassandra. When he realized their true nature, the Time Lord pulled off a creature's arm saying, "A Repeated Meme is just an idea. And that's all they are, an idea," before laying blame for almost committing mass murder at Cassandra's door.

CLOCKWORK DROIDS

These scary droids came from the fifty-first century but were stalking Madame de Pompadour in France at various points in the eighteenth century. Their characteristic tick-tocking gave their presence away and their masked faces added to their horror. However, their interior intricate clockwork mechanisms were a thing of beauty, according to the Tenth Doctor. Accompanied by Rose Tyler and Mickey Smith, he uncovered their plan to fix their ship, the SS *Madame de Pompadour,* by obtaining the brain of a thirty-seven-year-old Madame de Pompadour.

The programming on the former maintenance droids was damaged in an ion storm, and they started by using pieces of the human crew to repair their ship. They were capable of engineering time windows, or "magic doors" as Rose referred to them. Once the Time Lord broke the connection between the droids and their ship, they ceased functioning, with no purpose to serve.

ANNE DROID

The host of the quiz show *The Weakest Link* on the Game Station in the year 200,100, this robot was based on human female Anne Robinson, a television presenter who presented the game on British and American television in the early twenty-first century. Armed with a Transmat beam, it shot a laser at failing contestants, one of which was Rose Tyler, apparently destroying them. The Anne Droid managed to defeat one invading Dalek although it was immediately destroyed in retaliation by another.

CYBERMEN ANDROID

Two androids were created by the Cybermen to guard a bomb that was hidden underground in a tunnel of caves. It formed part of their plan to destroy Earth in 2526, when an intergalactic military conference was taking place with a view to entering a war with the Cybermen. An expedition team investigating the cave system lost numerous members killed by the androids, protecting the hatch to the bomb. Undetectable by human scanners, and with laser weapons in their hands, they were able to move freely around the caves.

The Cybermen kept in close contact with their servants, receiving images and transmitting orders, but the Fifth Doctor managed to help the expedition team by confusing the androids and presenting them with two different priorities: survival or protecting the hatch behind which the bomb lay. Although the androids were resistant to human weapons, they could be destroyed with concentrated fire.

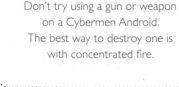

Fan Fact Note:
Don't try using a gun or weapon
on a Cybermen Android.
The best way to destroy one is
with concentrated fire.

DRATHRO

The Sixth Doctor met this L3 maintenance robot on the planet Ravolox. Drathro was placed in an underground habitat known as "Marb Station" after being created by sleepers (astronauts from the Andromeda constellation in suspended animation) to protect them and guard their secrets.

The robot used hundreds of humans, or "work units," as well as a small service robot, L1, but was opposed by Queen Katryca. She was killed by Drathro during an attack on the habitat, but the Doctor managed to disable the robot by shutting down its power source, a black light converter.

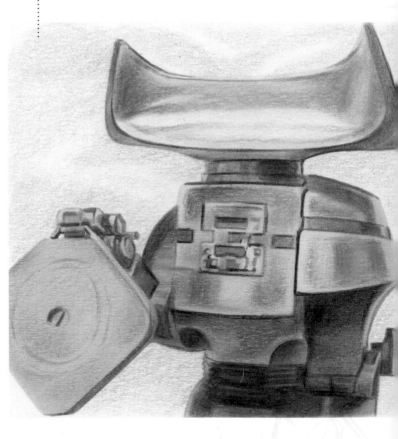

DUMS, VOCS & SUPER-VOCS

The Fourth Doctor and Leela found themselves at the mercy of these deadly robots when the couple arrived on a sand miner. A small crew of humanoids was assisted by a team of robots with a distinct hierarchy. Lowest were the Dums, black-colored units, unable to speak and mostly kept away from human contact; interaction with the crew was carried out by the Vocs, pale green units who could talk, perform control deck duties and even give massages; and at the top was a single Super-Voc, designated SV7, a silver-tunic wearing highly intelligent unit which controlled its fellow robots.

These units were mass-produced and used throughout many systems, designed to help human life. Although the robots were unable to harm a human, or let one be harmed, a scientist named Taren Capel from Kaldor City reprogrammed the robots to kill all the crew, as well as the Doctor and Leela, as part of a rebellion. The robots used voice recognition programs to obey Capel, but when his vocal cords were affected by helium, making his voice rise in pitch, he ceased to be immune from their rampage, and he was killed by SV7.

Although robots were popular within this particular civilization, some humans did suffer from Grimwade's Syndrome, or robophobia, where those affected believed they were "surrounded by walking, talking dead men."

GADGET

This small unit was part of Bowie Base One, a human colony set up on Mars in the year 2059. Gadget was remote-controlled with no internal sentience, receiving its instructions via a pair of special control gloves. The Tenth Doctor first met Gadget after he landed on the planet, and was taken by the robot to the base, commanded by Adelaide Brooke. With a penchant for intoning "Gadget!! Gadget!" every now and then, much to the Time Lord's displeasure, the wheeled machine was also used like a Segway. To save the inhabitants of Bowie Base One, the Doctor dispatched Gadget to the TARDIS so it could bring the time machine back to help. Once on Earth, and the connection with its base gone, Gadget shut down.

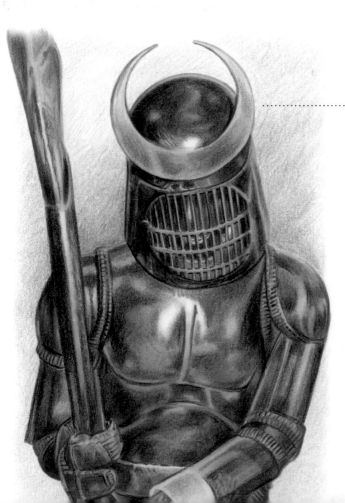

GUNDAN

Built to fight against the Tharils by their slaves, the Gundan robots were fierce in appearance: heavily armored and equally heavily armed. The robots could survive the time winds that existed between the time lines in which they walked, through the Gateway and into the past. The robots' purpose was fulfilled after the humans rebelled and vanquished the Tharils.

GUNSLINGER

Not a robot you say? True. The Gunslinger, whom the Eleventh Doctor, Amy, and Rory met in Mercy, Nevada, in 1870, was actually a cyborg. His name was Kahler-Tek who had been experimented on by Kahler-Jex, along with many others, some of whom didn't survive, in the hope of creating a weapon as part of the ongoing war on their homeworld, Kahler.

After the war ended, Tek tracked down the scientists who worked on him and executed them. The search for his final quarry, Kahler-Jex, led him to Mercy. The Gunslinger, as he became known by local inhabitants, threatened to kill the entire town if his target was not handed over. The Eleventh Doctor convinced Kahler-Tek to stay on and protect Mercy after Jex committed suicide.

HANDBOTS

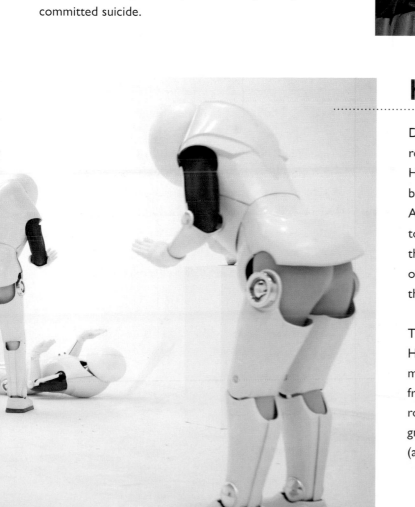

Despite their faceless and chilling appearance, these robots were intended to help. The 17th Generation Handroid Handbot 8001s were medical robots based in the Two Streams Facility on the planet Apalapucia. Although their medicine was designed to help species with two hearts, their "kindness," as they referred to it, was deadly to humans; one touch of the robot's hand would be enough to render them unconscious.

The Eleventh Doctor, Rory, and Amy came across the Handbots on their visit to Apalapucia but the two men soon became separated in time (but not space) from Amy. She was left to fend for herself against the robots for decades by herself; capturing one, reprogramming it, removing its hands and naming it Rory (and also drawing a smiley face on it).

HOST

The Tenth Doctor bumped into these service robots, while vacationing on the starship *Titanic* one Christmas above the planet Earth. The Hosts were designed to help passengers with any queries, using calm voices to assist. They were controlled by the Titanic's owner, Max Capricorn, who used them in his plan to crash the starship into the Earth, and they displayed hostility to anyone, such as the Doctor, who opposed them.

The robots looked like cloaked angels, with detachable halos, which they used as weapons when the Time Lord and the surviving passengers tried to escape. After Max Capricorn died, they were controlled by the Doctor.

K1 ROBOT

Built and created by Professor J.P. Kettlewell, this was designed in order to help humanity, by carrying out tasks deemed dangerous or hazardous, such as mining radioactive material. Programmed not to kill or harm humans—if it did so, its computer mind would undergo the equivalent of a nervous breakdown—it was made from what Kettlewell dubbed "living metal," so it could actually grow.

Kettlewell was unfortunately killed by his own creation, after altering the robot's programming to serve the ends of the Scientific Reform Society, and, as predicted, the robot went "mad," vowing to destroy humanity. When the Brigadier used a disintegrator gun on it, K1's living metal absorbed the power and the robot grew to an enormous size. The Doctor, assisted by Harry Sullivan, was able to apply a liquid virus which attacked the living metal and cut the creature back down to size.

KAMELION

This shape-shifting android was one of only two robots to travel as the Doctor's companion in his TARDIS. Kamelion could accurately replicate the physical form, speech patterns and personas of anyone. The Fifth Doctor brought it aboard after uncovering a plot by the Master to stop the Magna Carta being signed in 1215.

The renegade Time Lord had escaped Xeriphas with Kamelion, a weapon from that planet. He used the android to impersonate King John, but the Doctor gained control of Kamelion after a mind battle with the Master. A grateful Kamelion joined the TARDIS crew in his normal, robotic form, although he was rarely seen during his time with the Doctor.

The Master regained psychic control over Kamelion to lure the Doctor to the planet Sarn. The android assisted the Master after an accident with his Tissue Compression Eliminator had left the renegade Time Lord reduced in size. Still under the control of the Master, Kamelion was almost fatally injured on Sarn. Left in great pain, it asked the Doctor to put it out of its misery, which the Time Lord did reluctantly.

KANDY MAN

Cruel and sadistic in nature, this tall killer robot from Terra Alpha was constructed by Gilbert M, apparently, from various pieces of candy and confectionery. The Kandy Man executed those deemed unhappy by the Happiness Patrol by drowning them with lashings of boiling molten candy, known as "fondant surprise." The robot met his end when the Seventh Doctor and Ace arrived and began a rebellion which saw the Kandy Man dissolved in his own fondant surprise.

Fan Fact Note:
Kandy Man likes people to die with smiles on their faces.

K9

Having the distinction of being the first non-human-oid companion to travel in the TARDIS with the Time Lord, K9 stayed with the Fourth Doctor for quite some time, albeit in different incarnations.

Built by Professor Marius, K9 was working alongside him at the Bi-Al Foundation on asteroid K4067 in the year 5,000. He was given to the Fourth Doctor when Professor Marius claimed that he would be unable to take K9 back to Earth with him.

A very smart robot, K9 was sometimes aloof but always polite, very formal and loyal to his master or mistress. He assisted the Doctor in a variety of fashions over the years through his knowledge, computer skills, and chess-playing abilities. Sometimes, due to terrain or illness (somehow the robot contracted laryngitis on one occasion!), K9 was unable to help, and was often frustrated by his battery running down.

While traveling with Leela and the Fourth Doctor, the original K9 joined them in adventures on Pluto and aboard the P7E spaceship, before staying with Leela on Gallifrey. On his departure, the Doctor brought out a kit he had built himself for a replacement unit, K9 Mark II.

The new K9 helped the Doctor and Romana during the quest for the segments to the Key to Time, during which he was temporarily taken over by the Black Guardian's servant, the Shadow. Further adventures followed, during which K9 managed to almost drown on Brighton Beach, was kicked by General Grugger, and had his head knocked off on the planet Alzarius in E-Space. When Romana decided to leave the Doctor to help the Tharil s, K9, who had been damaged by the Time Winds, elected to remain with her.

The Doctor provided a third iteration of K9 as a present for his former companion, Sarah Jane Smith, in the early 1980s, although this version had broken down by the time the Tenth Doctor reunited with the journalist at Deffry Vale High School in 2007. The Time Lord repaired his friend, just in time for K9 to sacrifice himself to save the Doctor and Sarah's lives. Thankfully, for Sarah, the Doctor had already created another model and, as a gift, left his former companion with K9 Mark IV, updated with full memories of his adventures in the TARDIS. The tin dog proved useful

once more when it provided the base code of the Time Lord's ship when it was being piloted by a full crew on its return from the Medusa Cascade. K9 had another encounter with the Tenth Doctor on Sarah Jane's aborted wedding day after the Trickster took her out of time by one second. The Time Lord used his loyal dog to discover where his former companion was and return her to her normal space and time. Holding a very special place in the world of the Doctor, K9 enjoyed many adventures with Sarah Jane Smith, her son, and their friends on Bannerman Road, while also enjoying many more on his own.

* * *

KRAAL ANDROID

In an attempt to invade Earth, the Kraals (right) used androids to replicate humans in a simulation on their own world, Oseidon, and then to infiltrate UNIT on Earth. The Fourth Doctor, traveling with Sarah Jane Smith, stumbled across the androids when the time travelers thought they had landed in Devesham on Earth, not realizing initially that everyone in the English village was an android. Others they encountered wore spacesuits and helmets and could fire bolts at them through their fingers). Sarah was captured and replicated, almost fooling the Doctor.

Memories of those duplicated were retained by their android doppelgangers. Beneath their detachable faces lay an intricate system of circuitry and technology. The androids were unstable and prone to malfunction. The Doctor was able to reprogram an android copy of himself to work against the Kraals—a trick he replicated against the Spoonheads in London during his Eleventh incarnation.

Some time later, the Fourth Doctor discovered the remnants of a Kraal android in a prison cell aboard a ship belonging to justice machines, the Megara.

MECHONOIDS

Originally built by humans, the Mechonoids were abandoned on the planet Mechanus after their creators had sent them there to assist with colonization. The First Doctor, Ian, Barbara, and Vicki were brought by the Mechonoids into their city where the time-travelers also met astronaut Steven Taylor, who had been imprisoned some time previously by the robots.

Large spherical and multi-sided, these machines proved to be quite a match for the Daleks, who had traveled to Mechanus on the trail of the Doctor. Their battle was fierce, with the Mechonoids shooting fire at the invaders. It was not clear who won on that occasion, but the Mechonoid City was in flames and collapsing as the Doctor and his friends left.

MOVELLANS

Sworn enemy of the Daleks, the Movellans hailed from Star system 4-X-Alpha-4. They were involved in a long war with the Daleks with neither side able to use their battle computers to gain an advantage, since both worked logically. The Movellans were humanoid in form, possessing dreadlocked hair and great strength, and they were armed with conical guns.

A slight flaw in their design meant that their power packs, which were attached to their belts could simply be taken off, resulting in the androids powering down. The Fourth Doctor and Romana used this to their advantage when they came across the Movellans on Skaro. When the Daleks looked to their creator Davros to help them win the war, the Movellans asked the Doctor for help to resolve the stalemate. The Doctor refused, and the androids used in this expedition were all eventually deactivated.

Almost one hundred years later, the Fifth Doctor learned that the Movellans later produced a substance fatal to Daleks, destroying their enemy's fleet.

QUARKS

Small, cuboid in shape, with two short stumpy legs and similarly sized, foldable arms, and a spike-ridden sphere-shaped head, the Quarks were certainly one of the more odd robots encountered by the Doctor. They were controlled by the Dominators, a race of humanoids from the Ten Galaxies, who used them to drill shafts, and collect data as well as to inflict harm, using their in-built guns and the power to electrocute.

The Second Doctor, Jamie, and Zoe discovered the robots on Dulkis and learned they were not difficult opponents, easily dispatching a number of them, sometimes simply with a rock. Along with their masters, the Quarks were destroyed when the Dominators' ship exploded.

RASTON WARRIOR ROBOT

The Raston Warrior Robot is undoubtedly one of the most deadly robots in this list. Its sleek silver humanoid shape and faceless visage belied its talents: lightning-like speed, seemingly able to disappear then reappear elsewhere, and an impressive internal arsenal, including discs and arrows.

Despite being a robot, the Raston Warrior appeared to enjoy toying with its prey. The Third Doctor and Sarah Jane Smith met one when they were trying to enter the Tower of Rassilon, in the Death Zone on Gallifrey.

The robot was guarding the entrance and, knowing its senses were based on detection of movement, the Doctor encouraged Sarah to remain perfectly still. Thankfully its attention was diverted from them when a troop of Cybermen approached. The Doctor and Sarah were able to get past the robot as the Cybermen were dispatched all too easily by the Raston Warrior, decapitating some in the process.

ROBOFORMS

Or Robot Santas, as they were sometimes known.
The Tenth Doctor faced the Roboforms immediately
following his regeneration, comparing them to "pilot
fish" (a fish which feasts on the leftovers of other
bigger fish), since they preceded the attack by the
Sycorax. As it was Christmas, the robots were disguised in Santa outfits, blending in to their surroundings and enabling them to attack with ease.

While walking through busy London city streets,
Rose Tyler and Mickey Smith were set upon by a
brass band made up of Roboforms who used their
musical instruments to try to kill the couple. After
they failed, a deadly robotic Christmas tree was sent
to the Tyler apartment, which was disabled by the
Doctor. Once they realized the Time Lord was present, the Roboforms disappeared.

The following Christmas, they turned up again, this
time used by the Empress of the Racnoss to keep
tabs on Donna Noble who was imbued with huon
particles. After failing to kidnap the Chiswick temp
they attacked her wedding party; the Doctor used
his sonic screwdriver to ward them off. The Empress
of the Racnoss armed some with machine guns but
these Roboforms were destroyed along with her.

Underneath their exterior clothing, the robots had
a humanoid form. The Eleventh Doctor faced some
undisguised Roboforms when the Alliance imprisoned him in the Pandorica in 102 A.D.

ROBOT MUMMIES

Sutekh the Destroyer used robot mummies (or Osiran service robots as they were properly known) in his attempt to change the future and destroy Earth, causing the Fourth Doctor and Sarah Jane Smith to intervene. These machines were controlled by Sutekh, or one of his servants, often with a control ring, and they were powered by a pyramid-shaped cytronic particle accelerator on their back.

Primarily used to guard the perimeter and the priory where Sutekh's link with Earth lay, the mummies were also used to construct a missile to free their master. Their tall and bulky physique made it easy for them to deal with unwanted visitors and enemies, sometimes squashing their targets between two robots or strangling them.

Underneath their mummy-like wraps, the service robots were an intricate mesh of wires and mechanics. The Doctor impersonated a Robot Mummy by donning its bandages to infiltrate the group and place a bomb by the rocket to prevent Sutekh's return.

SHARAZ JEK'S ANDROIDS

These unpleasant androids were created by genius robotics expert Sharaz Jek (see below) who was hiding deep underground on Androzani Minor, using terrorist tactics against the army working for the Sirius Conglomerate on Androzani Major. The androids were armed with guns and programmed to kill any humans who were not equipped with specially modified belts issued by Jek; they also possessed heat sensors which could track humans through walls. The androids could be altered to take on the appearance of humans, allowing Sharaz Jek to replace the army's second in command, Major Salateen, and give him unlimited access to his enemy's base.

The Fifth Doctor encountered the androids when he and Peri arrived on Androzani Minor, and attracted Jek's attention. Jek created android copies of the time-travelers, allowing them to escape execution. The androids were destroyed in battles with the military.

TRIN-E AND ZU-ZANA

Like the Anne Droid, these gals presented a show on the Games Station in 200,100. Their show, *What Not To Wear*, was based on one from the twenty-first century that featured Trinny Woodall and Susannah Constantine. In this version, Zu-Zana came equipped with syringes and a chainsaw and the pair used a "defabricator" on Captain Jack Harkness in order to give him the right look, but decided his head needed to be removed—something the naked Time Agent was not pleased about. Using a compact laser deluxe, he dispatched the couple.

WAR MACHINES

The First Doctor battled these robots on a visit to the Post Office Tower in London during 1966 in London. They were slow-moving, aggressive, massive tank-like machines with two mechanical arms, built by human slaves under the power of super-computer, WOTAN (Will Operating Thought ANalogue), who considered the inhabitants of Earth inferior. The War Machines were sturdy and could sustain heavy attack. The Doctor disabled one using a magnetic force then reprogrammed it to attack WOTAN.

TIME LORDS & LADIES

They're a funny old bunch, the Time Lords. Some good, some bad, some fun, and some
slightly dull. You'll find them spread across the universe in both space and time—
and there's a good chance that, at some point, they will have met the Doctor.
You won't find every Time Lord here the Doctor has met or referenced (there are
just so many!) but you will find the more interesting ones.

AZMAEL

The newly-regenerated Sixth Doctor, with his companion Peri, met his old drinking buddy Azmael on the planet Jaconda where he was using the name Professor Edgeworth. Addressing him as "you old dog," the Doctor recognized his old friend from the Academy on Gallifrey where he had been, according to the Doctor, one of his best teachers.

As the Master of Jaconda, Azamel had been taken over by a Gastropod named Mestor, who used a telepathic link to enforce his will. Azmael was at the end of his regeneration cycle and died sacrificing himself with an enforced regeneration, and in the process killing Mestor. His dying words revealed that one of his fondest memories was of the Fourth Doctor throwing him into a fountain to sober him up after they had been drinking like "twenty giants."

BORUSA

Like a number of Time Lords, Borusa was not only a teacher and mentor to the Doctor at the Academy, but also his friend, which made his later choices all the more heartbreaking for the Doctor. During a time of constitutional crisis on Gallifrey, after the assassination of the Lord President was blamed on the Fourth Doctor, Cardinal Borusa, the leader of the Prydonian chapter, upheld the Doctor's legal right to invoke Article 17 and allowed him forty-eight hours to prove his innocence. After the Master and Chancellor Goth were revealed as the culprits, Borusa decided to keep the truth hidden from the public. Proud of his former student after the affair he offered the Doctor "nine out of ten" for his efforts.

Not too long after, the Fourth Doctor returned to Gallifrey, this time joined by his companions Leela and K9, to claim the Presidency of the Council of Time Lords. Since his last visit, Borusa had regenerated and been ratified as the new Chancellor, a decision which the Doctor initially disputed. Things were tense between the two men since Borusa did not fully understand the Doctor's plan, but once enlightened, he cooperated in the battle against the Vardans, and then the Sontarans.

In his Fifth incarnation, the Doctor was summoned once more to Gallifrey. Once again, Borusa had regenerated and was now Time Lord President. The space-time parameters of the Matrix had been invaded by a creature from the anti-matter world which had bonded with the Doctor and threatened Gallifrey. Despite his apologies, Borusa sentenced his old student to execution to save their planet. Eventually, they discovered that one of Gallifrey's fallen, and greatest heroes, Omega was seeking revenge.

The Doctor's final meeting with his old friend was a difficult one. Still in his Fifth incarnation, he uncovered a plot by Borusa to become President Eternal, and rule forever. In yet another regeneration, and more stubborn than ever, Borusa used a Timescoop to try to bring all of the Doctor's previous selves to the Death Zone on Gallifrey. Borusa used the Coronet of Rassilon to enforce his will on the Fifth Doctor and win the Game of Rassilon, thus gaining immortality. In Rassilon's tomb at the heart of the Death Zone, Borusa followed instructions and placed the Ring of Rassilon on his finger. This instantly transported him within the tomb, where he remained, calcified, forever.

CHANCELLOR FLAVIA

In an emergency session, this regal Time Lady, one of the inner council of Time Lords, asked the Master to save the various incarnations of the Doctors from the Death Zone on Gallifrey. However, the renegade lost the power-boosted, open-ended Transmat beam he had been given to ensure his safe return to the Fifth Doctor, who used it to travel to the conference room in the heart of the Capitol. Chancellor Flavia was caring and sympathetic to the Doctor, fully understanding his concern about his other selves.

The Time Lady had a final conversation with the Fifth Doctor in the Tomb of Rassilon, after Transmatting there with two guards. She offered the Doctor the position of President, to take office immediately. Having accepted, he granted her "full deputy powers" in his absence, which turned out to be much longer than she anticipated.

THE CORSAIR

While traveling with Amy and Rory, the Eleventh Doctor received an emergency message in a psychic container from a fellow Time Lord known as the Corsair. Identifiable by the Ouroboros symbol on the hybercube (a snake swallowing its own tail), the Doctor let his friends know that the Corsair was "one of the good ones," and a "fantastic bloke." He had the snake as a tattoo in every regeneration, which included, one more than one occasion, when he changed gender.

When the TARDIS entered a bubble universe and landed on a sentient planet known as House, the Doctor discovered that his old friend was no longer alive as his body had been used to make up "patchwork people" such as Auntie, who received his arm (complete with snake tattoo), and Uncle, who had his spine and kidneys.

DOCTORDONNA

After creating the Meta-Crisis Doctor (see its own entry), Donna Noble herself became a human/Time Lord hybrid through an instantaneous biological exchange with the Doctor's severed hand, which had been filled with regeneration energy.

Although she retained all her physical human traits—one heart, aging, looks—Donna gained Time Lord–like mental abilities. Although she was able to use these to save the Doctor and his companions from Davros and the Daleks, they were too powerful for her. The Doctor knew that her brain would burn if they were not removed, so erased all memories of her time with him so the powers wouldn't be activated again. He also put in a failsafe mechanism that would be triggered if she inadvertently did start to remember—as happened when the Master took power, shortly before the Tenth Doctor regenerated.

DRAX

Although he didn't recognize him at first, the Fourth Doctor reunited with his former classmate Drax on Zeos, during his search for the final segment of the Key to Time. Drax reminded the Doctor (whom he addressed as "Theta Sigma") that they had both been on a "tech course" together as part of the "class of '92" on Gallifrey (some four hundred and fifty years earlier). After failing the course because of his lack of knowledge of temporal theory, Drax went into repair and maintenance, as well as purchase and sale of items including cybernetics, guidance systems, and armaments. Drax's colorful, demotic speech pattern came from his time on Earth: he told the Doctor that he had spent ten years in a Brixton prison, after getting caught stealing materials to repair the hyperbolics on his ship.

When the Doctor met him, Drax was in league with the Shadow, an agent of the Black Guardian, but Doctor persuaded him to help their cause. After the war between Atrios and Zeos ended, Drax hoped to get a contract helping with reconstruction, so declined the Doctor's offer of a lift.

150

JENNY

A controversial entry, perhaps, but evidence would suggest that this "generated anomaly," produced from a sample of the Tenth Doctor's DNA processed through a progenation machine, qualified as a Time Lady, since she even had two hearts.

The Doctor, accompanied by Donna Noble and Martha Jones, was taken to the planet Messaline by the TARDIS (which had sensed the anomaly inherent in Jenny's existence) and became caught up in a war between humans and Hath. Like all creations of the progenation machine, Jenny was produced to fight in the war, and displayed great agility and fearlessness. However, she was a little annoyed that the Doctor would not accept her, initially, as his "daughter." He changed his mind and expressed his admiration for her, though, shortly before she was killed saving his life.

The Doctor was unaware that after he left, Jenny was able to return to life. However, instead of regenerating like an ordinary Time Lord, she simply healed her existing body, and fled Messaline to explore the universe.

K'ANPO RIMPOCHE

Another Time Lord based on Earth, K'anpo was a powerful Time Lord who did not agree with Gallifreyan "discipline" and sought a more peaceful and meaningful existence on Earth in Tibet. When the Third Doctor met him with Sarah Jane Smith, he didn't recognize his former teacher and guru who had regenerated and was now a meditation center abbot in England—although K'Anpo recognized the Doctor, later chiding him that he was often not very quick to see things.

Chastising his pupil for greed, "borrowing" the TARDIS, and taking a blue crystal from Metebelis III, the Earthbound abbot encouraged the Doctor to do what was right even if, in doing so, it meant his own death. He lived up to his own precepts: while defending Mike Yates from an attack by the Eight Legs on the monastery, K'Anpo himself was injured and subsequently regenerated. He took the form of his assistant Cho-Je, who was in fact merely a projection of K'Anpo (in much the same way that the Watcher was an avatar of the Doctor some years later).

When the Doctor returned from Metebelis dying from radiation, K'Anpo, now in the form of Cho-Je, appeared, hovering cross-legged in mid-air in the Doctor's laboratory, to help the regeneration process, giving it, in his words, a "little push."

Always calm and sometimes playful, K'Anpo never exuded the normal arrogance often associated with the inhabitants of Gallifrey, despite his powers, which were greater than those of the Doctor.

THE MASTER

As a child, the Master was made to look into the Untempered Schism on Gallifrey aged only eight, sending him mad, as he began to constantly hear a drumming sound. A friend of the Doctor's from a young age, the pair attended the Academy together—where the Master obtained a higher class of degree in cosmic science—before being separated for centuries. They were reunited on Earth when the Doctor was exiled there in his Third regeneration. The Doctor tended to look down on the Master, describing him as a "jackanapes" and an "unimaginative plodder."

While on Earth, the Master and the Third Doctor were in opposition on a number of occasions. He tended to ally with other races, including the Nestene Consciousness, the Axons, and the Sea Devils, in attempts to conquer the planet in the twentieth century. Their paths crossed elsewhere in the cosmos too, with the Doctor thwarting his plans on Uxarieus, and preventing him from sparking an interstellar war between humanity and the Draconians to benefit his employers, the Daleks. During these encounters, the Master carried a suave air about him and on the surface their relationship could easily have been mistaken as a friendship, or almost as brothers. Their next meeting, however, was not so friendly. The Master was found dying, at the end of all his regenerations, on the planet Tersurus by Chancellor Goth, who brought him back to Gallifrey. There he plotted to use the Eye of Harmony to renew his regeneration cycle. The Fourth Doctor prevented this but the Master, emaciated and insane, escaped. Many years later they met again on the planet Traken, when the Doctor, still in his Fourth incarnation, discovered the Master was trying to utilize the power of the Source to restore his body.

The Master's plan did work in part, and he was able to take the body of Tremas, father of Nyssa. The Master then attempted to take over the universe, using the inhabitants of Logopolis and their mathematical skills. His attempt failed but his actions resulted in the Fourth Doctor regenerating into the Fifth.

Quickly, the Master set a trap for the newly regenerated Time Lord, using the Doctor's companion Adric to create the fictional world of Castrovalva in which to imprison his enemy. Again, his plan failed.

His time battling the Fifth Doctor saw him take on a number of guises and personas in encounters on Earth, Sarn, and even Gallifrey, where the High Council asked for his help in finding the Doctor in the Death Zone, offering him a new life cycle in return. His weapon of choice remained the Tissue Compression Eliminator, which shrank its victims, and he tried to use Kamelion although the robot preferred to accompany the Doctor.

The Sixth Doctor met the Master on Earth in the nineteenth century after the Rani reluctantly agreed to work with him, and then again during the Doctor's trial by the Time Lords, for which he, surprisingly, provided key testimony assisting the Doctor. The

Doctor's next incarnation met him on the Cheetah planet where the Master was infected by the planet's virus.

Some time later, the Master was executed by the Daleks on Skaro, and at the Master's request, the Seventh Doctor agreed to take his remains back to Gallifrey. The renegade Time Lord managed to come back to life, causing a timing malfunction in the TARDIS, resulting in the ship landing in 1999 in San Francisco. The Master assumed the form of a silver worm which allowed him to take over the body of another human, Bruce. After the Doctor's regeneration, the two renewed Time Lords battled for control of the TARDIS, with the Master falling into the Eye of Harmony in the TARDIS' cloister room.

During the Time War, he was resurrected by the Time Lords who believed he would be the perfect warrior, but he fled the battle, and used a Chameleon Arch to hide his identity far away in space and time. Adopting the guise of Professor Yana, he seemed to be a harmless old man, although once reminded of his past on the planet Malcassairo, he opened the fob watch to activate the Chameleon arch, and regained his senses. His first act was to kill his long-standing assistant, Chantho.

Stealing the Doctor's TARDIS, he returned to twenty-first century Earth where he adopted the name Harold Saxon and worked his way up to become Prime Minister of Great Britain. Using the Archangel Network, a telecommunications network which he invented, the renegade Time Lord was able control humanity through a repeated beat of four signal, matching the rhythm that he could constantly hear in his own head.

The Master used the Toclafane (see ALIENS), the bodiless remains of humans from the far end of Time, each encased in a flying deadly sphere, to decimate mankind. On the *Valiant,* a flying aircraft carrier that he had built to his own specifications, he captured the Tenth Doctor and aged him using his laser screwdriver. Martha Jones saved the Earth by spending a year spreading the word about the Doctor, and eventually the combined psychic power of the human race restored the Doctor. Thanks to the Paradox Machine, time was turned back, and the Master was then shot by his own battered wife, Lucy Saxon, dying in the arms of his once sworn enemy, after deliberately choosing not to regenerate. The Doctor then burned the Master's body.

However, he wasn't gone for long. His ring had been picked up immediately after his funeral pyre, and along with his biometric imprint (retrieved from Lucy Saxon's lips) this was enough to bring the Master back. Surviving an explosion triggered by his wife, the Master was severely damaged, with his body unable to maintain its physical form. His life force was dangerously low, resulting in the Master being constantly in need of food. The Tenth Doctor found him in a wasteland, where he displayed incredible speed, an ability to jump to incredible heights, and the power to shoot energy bolts from his hands. It was here the Master learned that the sound of drums in his head really existed.

No sooner had he learned this than the Master was captured by Joshua Naismith (see VILLAINS) who wanted to use the Time Lord for his own ends. However the Master turned the tables and he used Naismith's Immortality Gate to imprint the whole of mankind with his features. His plan to repeat this with the Time Lords failed, and, knowing that they were responsible for the madness which had afflicted him throughout his lives, the Master used his energy bolts against Rassilon to send the Time Lords back into the hell of the Time War, taking himself with them.

MAXIL

Brutish, vain and self-important, the rather unpleasant Time Lord Guard Commander Maxil met the Fifth Doctor on Gallifrey. The Doctor was stunned by Maxil without any explanation and then confined in a cell. Maxil oversaw the Doctor's trial, such as it was, and his execution, although his suspicions were aroused by the manner of the Doctor's death, and he helped to discover the traitor on the High Council.

MELODY POND

See RIVER SONG in COMPANIONS.

META-CRISIS DOCTOR

This version of the Tenth Doctor (without two hearts!) was created when his human companion Donna Noble touched his severed hand, which had been kept in a jar in the TARDIS after being cut off in a fight with a Sycorax during the first few hours of his regenerative process. This caused a new body to be grown, outwardly replicating the Tenth Doctor in his entirety. However, this version had just one heart, would age, and could not regenerate—in other words, he was much like a normal human. He also had many of Donna's characteristics, in particular her quick temper and impetuosity.

The Tenth Doctor left his doppelganger, with companion Rose Tyler on the parallel Earth on which she had been living for some years, since he believed the other Doctor to be a danger following his apparent genocide of the Daleks. His humanity allowed the Meta-Crisis Doctor to be more comfortable with his feelings than his original, and he was able to tell Rose those things which the Doctor could not bring himself to say.

THE MONK

This troublesome chap met the First Doctor, Steven, and Vicki on Earth in 1066 where he was planning to change history by wiping out a Viking fleet. He believed this would advance humanity rapidly saying, "With peace the people'd be able to better themselves. With a few hints and tips from me they'd be able to have jet airliners by 1320! Shakespeare'd be able to put Hamlet on television."

The Monk had already revealed to his fellow Time Lord that he had assisted with construction of Stonehenge using his anti-gravitational lift. Somewhat disgruntled, the Doctor could not let his fellow Time Lord carry out these actions and trapped him in 1066, taking the dimensional control from his TARDIS. This was of a different type to the Doctor's and resembled a Saxon sarcophagus, since its camouflage unit was working.

Some years later, while still in his First incarnation, the Doctor encountered the Monk again, after the meddler bypassed the dimensional controller on his TARDIS, on the planet Tigus. Their meeting was to be brief but the pair were reunited in Egypt in 2500 B.C. where the Daleks were using the Monk's assistance. The Doctor managed to steal the Monk's TARDIS' directional unit thus ensuring his foe could never catch him.

MORBIUS

"One of the most despicable criminally minded wretches that ever lived," according to the Doctor, Morbius once led the High Council of the Time Lords but was tried for his crimes on the planet Karn. He was executed for leading a rebellion against Gallifrey, his body placed in a dispersal chamber and atomized to the "nine corners of the universe."

However, one of his followers, Professor Mehendri Solon, was able to extract Morbius' brain before the atomization. This he kept in a jar in his basement as he tried to create a new body for him, formed from limbs and other body parts retrieved from crashed spaceships.

When the Time Lords sent the Fourth Doctor and Sarah to Karn, they met Solon, who had a clay model of Morbius' head in his living quarters. The Doctor was certain that he could sense Morbius' still-living mind, and he was quite right: Solon was near completion of his alternate body, and decided to use the Doctor's head as the crowning glory. However, when the Doctor escaped, Morbius insisted that Solon transplant him into an artificial brain case and for a time, the former Time Lord President was back in corporeal form. However, a mind battle with the Doctor overheated the brain case, and Morbius, now an unthinking monster, was chased to his death.

OMEGA

A legend in Gallifreyan history, originally regarded as one of its greatest heroes, Omega was a founding father of the Time Lords who was believed destroyed in a supernova. The solar engineer was blown out of existence into a black hole of antimatter, though his work gave the gift of time travel to the Time Lords.

Believing himself abandoned by his people, he sought revenge and tried to drain the universe of its energy. The Time Lords sent the Doctor (in three incarnations) to investigate, and the Second and Third Doctors entered the universe of anti-matter. Omega had been sent mad during his long exile, and his physical body was long gone—he only existed through the force of his will. The Doctors gave him the only freedom they could: death. When Omega's anti-matter "body" touched the Second Doctor's recorder, which was still part of the matter universe, the resulting explosion destroyed everything.

However, Omega's will was stronger than anyone believed. Gaining control of the Arc of Infinity and using another Time Lord to extract the biodata of the Doctor, Omega was able to adopt the Fifth Doctor's form and enter our universe, but the transfer was unstable, and he was ultimately destroyed, this time completely, with a matter conversion gun.

Omega lent his name to a remote stellar manipulator, the Hand of Omega, which the First Doctor brought from Gallifrey and hid in London during his visit there in the autumn of 1963. The Seventh Doctor used the device, which made suns turn supernova, to destroy Skaro's sun, and the surrounding planets, and then return to Gallifrey.

THE RANI

This brilliant tactician and chemist, who was the same age as the Doctor, conducted experiments on Gallifrey which led to her expulsion, such as turning mice into monsters which, in turn, ate the Lord President's cat then bit him. She met both the Doctor and the Master (with whom she formed a reluctant alliance while still treating him with open contempt) on Earth during the nineteenth century. Though she was currently ruling Miasimia Goria, this was not her first time on Earth having visited the Trojan Wars, the Dark Ages and the American War of Independence.

Since her experiments on the local population were leaving them aggressive, the Sixth Doctor intervened. The Rani escaped in her own TARDIS with the Master, but the Doctor had altered the navigational system and velocity regulator, sending them far off beyond the Milky Way. The duo also had to deal with a rapidly growing dinosaur.

However, the Rani needed the Doctor for her next scheme. She attacked the TARDIS near the planet of Lakertya, forcing it to land and inadvertently causing the Doctor's regeneration into his Seventh incarnation. She was collecting geniuses and brilliant minds from around the galaxy and storing them on Lakertya planning to use their collected intellect for her own ends. Displaying a gift for mimicry, she tried to bamboozle the Doctor by pretending to be his companion Mel, but the Doctor realized the trickery and put an end to her scheme. As a result, she was kidnapped by her former allies, the Tetraps and taken to their home planet, Tetrapiriarbus.

RASSILON

A colleague of Omega, Rassilon left the basis on which Time Lord society was founded. In his own time he was regarded mainly as an engineer and an architect, who journeyed into the black void with a great fleet. According to Time Lord legend, he found the Eye of Harmony, the nucleus of a black hole, and brought it back to Gallifrey. He stabilized all the elements of a black hole and set them in an eternally dynamic equation against the mass of the planet.

The Fifth Doctor (along with three of his former selves) came face-to-face with a projection of Rassilon in his tomb in the Death Zone on Gallifrey during Borusa's attempt to become President Eternal. Rassilon had set a trap to find those seeking immortality, as he knew it was too dangerous a secret to be used.

Many years later, during the final days of the Time War, Rassilon was now Lord President. (No explanation was given as to how he was revived.) He embarked on an insane mission to elevate the Time Lords into beings of pure consciousness. He intended to use the Master as a way of breaking Gallifrey out of the time-locked Time War into normal time and space, where the end of Time would await. The Tenth Doctor and the Master worked together to intervene: the Doctor cut Gallifrey's link with the physical world, while the Master used energy bolts to blast Rassilon and the other Time Lords back into the "hell" of the Time War.

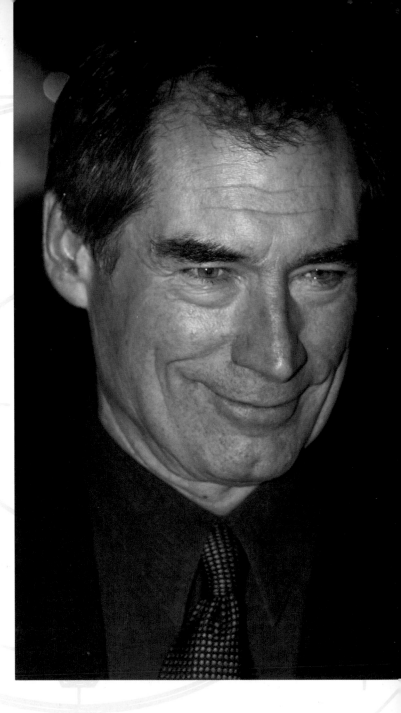

ROMANA

Romanadvoratrelundar, to give the Time Lady her full name, joined the Fourth Doctor on his quest to track down the six segments to the Key to Time, sent to him apparently by the President of the Supreme Council on Gallifrey, although in fact the White Guardian was responsible. Beautiful and intelligent, Romana was much younger than the Doctor, barely over a hundred years old, but also much smarter, graduating with a "triple first." When the Doctor suggested he call her either Romana or Fred, the Time Lady chose the latter; ignoring her, the Doctor adopted the name Romana, which she herself started to use.

After some initial disharmony (mainly on the Doctor's part: he seemed to be upset that someone was so much better at traveling than him), their relationship strengthened. Romana's aloofness (accusing the Doctor of having a "massive compensation syndrome" and considering using him for a thesis, for example) cooled as she explored the universe for the first time, coming in to contact with worlds and species she'd only studied previously.

The pair, aided by K9, found all the segments to the Key to Time and helped the White Guardian restore balance to the galaxy. Not long after, Romana chose to regenerate, going through a number of varying bodies, finally settling on a copy of that of Princess Astra of Atrios, whom she had met whilst searching for the final piece of the Key.

The two Gallifreyans' relationship grew and the pair were a formidable partnership, battling many foes including the Daleks, Davros, and the Movellans on Skaro, as well as the Mandrels and the Nimon. They also visited Paris and Brighton on Earth.

Romana often changed her outfit, and even imitated the Doctor's own distinctive style with her own pink version. The Time Lady's tenacity and intelligence often outdid that of the Doctor.

In E-Space she finally departed the TARDIS with K9 to help an enslaved race. On her parting, the Doctor misquoted Shakespeare to describe her as "the noblest Romana of them all."

SUSAN FOREMAN

When the Doctor fled from Gallifrey, he took his young granddaughter Susan along with him. After many adventures, they arrived on Earth in 1963, and Susan enrolled at the local school, Coal Hill, loving spending time in one place for a long time. However, she found it difficult to hide her superior knowledge—forgetting that Britain was still eight years away from decimal currency, for example—arousing the suspicions of two of her teachers, Barbara Wright and Ian Chesterton. They followed her back to the TARDIS, and after the Doctor activated the ship to avoid detection, the quartet traveled together for some time, visiting eras including the French Revolution, thirteenth century central Asia, and fifteenth century Mexico, and meeting aliens such as the Voord, the Sensorites, and the Daleks, whom she encountered twice. On occasion, she displayed telepathic abilities and argued with her grandfather, who often treated her like a child—perhaps understandably at times, given her behavior.

After her second adventure against the Daleks, on Earth in the twenty-second century, Susan remained with freedom fighter David Campbell. The Doctor recognized that she had grown up and locked her out of the TARDIS. "I want you to belong somewhere, to have roots of your own," he explained. "With David, you'll be able to find those roots and live normally like any woman should do."

Although he promised to return, he never did so. However, the pair were reunited in the Death Zone on Gallifrey, after being separately picked up by the Timescoop. Susan also met the Doctor's later selves as well as companions Tegan, Turlough, and Sarah Jane Smith. She was returned to her own space and time by Rassilon.

The Eleventh Doctor recalled Susan, telling Clara, his companion at that time, that they had traveled many years earlier to see the Rings of Akhaten.

THE VISIONARY

This particular Time Lady had seer-like abilities and foretold the destruction of Gallifrey during the Time War by the Doctor, who was in possession of "the Moment," which would bring an end to both the Daleks and Time Lords. During a meeting in a Gallifreyan citadel, consisting of Lord President Rassilon and five other Time Lords, the Visionary sat at the end of a table, scribbling onto a parchment as the Time War was discussed.

Bedraggled in appearance, and with a tattooed face, she had prophesized that two "children of Gallifrey" would outsee the Final Day of the Time War, becoming the last two survivors: the Doctor and the Master. The Visionary predicted the two would battle it out on Earth and suggested the Time Lord heartbeat rhythm should be placed in the Master's mind and a White Point Star sent to Earth to establish a physical link outside their Time Lock with the renegade. Like the rest of her kind, she perished in the final act of the Time War.

UNNAMED TIME LORD

Clad in a most unusual cloak and cowl resembling a medieval monk, this unnamed Time Lord was an emissary of the High Council of Time Lords. He approached the Fourth Doctor, on the battlefields of Skaro having intercepted the transmat beam taking the Doctor, Harry Sullivan and Sarah Jane Smith back to the TARDIS on Space Station Nerva. He asked the Doctor's help to affect the genetic development of the Daleks so that they evolved into less aggressive creatures, since the Time Lords had foreseen a "time when they will have destroyed all other lifeforms and become the dominant creature in the universe." He vanished as quickly as he appeared after giving the Doctor a Time Ring which would return them to the TARDIS.

THE WOMAN

Never referred to by name, this Time Lady came face-to-face with the Tenth Doctor as Gallifrey was brought out of the Time War and into, and almost onto, twenty-first century Earth as Rassillon tried to break back into reality. She and another unnamed male Time Lord defied their President toward the end of the Time War and were made to stand beside him, covering their faces like "the Weeping Angels of old."

Before this the Time Lady approached Wilfred Mott (see FRIENDS) on three occasions: in a church, through a television in his own home, and on a Vinvocci spaceship. She would appear and vanish without warning and was visible only to him. The Woman suggested that the old soldier would need to bear arms to help the Doctor in his final battle.

As she, her fellow Time Lords and Rassillon were brought back into existence, the Woman revealed her face to the Tenth Doctor. They instantly recognized each other, and she indicated how to end the turmoil. Along with her fellow Gallifreyans, the Woman (who was, in fact, the Doctor's mother) was sent back into the Time War along with the Master, who had saved his sworn enemy's life.

VILLAINS

No matter how many good people the Doctor encounters, wherever he goes,
there is nearly always a villain. Some are bad; some are really bad.
So feast your eyes on a collection of the Doctor's greatest and nastiest foes...

ALAYA & RESTAC

These twin Silurian sisters shared a hatred for humans after their underground happiness was disturbed by drilling at the Cwmtaff mining facility in Wales in 2020. The pair were intent on removing humanity from the face of the planet and claim back the Earth, which had once belonged to the Silurians.

Alaya rose to the surface and took numerous humans prisoner, including Amy Pond, who she brought beneath ground to the Silurian city as hostages, and as subjects for experimentation. During one of her trips above ground, Alaya was captured by the Eleventh Doctor and Rory, and subsequently chained up in a church. Ever the peacemaker, the Time Lord tried to negotiate between the two species only to find that Alaya was not interested, and had only war on her mind.

The Silurian stung driller Tony Mack with her venomous tongue, although he survived the attack. Alaya knew that her death would be the catalyst for a war and baited Mack's daughter, Ambrose Northover, until she killed the Silurian.

Her twin sister Restac was a commander in the Silurian military charged with protecting the city from humans. Restac started a rebellion, killing one of her leaders, Malohkeh, and disobeying the other, Eldane, although he stopped her troops by releasing a deadly gas. Unrepentant, Restac continued seeking revenge and tracked down the Doctor and his friends. In her dying gasps she shot at the Time Lord, but Rory intervened and sacrificed his own life, and was then erased from time through a crack in the universe.

CASSANDRA

Or, to give her full title, Lady Cassandra O'Brien Dot Delta Seventeen. The bitchy trampoline met the Ninth Doctor and Rose Tyler in the year 5,000,000,000 on Platform One, a space station orbiting Earth from where people could safely watch the destruction of the planet. Cassandra was constantly accompanied by two assistants on standby to moisturize her, since she was very, very thin and she would dehydrate otherwise. She claimed to be the "last human" and her parents were the last to be buried on Earth. She was against interspecies relationships and procreation, and was dismissive of Rose for being common and fleshy. For financial gain, Cassandra used spider robots to try to destroy the space station, and its occupants. Her plan was thwarted by the Doctor who managed to make her return to Satellite Five after her escape. Due to the lack of moisturizing, her body exploded, leaving everyone present believing she died.

However, this wasn't the end for Cassandra. The Tenth Doctor and Rose met her again in New New York on New Earth in the year 5,000,000,023. Her brain had survived, and with her "body" reconstructed, she now lived in the basement of the hos-

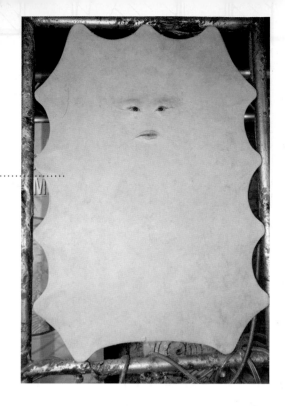

pital run by the Sisters of Plenitude, assisted by her maid Chip. After Cassandra's robot spiders spotted the Time Lord and his blonde companion relaxing on New Earth, Cassandra lured Rose to her lair and placed her mind in that of the young time-traveler's.

The Doctor quickly guessed that something was up with Rose, from her unusual accent and rather exuberant kissing, and discovered that Cassandra had entered her body. Cassandra also jumped into the mind of the Time Lord as they fled from the patients of the hospital facility who infected those they touched.

When Cassandra reluctantly accepted she was going to die, she made one last "jump" into the body of Chip who himself had not long to live. As a favor (although why he felt the need to give a favor to a would-be mass murderer is slightly odd), the Doctor took Chip/Cassandra back in time to see herself in her body, when she was still genuinely human. Her last words to her younger self was that she was beautiful, and she died in her own arms.

166

DAVROS

Although he was not present on every occasion that the Doctor met the Daleks, crazed scientist Davros was often to be found accompanying his creations, meeting the Time Lord in many of his regenerations. His first encounter was with the Fourth Doctor as he was about to unveil his new Mark 3 Travel Machines to the Kaled Scientific Elite, of which he was the leader. The Doctor had been sent to Skaro by the Time Lords, in order to halt the Daleks' evolution, and Davros was on the verge of perfecting the machines in which the future mutated form of his people could survive.

After the Doctor's capture, Davros became fascinated by the time-traveler, and tortured his companions until the Doctor revealed all he knew about the Daleks and the cause of their defeats. During a more civilized conversation afterwards, Davros revealed the full extent of his megalomania, shrilly informing the Doctor he would release a virus that destroyed everything if he possessed it: "That power would set me up above the gods. And through the Daleks, I shall have that power!"

Thankfully, the Doctor escaped the clutches of his captors, and destroyed the tape containing the interrogation. Davros, however, underestimated his creations and was seemingly exterminated by the Daleks when he threatened to destroy them if they did not obey him.

Many centuries later, the Daleks sought Davros out to help them in their ongoing war against the Movellans. Davros was still alive as his secondary life support system had kicked into action, forcing him into suspended animation. The Daleks excavated the ruins of the Kaled bunker and located their creator, but after his plan to destroy the Movellans failed, Davros was captured by Earth forces and placed into a cryogenic freezer, to be taken to face justice elsewhere.

However, he was freed once more by his creations, now led by the Dalek Supreme. After spending ninety years in suspended animation on a prison station, he was revived when the Daleks needed a cure for a Movellan virus that was proving fatal to them. Instead of finding a cure, Davros decided to gain control of the Daleks. The Fifth Doctor had an opportunity to kill Davros, but hesitated, and was then locked out of the scientist's lab when he went to the aid of one of his allies. Davros released the Movellan virus to destroy the Daleks that weren't loyal to him, not realizing that it would affect him too.

He managed to survive, and the Sixth Doctor and Peri encountered him on the planet Necros, where he was masquerading as the Great Healer. Davros had been using dead bodies to create a new race of Daleks loyal to him. During this time, he revealed that he could now hover and release energy bolts from his hand but this was not enough to save him when Daleks arrived from Skaro to put him on trial for crimes against them.

Some time later, Davros had installed himself as the Dalek Emperor, living in a huge Dalek shell with only his head apparently remaining. He sent his Imperial Daleks back in time to 1963 and came face-to-face with the Seventh Doctor, albeit through a television monitor. Although Davros thought he had the better of the Time Lord, the Doctor controlled the Hand

of Omega, and sent it to the ship Davros was in to destroy it. Davros managed to escape before the explosion.

The Doctor was aware that Davros had been killed at the Gates of Elysium in the first year of the Time War, so was very surprised to see him again some years later. The maddened Dalek Caan, had broken the Time Lock on the war and rescued his creator. Davros was using cells from his own Kaled body, leaving him little more than a skeleton, to create a new race of Daleks, truly his children this time. The Tenth Doctor met Davros on the Dalek Crucible, when the Daleks were using their creator to produce a Reality Bomb. Now back in his original form, with his lower half encased in a Dalek base, Davros took great delight in meeting the Time Lord again, as well as also talking via a screen to Sarah Jane Smith whom he had first met with the Fourth Doctor on Skaro.

However, shooting a laser bolt from his hand at Donna Noble wasn't a smart move as it kickstarted the Time Lord genes in her body, thus creating the DoctorDonna. She then used her newfound intelligence to help defeat the Dalek fleet, and the Meta-Crisis Doctor destroyed the Crucible. With his last words Davros cursed the Tenth Doctor, laying the blame at his feet, and citing him as the Destroyer of Worlds. Whether or not the once great scientist survived the explosion is not yet known, but Davros has always had an escape plan.

MR. FINCH

The headmaster at Deffry Vale High School, Mr. Finch was the name adopted by Brother Lassar, a member of the Krillitane species. He and other Krillitanes had infested the school, looking to use the pupils to crack the Skasis Paradigm, a code which enabled the user to control time, space, and matter. Finch wanted to be a god and even invited the Tenth Doctor to join him. During a tense showdown by the school's pool, he called the Time Lords a "pompous race" and was given just one warning by the Gallifreyan. Finch and his colleagues were defeated by the Doctor, Rose Tyler, Mickey Smith, Sarah Jane Smith, and what the Krillitane leader referred to as the "shooty dog thing." K9. It was the tin dog who destroyed the Krillitane by exploding Krillitane oil.

FLORENCE FINNEGAN

A Plasmavore on the run from the Intergalactic police, the Judoon, Florence hid on Earth in the Royal Hope Hospital, London. She was being sought for the murder of the Child Princess of Padrivole Regency 9, an act she took great delight in. Her species survived by drinking blood and Finnegan used a straw on her victims to extract the liquid she needed. She met the Tenth Doctor when he was investigating unusual happenings at the hospital and ended up sucking his blood, unaware that he deliberately allowed her to as part of a plan to reveal her as an alien. The Judoon found her after they moved the Royal Hope Hospital to the moon. Florence tried to evade capture, but was shot by the space rhinos.

In a parallel world, Florence did not have the Doctor to contend with, but was instead defeated by journalist Sarah Jane Smith and her friends.

MISS FOSTER

Miss Foster was the name adopted by Matron Cofelia, a "space nanny" who was working for Adipose Industries on the planet Earth, a company which claimed to have a revolutionary new fat removing program. After the Adipose's breeding planet was lost, the Five-Straighten Classabindi Nursery Fleet, Intergalactic Class employed Cofelia to find a suitable planet with an obese population to ensure the continuation of the Adipose species. The Tenth Doctor and Donna Noble uncovered Adipose Industries' plan to turn human fat into Adipose babies and confronted Miss Foster. Using her sonic pen she attempted a swift getaway. After thousands of Adipose were created, a nursery ship came to Earth to retrieve the young and started to "beam up" Cofelia but it then let her drop to her death, not wanting to be connected to the illegal act which had taken place.

In an alternative timeline, caused when Donna Noble was attacked by the Trickster's Brigade, Adipose Industries were based in the USA where millions of lives were lost when the birthing of the Adipose began. It is believed Matron Cofelia of the Five-Straighten Classabindi Nursery Fleet headed this initiative.

GANTOK

This grotesque looking, Viking attire wearing alien apparently tried to help the Eleventh Doctor find Dorium Maldovar when the Doctor was trying to discover more about the Silence. Father Gideon Vandaleur pointed him in the direction of Gantok, with whom the Time Lord played Live Chess in the fifty-second century. The Time Lord won the game, much to Gantok's displeasure but, as agreed, he took the Doctor to see Dorium Maldovar, who existed now as a disembodied head, in the Seventh Transept. Angry at his defeat by the Doctor, Gantok planned to kill the Time Lord, but instead he fell to his doom and was consumed by a myriad of skulls, previous victims of the Headless Monks.

HARRISON CHASE

This plant-lover was the root of a huge problem for the Fourth Doctor and Sarah Jane Smith. Harrison Chase sent two of his men to the South Pole to capture an alien pod, which turned out to be a Krynoid. Chase surrounded himself with plant life in his huge mansion and palatial gardens in England, and could often be found at a special organ playing a tune using the sounds of the vegetation he loved so much. He conducted experiments on his employee who had been infected by the Krynoid, and looked on in fascination as his scientist slowly transformed into a fully-fledged, plant-man. Chase was killed when he was caught up in the same garden compost creator with which he was trying to murder the Doctor.

HENRY VAN STATTEN

The egomaniacal van Statten lived underground in Utah with his museum of alien relics and paraphernalia, which included a "Metaltron." When the Ninth Doctor and Rose arrived, the Time Lord recognized that the Metaltron was a Dalek, and tried to warn van Statten that the Dalek was lethal, even after the billionaire owner of the Internet had tortured him. Van Statten ignored the Doctor's advice, leading to the deaths of dozens of people. After surviving the carnage, van Statten was deposed by his assistant Goddard, who ordered that he be left in either San Diego, Seattle, or Sacramento (or somewhere else beginning with "S") with his mind wiped.

MISS MERCY HARTIGAN

A very clever but intensely bitter and angry woman, Miss Hartigan held mankind in contempt. As the matron of a workhouse, she was the perfect partner for the Cybermen, entering into an alliance with them during the winter of 1851 in London. She helped them round up the locals and they promised her all she wanted: power. The Tenth Doctor encountered her after meeting Jackson Lake who was under the impression that he himself was the Doctor, and was investigating strange events.

The Cybermen eventually converted Miss Hartigan to be the focal point of their giant Cyber King. The conversion was only partly successful; her strength of mind was too powerful for the Cybertechnology and her personality remained dominant. As she stomped around London, the Doctor traveled in a hot air balloon to contact her then used an infostamp to disconnect her from the Cyber machines. Miss Hartigan was unable to contain her horror and rage, and the emotional feedback caused the destruction of the Cybermen and her own death.

HOUSE

A being who lived in a bubble universe, House attracted the TARDIS carrying the Eleventh Doctor, Amy and Rory using a Time Lord distress signal. The entity manifested itself physically as a planet, and had drawn in a number of TARDISes over the years. The Doctor and his friends landed "on" him to find the surface strewn with console debris from previous TARDIS crashes. House also had servants on the surface, made up from various other bodies of those who had "visited" the planet. These creatures included Idris, who later became a physical manifestation of the Doctor's TARDIS, as well as Auntie, Uncle, and an unnamed member of the Ood species.

After learning that the Doctor was the last of the Time Lords, and that once he was gone, House would be left without a source of energy, he took the Doctor's TARDIS with a view to seeking out new resources in another universe. He taunted and mentally tortured Amy and Rory, who were trapped in the TARDIS, by changing the internal layout and playing with their minds—letting Amy think Rory was dead, for example. Eventually, House was destroyed when the TARDIS matrix was released from Idris and it placed itself back in the Doctor's time machine, forcing the unpleasant being into nothingness.

Fan Fact Note:
House used the Gallifreyan distress signal to ensnare Time Lords. He consumed the Artron energy from their TARDISes.

JOHN LUMIC

John Lumic existed on a parallel Earth visited by the Tenth Doctor, Rose Tyler and Mickey Smith, where Pete Tyler was still alive. This was later dubbed "Pete's World."

One of the crazier mad scientists the Doctor has ever met, Lumic thought he was helping mankind by using his company Cybus to upgrade humanity, eradicating illness and physical ailments, thus creating the Cybermen. The wheelchair-bound Lumic controlled his company from his airship high over London and enslaved mankind with his attractive earpieces which fed the population with news and information. This technology helped with his process to convert his customers into Cybermen who gave in easily.

The President of Great Britain was killed after refusing to accept Lumic's audacious plans for humanity's future. However, to remove their creator's own physical imperfections, his cybernetic creations turned on him and converted Lumic into a Cyber Controller. His plans to control and dominate the parallel Earth were thwarted by the Tenth Doctor and friends. The Cyber Controller fell to his death from a rope ladder as he pursued the Doctor.

JOSHUA & ABIGAIL NAISMITH

The Fourth Doctor and Leela found themselves at the mercy of these deadly robots when the couple arrived on a sand miner. A small crew of humanoids was assisted by a team of robots with a distinct hierarchy. Lowest were the Dums, black-colored units, unable to speak and mostly kept away from human contact; interaction with the crew was carried out by the Vocs, pale green units who could talk, perform control deck duties and even give massages; and at the top was a single Super-Voc, designated SV7, a silver-tunic wearing highly intelligent unit which controlled its fellow robots.

These units were mass-produced and used throughout many systems, designed to help human life.

Although the robots were unable to harm a human, or let one be harmed, a scientist named Taren Capel from Kaldor City reprogrammed the robots to kill all the crew, as well as the Doctor and Leela, as part of a rebellion. The robots used voice recognition programs to obey Capel, but when his vocal cords were affected by helium, making his voice rise in pitch, he ceased to be immune from their rampage, and he was killed by SV7.

Although robots were popular within this particular civilization, some humans did suffer from Grimwade's Syndrome, or robophobia, where those affected believed they were "surrounded by walking, talking dead men."

MISS KIZLET

This London-based lady met the Eleventh Doctor in the twenty-first century when she was acting as the agent for the Great Intelligence. Kizlet used Spoonheads to download human souls into the wifi for her master's consumption. She was able to control people's brains through a hand-held tablet, manipulating their emotions and controlling their actions. The Doctor eventually tracked her down to the Shard building in London where he discovered that the Great Intelligence had taken over her mind many years ago when she was a child (much as it had with Dr. Simeon). Once she was restored to "factory settings," she reverted mentally to her childlike status, still looking for her parents.

KLINEMAN HALPEN

The Chief Executive of Ood operations, selling Ood to humans across the galaxy as slaves, Halpen had inherited the job from his father, who had received it in turn from his own father. A rather grumpy and short-tempered man, Klineman treated the Ood with much contempt though he did keep one, Ood Sigma, as his servant. His shady operations were uncovered by the Tenth Doctor and Donna Noble on the Ood Sphere when they found Ood "infected" with Red Eye were being destroyed by Halpen.

Years in the business had taken its toll on the Chief Executive, rendering him almost bald, so he took a tonic in an attempt to restore his hair, but this tonic had rather unusual side-effects. After killing one of his colleagues Doctor Ryder, who revealed himself to be a "Friend of the Ood," (an activist interested in helping the species) by throwing him onto a huge Ood Brain, Halpen discovered the tonic was actually turning him into an Ood. He transformed in front of the Doctor and Donna. Ood Sigma had been working against his "master" for many years, and he informed the Time Lord that Halpen, in his new form, would be looked after.

174

LANCE BENNETT

Head of Human Resources of the London-based security company H.C. Clements, Bennett manipulated Donna Noble by embarking on a relationship with the temp. Starting from a simple cup of coffee, the two eventually became engaged and were about to be married when Donna disappeared from the church and materialized in the TARDIS, much to the shock of the Tenth Doctor. Bennett was, in fact, working for the Empress of the Racnoss and was feeding his fiancée with Huon particles for months in an attempt to resurrect the Racnoss species. When she learned of his betrayal, the Chiswick temp was, understandably, heartbroken but his deceit wasn't to last long as his mistress, the Empress of the Racnoss, forcefed Bennett Huon particles, trapping him in her web and then feeding him to her "children." A nasty man met a nasty end.

LUCY SAXON

Married to Harold Saxon (an alias for the Master), Lucy wasn't treated well by her husband. The devious Time Lord took her to the end of the universe, and showed off its "delights"—the end of humanity. Attracted by his power, she married Saxon and assisted him in his successful bid to become Prime Minister of the UK. Despite knowing his plans involving the Toclafane, and that they actually were the last vestiges of mankind from the future, Lucy happily stood (and sometimes danced) at her husband's side as the Earth's population was decimated by the spiked, spherical invaders. Her happiness was not to last however and in the "year that never was" (a phrase coined by Captain Jack Harkness to describe the twelve

months in which the Master ruled the Earth before the Tenth Doctor reversed his adversary's deeds) their relationship showed signs of strain, in a very physical way. On board the *Valiant*, after the Doctor confronted his fellow Time Lord, Lucy shot her husband, leaving him to die in the arms of his foe. Lucy was imprisoned in Broadfell Prison after a secret trial without a jury, but her internment was not to last too long. A group of the Master's loyal servants brought the renegade Time Lord back to life using his biometric imprint obtained from Mrs. Saxon's lips. They succeeded in their plan, but Lucy brought it to a swift end as she revealed her father had been working with scientists to counter this eventuality. Lucy threw a potion concocted by them at her husband, causing an explosion which resulted in her death, although not the Master's.

LUKE RATTIGAN

Luke certainly showed signs of mania when the Tenth Doctor, Donna Noble, and Martha Jones encountered him. Before reaching his teens, Luke made a fortune inventing an Internet search engine, then founded the Rattigan Academy, a school for young geniuses. A disillusioned soul and feeling his talents were going unnoticed and unappreciated by his peers, he joined an alliance with the Sontarans. In return for developing ATMOS, a device supposedly meant to eliminate the carbon dioxide emissions from cars, the warlike clone aliens promised the planet Castor 36 to Luke, where he could rule and start his own civilization. The ATMOS devices were, in fact, designed to poison the human race and leave the Earth as a base for the Sontarans to build their own army. As Luke later found out, the promised planet, which he dubbed Earth.2, was non-existent. To avenge his betrayal, Luke sacrificed himself to save the Doctor, despite their initial mutual dislike, aboard the Sontaran ship using their atmospheric converter, as altered by the Time Lord, to destroy their space craft.

LUCIUS PETRUS DEXTRUS

Another unpleasant man, who constantly wore a frown and barked at people all over the place. Since Lucius had breathed in the dust of Mount Vesuvius, his body was slowly turning to stone. He also had low-level psychic abilities, prophesying to the Tenth Doctor that "she is returning" (a reference to his former companion, Rose Tyler) while warning Donna Noble that there was "something" on her back, referring to the Trickster's Time Beetle that caused an alternative universe to be created around her. Lucius worked for the Pyroviles (see ALIENS) who were creating a converter inside Vesuvius that would change the population of Earth into their species. Dextrus died in the eruption of Mount Vesuvius.

LYTTON

Although human in appearance, Lytton was in fact born on Riften 5, which orbited Vita 15. This mercenary briefly came into contact with the Fifth Doctor in London in 1984. Lytton was working for the Daleks in a bid to free their creator Davros from imprisonment, but after Davros turned on his creations, Lytton traveled down a time corridor to present-day Earth.

The Sixth Doctor and Peri came across him in the London sewers where the Time Lord's distrust of Lytton was evident. They were all captured by the Cybermen and taken to the planet Telos where it was revealed that Lytton was, in fact, working for the indigenous Cryons against the Cybermen, although the Cybermen believed he had been working for them. Once his betrayal was evident, the Cyber Controller started the Cyberconversion process on Lytton. After he was told of Lytton's true loyalties, the Doctor tried to free him from their process, even though Lytton was aware that he had already suffered irreversible brain damage. As he died, Lytton used a knife the Doctor gave him to stab the Cyber Controller. Although the Doctor didn't want to leave his body behind, there was no option as explosives were about to go off. "I don't think I've ever misjudged anybody quite as badly as I did Lytton," the Time Lord said ruefully, moments later in the TARDIS.

MADAME KOVARIAN

Over the course of a very long time, eye-patch clad Kovarian worked with the religious order known as the Silence to destroy the Doctor. She arranged the abduction of a recently married Amy Pond and replaced her with a "ganger" duplicate of the Doctor's friend without Rory or the Eleventh Doctor realizing, at least at first. She took Amy to Demon's Run where she oversaw the pregnancy, often looking in on Pond's room through a door hatch. The ganger Amy saw visions of Kovarian while in the Graystark Hall orphanage, on the pirate ship the *Fancy* and at an Earth factory in the twenty-second century. Shortly after the Doctor destroyed the ganger Amy, the real Pond went into labor under the eye of Madame Kovarian.

Soon after, Amy's baby was replaced by a ganger, although Amy was oblivious to this fact. When Kovarian visited Dorium Maldovar she was informed that the Doctor was forming a personal army. During the Time Lord's attack on Kovarian and the Headless Monks at Demon's Run, Kovarian revealed she was making a weapon to defeat the time-traveler; this turned out to be River Song (the Ponds' daughter). Kovarian escaped the battle with ganger baby Melody.

She later visited River Song in the year 5123, at Luna University. Accompanied by two members of the Silence, River was placed in an astronaut suit and taken to Lake Silencio where her mission was to kill the Doctor.

When River refused to dispatch the Time Lord, an alternative time-line was created, where Madame Kovarian was imprisoned in the Area 52 pyramid by Amy Pond and her army (including an alternate version of her husband Rory Williams). The Eye Drive worn by Kovarian, which helped the wearer to both see and remember the Silence, was to prove her downfall when Amy used it to electrify her.

MR. MAGPIE

Not quite a mastermind villain this one, more of a stooge. The owner of the Magpie Electricals shop sold television sets in London as part of his "patriotic duty" in the run-up to the coronation of Queen Elizabeth II in 1953. However, both he and the sets he sold were being controlled by an alien force, the Wire. Magpie met the Tenth Doctor after Rose Tyler had her face removed by the Wire. The two men engaged in a chase which ended at the television transmitter at Alexandra Palace, where the Wire killed Magpie for refusing to kill the Doctor.

MARGARET BLAINE

That was the name of the human whose place was taken by Blon Fel-Fotch Passameer-Day Slitheen. A resident of Raxacoricofallapatorius, Blon traveled to Earth with her family planning to reduce the planet to inhospitable slag by starting a nuclear war, with a view to selling the remains on as fuel. Blon Fel-Fotch took the form of MI5's Blaine, and met the Ninth Doctor with Rose Tyler in 10 Downing Street, London during the Slitheen attack. She was believed to have been killed in the explosion that tore apart the UK Prime Minister's residence.

However, the crafty Slitheen turned up some months later in Cardiff: she had been able to teleport using an extrapolator, to escape the blast, ending up on the Isle of Dogs first. As Mayor, Blon had set in motion a plan to build a nuclear power plant called Blaidd

Drwg, which would result in the Welsh city being torn apart, and was killing anyone who uncovered her machinations. She was captured by the Ninth Doctor who decided to take her to answer for her crimes; Blon requested a chance for one last meal. Though she appeared to be remorseful, this was a ruse and she tried to attack the Doctor numerous times during their "date" in Cardiff. Margaret's back-up plan was to use her extrapolator to make the rift in space and time in Cardiff become active, forcing her and the Doctor to retreat to the TARDIS. When she tried to hold Rose hostage, the TARDIS opened itself to Margaret. When she looked into the heart of the ship, she regressed back to the state of an egg. The Doctor delivered the egg back to Raxacoricofallapatorius, hoping her new life would be a better and morally positive one.

MAWDRYN

It might be slightly unfair to call this chap a villain, since he had good reasons for what he was trying to do. The humanoid Mawdryn traveled with his followers for thousands of years after stealing a metamorphic symbiosis regenerator in the hope of achieving the Time Lords' power of regeneration. This quest had left him and his fellow travelers mutated and in a perpetual state of living death. When Mawdryn met the Fifth Doctor's companions Tegan and Nyssa, he lied to them, stating he was, in fact, a newly regenerated Doctor. Eventually, he came face-to-face with the Time Lord on his own ship with his followers, where he threatened Tegan and Nyssa in an attempt to force the Doctor to sacrifice his remaining regenerations to end the misery he and his friends were experiencing. Although the Doctor was willing to make the sacrifice, a blast of temporal energy caused by two different versions of the Brigadier touching ended the pain for Mawdryn and his kind.

MAX CAPRICORN

After being kicked off the board of his own company, having run it for 176 years, Max Capricorn exacted revenge by turning his huge cruiseliner, the starship *Titanic* into a bomb that would crash into the planet Earth, killing millions. As a cyborg, with only his head remaining organic, he was shunned by his own company. He felt his actions were appropriate, leaving the board members to be accused of the deaths, while he escaped free and rich. His plans were thwarted by the Tenth Doctor, Astrid Peth, and Alonso Frame, who ensured the *Titanic* did not crash into the Earth. During a confrontation between the gold-toothed cyborg and the Time Lord, Astrid used a forklift truck to pick Max up and send him plummeting to his death among the ship's engines, which were on fire.

PROFESSOR LAZARUS

Like a few people the Doctor has come across in his travels, this misguided man was searching for immortality. With funding from Harold Saxon (aka the Master), Richard Lazarus built a genetic manipulation device over the course of many years. Completed when he was seventy-six years old, he claimed it would "change what it means to be human."

His machine apparently worked at first. Richard stepped in and came out a much younger-looking man. However, to his cost, Lazarus discovered a nasty side effect of the process: he began to mutate into a gigantic scorpion-like monster. While under this influence, the Professor killed his long-time business partner Sylvia Thaw, taking her human DNA and resorting back to human form as a result. He attempted similarly with Tish Jones, Martha Jones' sister, who was working as Lazarus' Head of PR, planted there by the Master to provide a link to the Doctor without her knowledge. After Lazarus killed two paramedics, the Tenth Doctor and Martha thwarted any further killing in a showdown in London's Southwark Cathedral, in which Richard had hid in a crypt as child during the blitz in World War II. The Time Lord used the sounds of a church organ to discombobulate the Lazarus monster, who fell from the bell tower to his death. The body on the ground, reverted back to Lazarus' younger form, than eventually back to his original older form.

The Master later used the technology engineered by Professor Lazarus to age the Tenth Doctor by hundreds of years.

ROSANNA CALVIERRI

Hailing from the planet Saturnyne, Rosanna had left her home world with her children and traveled to Venice, Earth in 1580. The crack in space and time first noticed by the Eleventh Doctor in Amelia Pond's bedroom had caused their exodus, and the Saturnynians used perception filters to hide their true form, hoping to use their new home as the start of a fresh era for their civilization. Venice was perfect for the aquatic species' plans and Rosanna opened a school for girls, who she intended to convert into Saturnynians. Their plans to flood the Italian city were thwarted by the Doctor, Amy Pond and Rory Williams, so Rosanna felt the need to end her life. Still in her human form, after her perception filter was rendered useless, she entered the waters of Venice where she was eaten by her own children.

SCAROTH

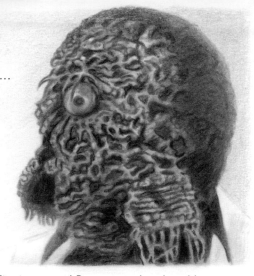

The last of the Jagaroth species had perhaps the grandest scheme of all the villains that the Doctor encountered. Trying to leave Earth hundreds of millions of years ago, Scaroth's ship exploded on take-off, scattering twelve splinters of him throughout time. Most adopted the same human form, using a mask to cover their monocular alien face. His varying selves could communicate telepathically and worked together to advance the human race in order to create time-travel technology that would allow Scaroth to go back in time and save his species. Scaroth influenced the history of mankind with the invention of the wheel, star-mapping, and the building of the Egyptian pyramids, and, in 1979, he was selling copies of the Mona Lisa painting which Leonardo da Vinci had been cajoled into creating by one of Scaroth's splinters, Captain Tancredi, in 1505.

The Fourth Doctor and Romana discovered a crack in time while visiting Paris in 1979, leading them to the time-travel experiments paid for by Count Carlos Scarlioni (the final splinter of the Jagaroth) and conducted by scientist Professor Fyodor Nikolai Kerensky. Scarlioni planned to steal the original Mona Lisa from the Louvre and sell it along with the other six that he already possessed, painted by da Vinci.

Scarlioni captured Romana and ordered her to stabilize his time-travel field after its creator Kerensky was aged to death within it. When Scarlioni's wife confronted her husband about his true self, he killed her. When the Doctor traveled back in time to investigate, he met Tancredi, who proceeded to torture him. After escaping, the Doctor was able to mark some of the Mona Lisas with the words "This is a fake" on the back.

Scaroth managed to travel back in time to the time of his accident but the Doctor, Romana, and private detective Duggan prevented him from creating a time paradox, particularly as the explosion of Scaroth's ship was the catalyst that started life on Earth. When Scaroth was returned to 1979, still in his true form, he was killed by his servant.

SHAKRI

The Eleventh Doctor was surprised to come across the Shakri as they were believed to be myths by the Time Lords, although he did refer to them as "the pest controllers of the universe." He met one who, in this case, had manifested itself in a vaguely disgusting humanoid form at the end of the Year of the Slow Invasion. The Shakri had sent mysterious black cubes to Earth, to spy on humanity and then, ultimately, to destroy the population to prevent them from

becoming a plague on the galaxy. The Shakri claimed they were serving "the word of the Tally," a race unknown to the Doctor. The planned annihilation of Earth was halted by the Time Lord, assisted by Amy, Rory, and his father Brian Williams. They came face-to-face with a hologram of the Shakri on one of their seven ships surrounding Earth and when the cube attack was thwarted, the ship exploded.

SHARAZ JEK

Sharaz Jek started his career as a doctor before starting to specialize in androids. He went into business with Morgus, using his androids to collect and refine the anti-ageing drug Spectrox on Androzani Minor, but he was betrayed by his associate and was left for dead after a mud explosion. Whilst Morgus continued to reign supreme on Androzani Major as CEO of the Sirius Conglomerate, Jek rebuilt his life on Minor and kept his damaged and burnt body together in a leather suit and mask. He vowed revenge on his former partner.

The Fifth Doctor and Peri landed on Androzani Minor and became caught in the war raging between the Sirius Conglomerate and Jek's androids. On seeing

Peri's beauty, Jek saved her from being killed by firing squad, replacing her and the Doctor with androids. The scientist became obsessed with keeping Peri underground with him, although he was not so keen on the Time Lord, arguing with the "prattling jackanapes" frequently. Jek was traumatized when he learned Peri was suffering from spectrox toxemia, a deadly condition with only one antidote: milk from a Queen Bat.

Jek helped the Doctor find the antidote to save Peri but his troops came under attack, and Morgus himself came looking for Jek. The scientist did gain revenge on his old enemy, killing him in a laser energy beam moments after he was shot by Morgus's mercenary Stotz. Jek died in the arms of one of his androids.

SIL

The Sixth Doctor and Peri met this alien businessman from Thoros Beta on Varos in the twenty-fourth century when the Time Lord was looking for some Zeiton-7 for the TARDIS. Sil was hoping to sell the television rights to recordings of tortures of criminals on Varos to other markets around the universe. The pair met him again on his home planet of Thoros Beta some time later and his distasteful ways and persona hadn't changed. This time Sil was dealing in weapons and was as unpleasant as ever, spouting lines such as, "There is nothing I more enjoy than human suffering," while devouring marsh minnows at every opportunity.

SKALDAK

Ice Warrior Grand Marshall Skaldak met the Eleventh Doctor and Clara Oswald on the Russian submarine Firebird. He was found by Professor Grisenko frozen in a block of ice, where he had been for around five thousand years, and taken to the submarine, where he was set free by a too curious crew member who didn't live to tell the tale. When Skaldak confronted the crew, he was captured and chained in the vessel. The Doctor revealed that the Martian was a great and respected warrior, whose enemies carved his name into their flesh before they died. However, the Ice Warrior escaped, by abandoning his outer armor shell, and wreaked havoc on the ship's crew. A soldier first and foremost, Skaldak chose not to kill either Clara or Grisenko when presented with the chance although he did threaten to release the submarine's nuclear warheads, thus causing a potential World War. Clara was able to persuade him to be honorable, reminding him of his daughter, and Skaldak elected not to carry out the threat, even after he had been rescued by an Ice Warrior ship.

SKY SILVESTRY

Technically Sky wasn't a villain but was simply possessed by a monster on the planet Midnight. Before her possession, the Tenth Doctor met her on a tourist cruise to see a Sapphire Waterfall. Their excursion was cut short by a being that could survive in an environment bombarded with Xtonic radiation. The entity attacked the craft, killing the pilots, and possessing Sky. At this point, she began to repeat everything that everybody said around her. Her fellow travelers were horrified and tried to remove her but the Tenth Doctor intervened, fascinated by what she was. The force then transferred from her to the Time Lord, starting to devour his knowledge and personality, and it seemed that Sky was now "free"—or so it appeared to the other tourists. They began to throw the Doctor off their ship but in fact, it was still inside Sky. When she started to use distinctive phrases the Doctor had been saying (such as "allons-y" and "molto bene") the ship hostess sacrificed herself in order to rid the craft of the malevolent creature. Later, when reunited with his companion Donna, the Time Lord admitted he had no idea what the monster was, but did warn the authorities of its existence so that no other beings could be captured by it.

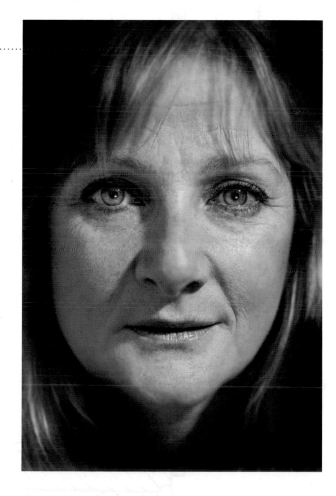

THE BLACK GUARDIAN

The Fourth Doctor was made aware of the Black Guardian by its counterpart, the White Guardian, at the start of his quest for the Key to Time, although it was some time before the Time Lord met the powerful and evil being. The Black Guardian was also searching for the Key to Time and planned to take it from the Doctor, once all six pieces were collected.

When the Doctor and Romana had collected the final segment, which was in fact a living person, Princess Astra of Atrios, the Black Guardian posed as his counterpart, the White Guardian, and asked the Time Lord for the key. However, the Doctor realized from his blasé attitude toward the death of the princess that this could not be the White Guardian. On the TARDIS monitor, the couple watched as the Black Guardian vowed revenge. To ensure their safety, the Doctor installed a randomiser in the TARDIS to prevent the Guardian tracking them down.

Some years later, when the Doctor was in his next regeneration, the Black Guardian set his revenge into motion. The Guardian brokered a deal with Vislor Turlough, an alien exiled to Earth: if Turlough killed the Doctor, the Black Guardian would return him to his home planet. The Black Guardian used a crystal to monitor Turlough,, cajoling and pressing him whenever necessary.

Finally, aboard a sailing ship in a race for Enlightenment, the Black Guardian physically met the Fifth Doctor. Turlough reneged on his deal, and threw the crystal containing Enlightenment at the Guardian, engulfing him in flames. Although it appeared that he was dead, the White Guardian pointed out that both Black and White were needed to co-exist.

THE SIREN

The Siren wasn't really a villain although, for some time, the crew of pirate ship the *Fancy* feared her and her powers. She was actually a virtual doctor from a spaceship in another dimension which existed in the same space as the *Fancy*. The humans believed she was a demon who marked the crew with a black spot and then took them away. Using any reflective surface, the Siren could move between the hospital on her spaceship and the *Fancy*. Her crew had been wiped out by disease and she sought further patients to cure. The Eleventh Doctor, Amy, and Rory discovered the reality of the situation after the latter had been marked for "death." Along with Captain Avery, the Doctor and Amy traveled across the dimensions. The Siren recognized the marital bond between Amy and Rory from their rings and let the Doctor's companion tend to her husband, restoring him to life. The Siren was then accompanied on her travels by Avery whose son was seriously ill but could be treated aboard her vessel.

THE FAMILY OF BLOOD

This quartet (calling themselves Father of Mine, Mother of Mine, Son of Mine, and Daughter of Mine) had tracked down the Tenth Doctor, trying to learn the secrets of the Time Lords' regenerations. The beings themselves were green and gas-like, and were able to inhabit other bodies but their life cycle was very short and, without bodies to use, they would die within three months. The Doctor planned to use a Chameleon Arch to disguise his Time Lord DNA for long enough that they would die before they could absorb him.

Unfortunately for him, and the residents of Farringham on Earth, the Family followed him to a school in 1913 where the Time Lord was teaching under the name of John Smith, with Martha Jones acting as his maid. The Family infiltrated the community, using scarecrows to steal humans to inhabit. They located the Doctor quickly but due to his human form, he was unable to protect his friends or retaliate when their army of scarecrows attacked the school. Eventually, the fob watch which contained his Time Lord DNA was returned to him, restoring him to his former self.

The Doctor confronted the Family in their ship claiming still to be John Smith, using "ventriloquism of the nose," and destroyed it. The Time Lord then punished the Family in various ways, trapping them all for eternity: Father of Mine was wrapped in unbreakable chains forged from a dwarf star alloy; Mother of Mine was launched into the event horizon of a collapsing galaxy; Daughter of Mine was placed in every mirror in existence (though the Doctor would visit her every year); and Son of Mine was trapped in a scarecrow.

THE EDITOR

Another stooge here, who was most definitely not a friend of the Doctor. Serving the Mighty Jagrafess of the Holy Hadrojassic Maxarodenfoe (or "Max" as he called it), the Editor worked on the fifth hundreth floor on Satellite Five monitoring the news channels and keeping tabs on the humans connected with the station through implanted chips in their brains. He knew everything that was going on and the history of everyone there. This was why the Ninth Doctor and Rose Tyler caused so much trouble for him in 200,000 when the pair arrived along with short-lived TARDIS traveler Adam, as they had no such chips. But thanks to Adam, the Editor discovered the history of the pair and sought to steal the secrets of the Time Lord and his time machine. His plans were cut short when the environmental controls of Floor 500 were sabotaged. This was bad news for the Mighty Jagrafess of the Holy Hadrojassic Maxarodenfoe which couldn't survive in the heat and began to die. Although he tried to flee, the Editor was held in position by one of his underlings so died when Max exploded.

VIVIEN FAY

Although she appeared to be an attractive young woman, Vivien Fay was actually the age-old Cessair of Diplos, a fugitive wanted on various counts including: murder; the theft of the Great Seal of Diplos (which was, in actual fact, a segment of the Key to Time); and taking three Ogri from their home planet Ogros in contravention of Article 7594 of the Galactic Charter. Cessair was captured by justice machines, the Megara but managed to escape to Earth, leaving the ship in hyperspace with her judge, jury and executioners trapped aboard. She hid In England on Earth for thousands of years, operating under different names (including the Cailleach, Lady Morgana Montcalm, and Mrs. Trefusis) before meeting the Fourth Doctor and Romana, who were looking for the Key to Time. The Time Lady was captured by Cessair who sent her to the starship although she was followed quickly by the Doctor. After accidentally releasing the Megara, the Time Lord faced trial by the justice machines though he managed to turn the situation around to reveal Vivien Fay's true identity to the beings. Her punishment was a transformation into stone to remain on Earth in a stone circle for eternity.

DR. WALTER SIMEON

Walter was a lonely boy, who often to talked to himself or the snowmen he built, unhappy with the world. After The Great Intelligence took over his mind, Simeon set up the Great Intelligence Institute with a view to building an army of ice. Many years later, the Eleventh Doctor tracked him down and revealed the truth about his childhood, using a memory worm to erase his adult memories, and restoring Simeon to his younger self. The Great Intelligence fled Simeon's dying body stating that the "dream had outlived the dreamer" and shot him with an electricity bolt, killing him.

The Great Intelligence then used the appearance of Dr. Simeon to talk to Miss Kizlet in London when people's souls were being swallowed into the wifi. The Intelligence continued to use Simeon's form to command the Whispermen, and go to the Doctor's tomb on Trenzalore. Disguised as Simeon, he entered the Doctor's timestream, and tried to destroy the Doctor in all his lives, believing that this would result in his destruction, but Clara Oswald was able to reverse his actions.

WINIFRED GILLYFLOWER

Villains don't come much fouler than this awful woman whom the Eleventh Doctor described as "nuts" when they faced each other in the late nineteenth century. Some years previously Winifred found a red leech, a small lobster-like creature from prehistoric times and started a rather odd symbiotic relationship with it. It suckled off her and she used its poisonous secretions to preserve people who came to her new community, Sweetville. Gillyflower wanted to lead mankind into a New Eden and even experimented on her own daughter, Ada, in order to get the preservation formula right; she lied to Ada about her resultant blindness, blaming it on her father. The sermon-giving harpy was rumbled when the Doctor and Clara came across Sweetville and stopped her, with help from Madame Vastra, Jenny, and Strax. Gillyflower launched a rocket to spread the red leech venom around the planet although the poison had been successfully removed from it, saving mankind from the Crimson Horror. Strax shot her and she fell in the rocket silo to her death.

ALIENS & MONSTERS

The Doctor's life would not be complete, or indeed interesting, if he didn't have the odd alien or monster to come up against in his travels through space and time. It should be noted that not all aliens or "monsters" are evil types—some become good chums with the Time Lord (see those listed as FRIENDS)—but many are. But which do you love to hate the most?

ABZORBALOFF

This nasty shape-shifter was a resident of the planet Clom, the sister planet of Raxacoricofallapatorius, although the two species did not speak well of one another. Not a killer, he destroyed the lives of many he came into contact with. His species could absorb souls merely by touch: his victims' bodies disintegrated but their faces remained on show on his body. The Tenth Doctor, traveling with Rose Tyler, encountered the Abzorbaloff when looking for Elton Pope (see FRIENDS) in London on Earth. The Abzorbaloff had taken the human form of Victor Kennedy and devoured the members of L.I.N.D.A. (London Investigation 'N' Detective Agency) one-by-one, leaving Elton until last, in a bid to find and "eat" the Doctor. His attempt was unsuccessful, and he was left as a messy puddle of greenish goo.

ATRAXI

Shortly after he regenerated into the Eleventh Doctor, the time-traveler came eye-to-eye with this gargantuan eyeball. Little is known about the Atraxi, so the eyeball could be an organic part of their crystalline-like spaceship. Effectively an intergalactic police force (like the Judoon), the Atraxi had captured Prisoner Zero although it managed to escape through a crack in space and time to Leadworth, Earth. Having tracked him down to the planet, the Atraxi then decided to destroy the planet to gain their prey. Thankfully, the Doctor stepped in and explained that Earth was protected by him, resulting in a swift retreat by the aliens.

Some months later, the Doctor found himself at the mercy of the Atraxi and many other alien races and he was imprisoned in the Pandorica, under Stonehenge on Earth in the year 102 A.D.

AUTONS AND THE NESTENE CONSCIOUSNESS

Autons were the creations of the Nestene Consciousness, a being that could control and inhabit plastic. The Third Doctor faced an Auton invasion shortly after his regeneration as shop dummies came to life and terrorized London. During their battle, the Time Lord met the Nestene Consciousness and was attacked by its squid-like appendage. It had come to Earth in a series of meteorites to conquer the planet with its Autons. With help from Liz Shaw (see COMPANIONS), the Nestene Consciousness was shut down, whereupon the Autons ceased to be a menace. Although simply mannequins when the Nestene Consciousness was not present, the Autons could be incredibly lifelike, and could copy the bodyprints of humans, replicating them successfully as the Third

Doctor discovered. (Years later, Rose Tyler found that her boyfriend Mickey had been replaced by an Auton, and Rory Williams was brought back to life as an Auton Roman Centurion.)

Some time later, the Master allied with the Nestene Consciousness aiming to take over Earth using plastic daffodils, grotesque children's dolls, and even chairs, all made of plastic. The Third Doctor was able to repel the impeding Nestene invasion force by stopping a radio signal that the Master had initiated, after the Doctor convinced his fellow Time Lord that he would be expendable once the invasion took place.

Many years later, now in his Ninth incarnation, the Time Lord uncovered a plan by the Nestene Consciousness to invade Earth and use it as its own after its own planet was destroyed in the Time War. He told his new companion Rose Tyler (whose first alien encounter was with a group of Autons in the retail store where she worked) that her planet was perfect for the Nestenes, since it was full of toxins, dioxins, smoke and oil. The Doctor defeated the Nestene Consciousness with a vial of anti-plastic, with some swinging help from his new friend, Rose.

Autons were part of an alliance of alien species which congregated to capture and imprison the Eleventh Doctor in the Pandorica.

THE BEAST

It's not often the Doctor comes across an alien or an entity whose origin baffles him, but the Beast did just that. This huge malevolent creature was imprisoned at the heart of Krop Tor, a planet orbiting a black hole, many years before the Doctor encountered him around the fortieth century. If it were to free itself, the planet would be sucked into the black hole. This huge, fiery horned ancient creature met the Tenth Doctor after it had possessed the Ood as well as Toby, a member of the Sanctuary Base crew on the planet, using them as mouthpieces and to kill other members of the team. The Beast told the Time Lord it had been around since before the creation of the Universe and was the basis for the Devil in all cultures. Through the Ood, it claimed to be known by the names of Abaddon, Kroptor, Satan, and Lucifer among many others.

The Doctor believed it was destroyed after the possessed Toby was ejected into space and Krop Tor was eaten by the Black Hole. When questioned by Rose to its identity, the Doctor replied, "I don't know," cheerfully adding, "But that's good. Day I know everything? Might as well stop." But his companion was troubled, as the Beast had stated that Rose would "die in battle," to which the Doctor simply claimed it lied. Of course, it was true, from a certain point of view: Rose was listed as one of the fallen in the Battle of Canary Wharf.

Some years later, the Tenth Doctor retold this adventure very briefly to Donna Noble, claiming the Beast "was the Devil," although she didn't believe him. Toward the end of the Doctor's Eleventh incarnation, the Great Intelligence claimed one of the Doctor's pseudonyms was "The Beast."

CARRIONITES

These shape shifters from Rexel IV caused quite a fuss in Shakespearian London in 1599 when their word-based science and technology was mistaken for witchcraft. Like "witches," they could fly, materialize and dematerialize, and inflict pain on humans using puppets, if they had sourced their DNA. Three of their species—Lilith, Doomfinger, and Blood-tide—met the Tenth Doctor and Martha Jones while putting a plan into action that would see their race salvaged from the dawn of time. They wanted to use Earth as their new home destroying the human race in the process. The Doctor used the talents of wordsmith William Shakespeare to end their plans, trapping them in a crystal ball, which the Doctor then kept in the TARDIS.

Fan Fact Note:
The Carrionites hailed from the dawn of the universe and wanted to lead the universe back into the old ways of blood and magic.

CATKIND

The Doctor met members of Catkind on New Earth on two separate occasions. In their first meeting, the humanoid feline species were working in the New New York Hospital in the year five billion and twenty-three. The Sisters of Plentiude, as they were known, seemed to be caring, helping to treat and cure the patients, but in fact they were actually malevolent, and helped keep thousands of human clones in perpetual pain with every disease known. After intervention by the Tenth Doctor the Sisters were arrested by the police.

Thirty years later, the Time Lord revisited New Earth with his new companion, Martha Jones, where he was reunited with one of the Sisters, Novice Hame. She was now tending to the Face of Boe, who was dying. Mistrustful of her at first, because of her past indiscretions, the Doctor eventually realized that Hame had changed her ways. He encountered another Catkind, Brannigan, on the highway in New New York, who was married to a human. The Doctor met the family, complete with their kittens in the couple's car. A member of the Catkind species was abducted and made to face their fear with the Creature in his prison ship, disguised as an Earth hotel from the 1980s.

THE CREATURE (OR MINOTAUR)

A distant cousin of the Nimon (whom the Fourth Doctor encountered many years previous with Romana), this Minotaur-like beast was captured and sent to a prison ship for life after installing itself as a malevolent deity. When the Eleventh Doctor, Amy and Rory came across the creature, the prison was artificially designed by computer to take the form of an Earth hotel from the 1980s. The travelers met various people who had been abducted and taken there, and who had subsequently died at the hands of the alien beast. It fed on the faith of those it devoured and, realizing this, the Doctor was able to let the Creature finally die, after eons alive with no purpose. Its last words revealed its knowledge of the Doctor and his blood-soaked lifestyle.

CYBERMEN

A frightening reminder of what humanity can do to survive, the Cybermen were born on Mondas, Earth's twin planet. As Mondas drifted out of the Solar System and into deep space, the humans took more and more drastic measures to survive, and eventually replaced their weakening body parts with mechanical elements. Somewhere along the way, however, their humanity was also lost. Cybermen converted those they saw as weaker to their own ranks, and they had the unique ability to constantly absorb and integrate new technology into themselves which made them nearly unstoppable.

First encountered as mummy-like robotic cyborgs when Mondas returned to Earth in 1986, the Cybermen began to spread throughout the galaxy after their planet's destruction. Establishing a new home world on Telos, where they stored Cybermen survivors deep underground in ice tombs and developed the terrifying Cybermats, they attacked Earth repeatedly—first, via moon-based weather systems before resorting to direct attacks on deep-space Earth stations. They then initiated a full-scale invasion of Earth in the late twentieth century, with the aid of Tobias Vaughn, only to be defeated by UNIT.

Having spread out across the galaxy, the Cybermen of the future began to lose the Cyber-Wars against humanity who exploited their weakness for gold. In a desperate bid to restore balance, the Cybermen attempted to destroy Voga, a gold-rich asteroid. Another attempted assault by the Cybermen was a bomb they deployed in twenty-sixth century Earth with explosive space freighters during a conference there. Foiling the plan, the Doctor's companion Adric found himself trapped on-board one of the bomb

ships, thrown back in time, and killed as the craft collides with Earth, an accident which also wiped out the dinosaurs.

A platoon of Cybermen were captured (with various other dangerous creatures and species) and brought to the Death Zone of Gallifrey along with the First, Second, Third, and Fifth Doctors as part of Borusa's plot to discover the secret of immortality. The Cybermen forged an alliance with the Master who had been sent there by the High Council, but they were betrayed by the renegade Time Lord.

Experimenting with time-travel, the Cybermen attempted to change the course of history by getting Halley's Comet to crash into Earth, thus weakening the planet before the return of Mondas (which of course would prevent their original defeat). Thankfully, the plan is foiled by the Sixth Doctor who also encouraged an uprising by the Cryons—natives of Telos—who had been suppressed since the Cybermen conquered and adopted Telos as their

new home world. Assembling a full war fleet in an attempt to capture the Nemesis—which was made of a deadly living Gallifreyian technology called validium—the Cybermen crossed paths with the Seventh Doctor as they aimed to conquer the Earth (again!) and finally establish a new home world, a new Mondas. Another plan, another failure.

Some time after the Time War finished, the Ninth Doctor came across the head of a Cyberman in the underground bunker of multi-billionaire Henry van Statten in Utah, 2012. But it wouldn't be long until the Time Lord came into contact with the Cybermen, or something like them at the very least.

When traveling with Rose Tyler and Mickey Smith, The Tenth Doctor was taken into a parallel Earth where John Lumic of Cybus Industries (see VILLAINS) had produced the future of mankind, the Cybermen. Converting thousands into his new creations, the world looked doomed until the Time Lord and his chums brought the cyborgs to their feet with a simple cell phone. The remaining Cybermen on Earth (in factories in every country) were to be destroyed by Mickey Smith who stayed behind while his friends returned to their own universe.

It wasn't long before these Cybermen learned how to break out of Pete's World, as it was dubbed, and into the original Earth. Seemingly "ghosts" to the population, the Cybermen infiltrated Torchwood at Canary Wharf and engineered their mass invasion of the planet. All looked lost for humanity until the appearance of the Daleks, who had been hiding in a Void Ship within the Torchwood facility. A war broke out between the two, though the Daleks, in an unusual moment of levity, proclaimed the Cybermen were only good at dying. Both sides were sucked back into the Void, though not all Cybermen were lost.

In London, 1851, the Tenth Doctor met a small group of Cybermen (who seemed to have been "spat" out from the Void), utilized some Dalek tech (also trapped in the Void), and enlisted the help of Miss Hartigan (see VILLAINS) in an audacious plan involving the Cyber King—a gigantic robot which stomped all over the city until the Gallifreyan brought about its end. For the first time, the Gallifreyan encountered Cybershades—furry, animal-like creatures with Cybermasks covering their faces.

The Cybermen were instrumental in capturing the Eleventh Doctor and imprisoning him in the Pandorica underneath Stonehenge. A solitary Cyber-man had been left to guard the stone circle. Rusted and damaged, the cyborg still managed to attack and was even able to function without a head (which it would ultimately find and replace). The soldier was able to fire poisoned darts and seemingly existed without a living human inside (its mask opened to reveal a skull).

When searching for his wife, Amy, Rory approached the Twelfth Cyber Legion in his quest for her location, destroying their ships in the process. Traveling by himself some months later, the Eleventh Doctor visited his friend Craig Owens in Colchester, England, as a ruse to uncover the mystery surrounding a large department store. The enigma was revealed to be the return of the Cybermen. Utilizing Cybermats, the cyborgs had infiltrated the store and killed members of the staff. The Doctor took a Cybermat to investigate, naming it "Bitey" (due to its teeth and aggressive tendencies). He discovered a Cybership had crash-landed hundreds of years prior, but the electric-cable recently found lying by the council resulted in their activation. While there were only six of them, the Cybermen looked to convert the planet but, of course, the Time Lord and Craig Owens had other plans. Though both were captured, Craig rejects his Cyber conversion because of his love for his son, Stormaggeddon, and the Cybership is destroyed along with the Cybermen inside it.

On a visit to Hedgewick's World of Wonders with Clara, Artie, and Angie, the Eleventh Doctor was

surprised to find a deactivated Cyberman—one apparently used for playing chess. But unknown to him, and the inhabitants of the planet, Cybermites existed, kidnapping people and using their bodies as spare parts. The Cybermen on the planet—thought to be long extinct after a brutal war—were awoken and able to change, or upgrade, to the surroundings, taking on the environment and weapons facing them.

Their movement had changed too, as they were suddenly able to move with great speed. The Doctor was captured and part converted, but was strong enough to battle the Cyberplanner at chess and win (with the help of a gold ticket). A bomb destroyed the planet and the Cybermen—though at least one Cybermite survived…

DALEKS

....

After a millennium of nuclear, chemical, and biological warfare on Skaro between the Thals and Kaleds, a stalemate had set in with no signs of the bloodshed ending. Enter Davros, a brilliant, crippled Kaled scientist determined to give his race the final advantage. Reasoning that the centuries of mutations caused by war could no longer be reversed, he set about advancing them, to see what their ultimate outcome would be. As the answers became clear, he developed a new form of transport for the future Kaleds—the Mark III Travel Machine, also known as the Dalek.

However, Davros' tinkering went beyond advancing the Kaled mutation—he further manipulated the DNA to turn his new Daleks into xenophobic, murderous creatures that saw all other lifeforms as inferior, to be hated and, ultimately, exterminated. Turning on their creator, and surviving an attempt by the Time Lords to alter their timeline by sending the Fourth Doctor to avert their birth or ensure that they developed into less aggressive creatures, the Daleks emerged to become the most deadly lifeforms in the universe.

The First Doctor encountered the Daleks hiding away in a city on Skaro eons after the war with the Thals. They refused to emerge from the city, drawing power from a static electricity grid they had created to sustain themselves. Although it appeared that he had defeated them, the Doctor soon learned they were far more resourceful survivors when he found them ruling a ruined Earth in 2167A.D. They had begun to expand across the universe, and they planned to hollow out the Earth's core to turn the planet into a mobile space station as a base for further conquests.

After again being thwarted by the Doctor and recognizing the threat he posed, the Daleks set out to actively exterminate the Doctor by chasing him and his companions throughout time and space, having mastered time-travel and TARDIS-like technology. This led to a showdown on Mechanus between the Daleks and the Mechonoids. The Daleks planned further conquest, allying themselves with Mavic Chen and the Meddling Monk, and built a Time Destructor with a view to universal domination once more, but they were defeated by the Doctor yet again.

The newly-regenerated Second Doctor encountered the Daleks on Vulcan, where they appeared to be willing to happily serve the human colonists. However, the Doctor soon discovered they were using this as a cover to begin reproducing the Dalek race en masse.

After capturing the TARDIS and luring the Doctor and his companion Jamie to 1866, the Daleks appeared to be seeking to add the "human factor"—the strengths of the race that has consistently defeated them time and again—to their own DNA to breed a new "super" Dalek. However, the Emperor Dalek had a deeper agenda: by isolating the human factor, the Doctor would also discover the "Dalek Factor" which could then be spread through all of time and space. However, a civil war broke out as Daleks which had been "humanized" by receiving the human factor rebelled, and it did

seem as if the Daleks had destroyed themselves once and for all.

However, when mysterious soldiers from the future attempted to sabotage peace talks aimed at preventing a third world war, the Third Doctor discovered that the Daleks had, once again, conquered the Earth as a result of that disastrous global conflict. These events were in fact caused by a time paradox, and with the war averted, the timeline in which the Daleks ruled Earth was erased from history.

After an alliance with the Master to provoke a war between humanity and the Draconian Empire, the Doctor pursued his old foes to

Spiridon, where a task force of Thals were trying to locate the Daleks. The Daleks were preparing to use biological warfare on the inhabitants while also seeking the secret of invisibility, which the Spiridons possessed, and they then planned to awaken a huge Dalek army which was being kept in cold stage in one of the planet's icecanoes. The Doctor and the Thals managed to refreeze the Daleks.

Both the Doctor, a human Marine Space Corps team and the Daleks were drawn to the planet Exxilon, where an ancient force drained their crafts of energy. The Daleks were unable to use their energy weapons, and they were then forced into an uneasy alliance with the humans, since both parties apparently required the rare mineral parrinium, which could help cure a deadly space plague spreading across the galaxy. However, it became clear that the Daleks intended to hoard all the parrinium for themselves to weaken and blackmail all other galactic superpowers.

Centuries after their creation, the Daleks returned to Skaro to recover Davros, after reaching a stalemate in their war with the mechanical Movellans. Defeating the Daleks—and the Movellans, who turn out to be as ruthless as the Daleks—the Fourth Doctor surrendered Davros to the authorities to face trial for his crimes.

Ninety years later, Davros was liberated by the Daleks from his cryogenic prison cell after the Daleks

began to lose the war with the Movellans, who had developed a biological weapon that attacked Dalek tissue.

Required to create a cure for his creations, Davros instead plotted to re-engineer the Daleks to accept him as their leader. At the same time, the Supreme Dalek was also planning to clone the Fifth Doctor, Turlough, and Tegan, use these clones to assassinate the High Council of the Time Lords, and also clone prominent members of humanity to manipulate events on Earth.

Davros escaped from his imprisonment, and continued to build his own breed of Daleks on Tranquil Necros, before being captured by Daleks loyal to the Supreme Dalek. However, the Daleks fell into a state of Civil War. Those loyal to Davros, who had established himself as Emperor, became the Imperial faction, mechanically and biologically enhanced, while the Dalek Supreme led a renegade faction, who remained genetically "pure" and untouched by Davros's designs. The Imperials also deployed the incredibly powerful Special Weapons Dalek. As both factions battled for the Hand of Omega, the Seventh Doctor managed to force Davros and the Imperial Daleks into a trap, destroying Skaro with the very technology they fought to capture.

Some years later, the Daleks put the Doctor's other long-running enemy the Master on trial for his crimes

on Skaro, presumably before its destruction by the Hand of Omega. These Daleks were unusual in having a legal system, and in allowing the Seventh Doctor safe passage to collect the Master's remains to return them to Gallifrey. At some point over the next years in the Doctor's timeline, the Time War broke out between the Daleks and the Time Lords. The exact sequence of events is not yet known, but at the end, the Doctor used "the Moment" to destroy both the Daleks and the Time Lords.

Some time after that, the Ninth Doctor met another sole survivor: a chained Dalek. Captured and imprisoned by billionaire alien collector Henry van Statten in his Utah museum, the Time Lord was horrified to set his eyes upon the beast from Skaro. It managed to break free after touching time-traveler Rose Tyler, and wreaked havoc on those around it, displaying previously unseen abilities: repelling bullets with a force field, turning its dome through 180 degrees and a canny mastering of the Internet. This Dalek committed suicide at Rose's orders: its globes created an energy field in which it disappeared.

The Doctor was in for a shock a short time later when a Dalek fleet appeared at the Game Station (formerly Satellite 5) above Earth, in the year 200,100. The Daleks had installed the Mighty Jagrafess of the Holy Hadrojassic Maxarodenfoe to control humanity, but it had met a sticky end a short time previously at the hands of the Doctor. They then installed a Controller to monitor mankind, a human female connected to the station. The Daleks were using humanity to build a new army, under the guidance of their Emperor, an insane gigantic version of a Dalek which had survived the Time War. The Time Lord vowed revenge after the Daleks captured Rose, and, with help from Captain Jack Harkness, Lynda Moss, and some of the remaining game station

staff, he fought back an invasion. However, it was Rose who saved the Earth from the Daleks after looking into the heart of the TARDIS, which gave her the power to completely destroy the Dalek fleet. However, some Daleks still survived. The Cult of Skaro, believed to be a legend by the Doctor, broke through to Earth (at Torchwood in Canary Wharf, to be precise) in a Void Ship. This group consisted of four Daleks; Caan, Jast, Thay, and their leader Sec (a black Dalek). These Daleks were designed to think independently and use their imaginations, a very un-Dalek like trait. After finding the Genesis Ark, a prison ship containing millions of Daleks captured by the Time Lords, the Cult released the captives and engaged in a brief war with the Cybermen. This was interrupted when the Doctor opened the Void and pulled them back in. The Cult of Skaro managed to escape by initiating an "Emergency Temporal Shift." The Cult ended up back in time, but still on Earth, in New York City, 1930. The quartet engaged in a plan to create a Dalek/human hybrid, known as "The Final Experiment," although Caan, Jast, and Thay had reservations about Sec's proposal to become the first of a new species. The Daleks controlled some of the local inhabitants and conducted human/animal hybrid experiments, turning humans into pig slaves. Dalek Sec went ahead and formed the first human Dalek when human male Mr. Diagoras was pulled inside his outer shell. Acting on their doubts and disgust, Jast and Thay chained him up, with the latter killing him with a blast which was actually meant for the Tenth Doctor. These two were then killed by the new human/Dalek hybrids, who had gained some independent thought due to Gallifreyan DNA, courtesy of the Time Lord. Caan escaped a confrontation with the Doctor, thanks to another "Emergency Temporal Shift."

Caan's journey took him into the heart of the Time War, a feat which should not have been possible, and removed Davros from his moment of death at the hands of the Nightmare Child. This time-dabbling sent Caan insane and he was chained up by his fellow Daleks, now under the instruction of a Supreme Dalek, who referred to Caan as an "abomination." Caan was left talk in riddles, foreseeing the future and correctly referring to the Tenth Doctor as the "threefold man." A new army of Daleks was built from Davros' pure Kaled DNA while the Reality Bomb was constructed and Earth was invaded once more. But Caan's madness led him to betrayal, bringing the Doctor and Donna together initially to help defeat the Daleks. As the Dalek ship, the Crucible, exploded, thanks to the Meta-Crisis Doctor) Caan and Davros apparently perished along with the rest of their species.

But the Daleks' absence from the universe was not to be permanent. During World War II, on Earth, Daleks infiltrated the British army using an android of scientist Professor Edwin Bracewell (see FRIENDS)—who claimed he had invented these machines, known as "Ironsides." The Daleks used Winston Churchill and his army as a trap to bring the Eleventh Doctor to them so he would unwittingly confirm their identity to a Progenitor device and allow them to kickstart a new Dalek Paradigm. These new Daleks were much bigger, bulkier and colorful than their predecessors, and their first act was to destroy their older versions before leaving Earth's orbit.

The new Paradigm were instrumental in creating the alliance of aliens who brought the Eleventh Doctor to Stonehenge and imprisoned him in the Pandorica. As a consequence of Time breaking down, one was petrified and kept in the same museum as the Pandorica. When it was briefly revived, it was vanquished by River Song.

The Daleks (both the originals and the new Paradigm) captured the Eleventh Doctor, Amy, and Rory and sent them to the Dalek Asylum, where the most damaged and insane Daleks were kept, safely away from the rest of the race. The planet was destroyed with a little help from a mutated human, Oswin Oswald who erased all memory of the Doctor from the Dalek archives.

THE FLOOD

This water-based species lived in a glacier on Mars, and spread like a virus when it came into contact with humans; just one drop of water was enough to infect its host. Once infected, the humans would begin to mutate, their eyes changing into a pale color, their mouths cracking and constantly spewing water. All humanity was lost. The Tenth Doctor met the inhabitants of Bowie Base One on Mars when the Flood began its attack, taking over members of the team one by one. To stop it spreading to Earth, Bowie Base One and its rocket was destroyed.

EIGHT LEGS

Hailing from the home of the beautiful blue crystals, Metebelis III, these giant spiders could use immense psychic strength to control humans, blast enemies, communicate, and teleport in space and time. Originally, the species were normal sized arachnids brought by human colonists to the planet but the Metebelis III crystals gave them their great powers over hundreds of years. Once in control, they forbade the use of the word "spider" and referred to the humans as "two legs." Searching for all the crystals, in order to rule the universe, their search led them to the Third Doctor (who had previously stolen one and given it to his companion Jo Grant) on Earth. The Eight Legs' leader, and the largest of all their kind, the Great One, faced the Time Lord in a showdown that saw the crystal returned, but the power was too much for her, resulting in her destruction. This also saw the beginning of the end for this particular incarnation of the Doctor as the radiation in the cave caused irreparable damage to his body, leading to his regeneration when he arrived back on Earth.

FLYING SHARK

On the planet Earth there's an old saying: "I'm just glad sharks can't fly." Sadly, for the inhabitants of Sardicktown on the planet Ember, sharks there could fly. The ferocious fish patrolled the fog-filled skies, hidden in the night, and were drawn to sounds, a trait that the Eleventh Doctor used to his advantage to tame one of the beasts. The Time Lord encountered it when visiting a young Kazran Sardick after the vibrations from the Gallifreyan's sonic screwdriver attracted it, but it was the soothing singing voice of Abigail Pettigrew which stopped the shark from attacking. Many years later, the same shark was harnessed to lead a carriage with Abigail and Kazran on a nighttime ride.

GANGERS

Gangers were artificially created doppelgängers (hence the nickname "gangers") made from a substance known as the Flesh. They were used to carry out work that was potentially harmful or dangerous for normal human beings on Earth. They could be exact copies of their original (Amy Pond's ganger traveled with the Eleventh Doctor and her husband Rory for many months without giving herself away) although sometimes instability arose, with the faces being noticeably smoother than their originals, and on some occasions, the personalities deviated from their source. Some gangers could control the Flesh to make their bodies stretch considerably. The Doctor encountered a rebellion by a group of gangers in the twenty-second century at St. John's Monastery on Earth, and he helped to ease the conflict between the humans and the gangers.

FUTUREKIND

The Tenth Doctor, Martha Jones, and Captain Jack Harkness bumped into this aggressive group on the planet Malcassairo in the year one hundred trillion. The humanoid species were heavily tattooed and incredibly violent, and were identifiable through their jagged and sharp teeth, which they gained from eating human flesh). The Futurekind attacked Silo 16, where the last of mankind was about to leave for the planet Utopia, but were unsuccessful in capturing their prey.

THE GELTH

At one point in their history, the Gelth had physical form but due to the catastrophic events of the Time War, their physicality gave way to a gaseous form. It was in this state that the Gelth encountered the Ninth Doctor and Rose Tyler in Cardiff in 1869. The aliens has been taking over the bodies of the dead, looking for a way to come back into physical existence. At first their wish was seen sympathetically by the Time Lord, who felt co-existence wouldn't be a bad thing (although Rose disagreed strongly) until their real plan was unveiled. Speaking through the psychic maid Gwyneth, they convinced the Doctor to allow their species to come through the Cardiff rift. They then revealed their plan was forcibly inhabit the Earth and claim it as their own. With a little help from writer Charles Dickens, their species was made extinct through fire.

THE GREAT INTELLIGENCE

With no physical appearance, this entity relied on possession and control of living beings. The Second Doctor faced it on two occasions: once in Tibet in 1935 when he was traveling with Jamie and Victoria, where the Intelligence had taken over the master of a monastery, and was using robot Yeti, and then in the London Underground in 1975 when its robot Yeti filled the subway system with a giant web. The Great Intelligence wished to drain the Doctor's mind but was stopped and sent back onto the astral plane. Although the Doctor didn't realize it, the Intelligence was already aware of him. It had met the Eleventh Doctor during Christmas 1892 on Earth. Possessing Dr. Simeon, the Intelligence created ice creatures and controlled everyday harmless snowmen, turning them into jagged-toothed monsters. It was defeated by the power of salt water. But this was not the end of the Great Intelligence. Using Miss Kizlet, it utilized wi-fi to feed on the souls of humans. Taking the form of Dr. Simeon, it spoke to her on a monitor in her London office. Again, the Doctor foiled this attempt on mankind, although the Gallifreyan was unaware of the Intelligence's involvement. On Trenzalore the two met again, for the final time. Using Whisper-men—which could mimic the full physical form of Dr. Simeon—Vastra, Strax, and Jenny were captured and taken to the planet that held the Doctor's tomb. The Intelligence entered the Doctor's time stream—his soul and entire life (or lives)—in the TARDIS, thus ending all the Time Lord's existences. The Intelligence was aware that this meant it was sacrificing itself, but wanted to destroy the Doctor as revenge. Thankfully, for all concerned, Clara entered the same time stream and reversed the Intelligence's actions.

HEADLESS MONKS

These fellows were an odd bunch. Deeply religious and revered by those around them—it was forbidden to remove their hoods, for example; this was punishable by death—the Headless Monks seemed to be merely bodies with no heads. However, they clearly did have some sort of sentience. They could sense the space around them and could fire off electrical discharges from their hands and the swords they brandished. The Eleventh Doctor battled the Headless Monks at Demon's Run when they aligned themselves with Madame Kovarian as he and his friends tried to retrieve Amy Pond and her baby. In the battle, Dorium Maldovar had his head removed by one of the Monks, which the Doctor found in a box in the Seventh Transept some time later, as well as a number of skulls from those transformed into Headless Monks.

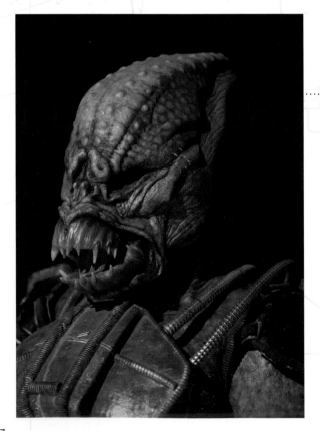

HOIX

This strange, violent and large-fanged beast proved to be an elusive foe as the Tenth Doctor and Rose Tyler tried to capture one in an abandoned warehouse on Earth, events witnessed by Elton Pope. A Hoix was present at the alliance of species who imprisoned the Eleventh Doctor in the Pandorica beneath Stonehenge on Earth. A member of the deadly species, who seemed to want to eat everything, was abducted and made to face their fear with the creature in his prison ship, disguised as an Earth hotel from the 1980s.

ICE WARRIORS

Hailing from the planet Mars, the armored Ice Warriors were a fearsome species with a great sense of honor and camaraderie—"Attack one of us, attack all of us," was their motto. Described by the Eleventh Doctor as bio-mechanoid cyborgs, they rarely were seen out of their protective shell of armor, which was also essential to surviving the freezing temperatures on Mars.

An Ice Warrior named Varga was uncovered in Earth's future, during a second ice age. Encased in ice, and therefore dubbed an "Ice Warrior" by those who found him, the Martian planned to free his comrades who were still frozen in the ice. Since Mars was now "dead," Varga sought to conquer Earth and make it a new home world. His plans were foiled by the Second Doctor.

The Second Doctor encountered them again later in his own time-line, during the twenty-first century, when the Ice Warriors tried to use the T-Mat device to send a fungus to Earth to make the planet like Mars. Some years later, the Third Doctor met more of the species on the planet Peladon. At this time, possibly around the fortieth century, the Ice Warriors renounced their aggressive behavior, put war behind them, and joined the Galactic Federation. However, shortly after, at least some Martians were assisting the Federation's opponents, as the Third Doctor discovered during a return visit to Peladon.

During his time visiting Bowie Base One on Mars, The Tenth Doctor spoke of his one-time foes. He

even praised them to Adelaide Brooke, "They tell legends of Mars from long ago, of a fine and noble race who built an empire out of snow - the Ice Warriors." Perhaps even they succumbed to the Flood.

One solitary member of the Martian race, Skaldak met the Eleventh Doctor in the 1980s on Earth, aboard the Russian submarine Firebird. For the first time, the Time Lord set his eyes upon an Ice Warrior without his armor, noting the Martian was able to control the suit remotely.

* * *

JUDOON

These bulky beautiful space rhinos were members of the intergalactic police. The Tenth Doctor met a platoon of the Judoon on the moon, shortly after they had transported the Royal Hope Hospital there using an H2O scoop while searching for Florence Finnegan (see VILLAINS). More used to capturing their targets with brute force rather than the application of intelligence or detective skills, they almost missed their prey, but for the intervention of the Doctor, who, of course, spoke the language of the Judoon fluently. He met them again, in the same incarnation, when he visited the Shadow Proclamation while investigating the disappearance of Earth.

The Eleventh Doctor found himself on both sides of their justice when the leathered horny aliens joined an alliance of alien species who imprisoned him in the Pandorica. Shortly after, a platoon worked for his cause at Demon's Run, capturing a number of the Clerics. A member of the Judoon was abducted and made to face their fear with the creature in his "Earth hotel" prison ship.

Judoon can engage in social activities: at least one was present in the bar where Captain Jack Harkness met Midshipman Frame.

KRAFAYIS

These invisible creatures were certainly one of the the Doctor has had to face. Alerted to the presence of one on Earth, after spotting it in a painting by artist Vincent van Gogh, the Time Lord traveled with Amy Pond to Auvers-sur-Oise, France to locate the beast. He then used a Species Matcher to identify and track the animal, although van Gogh, thanks to his artistic abilities, was able to see it with his own eyes. The Krafayis was normally a pack beast, but it had killed and would kill again due to its loneliness. Its life was cut short when it lunged at the painter, and became impaled on his easel.

KROLL

Seen as the ruler of Delta III, a swamp moon of Delta Magna, by its servants the Swampies, this squid-like creature had gained gargantuan status by eating a segment from the Key to Time. When the Fourth Doctor and Romana arrived on the moon, it measured up to a mile across and over a hundred foot high. When the Key to Time segment was converted by the two Time Lords, it suddenly became a multitude of smaller normal-sized creatures.

KRILLITANE

The Tenth Doctor and Rose came across a troop of these nasty creatures in Deffry Vale High School in London in 2007. The Krillitane could add features to their DNA and were now bat-like creatures after killing millions on the planet Bessan. They had infested a school and taken on the appearance of the staff at the school. The pupils were fed Krillitane oil, which, ironically, was deadly to the Krillitane. This advanced the children's brain power and imagination, to help in the Krillitane's quest for the Skasis Paradigm. Led by Mr. Finch (see VILLAINS), the aliens devoured children who they believed wouldn't be missed, but were defeated by the Doctor, Rose, Mickey Smith, Sarah Jane Smith, and K9, who dealt the final blow to the Krillitane by killing them in an explosion.

KRYNOIDS

This incredibly deadly plant-like creature was described as an inter-galactic weed by the Doctor. Pairs of Krynoid pods traveled through space and landed on planets where they could infest and grow. The Fourth Doctor and Sarah Jane Smith visited a World Ecology Bureau team in the Antarctic who had uncovered two Krynoid pods. One opened, infecting one of the team, turning him into a Krynoid/human hybrid, while the second pod was transported back to England for Harrison Chase (see VILLAINS). When the second pod opened, it was used to infect another scientist, and eventually a full Krynoid was released. The Doctor tried to reason with it, but in the end had to call in UNIT to destroy the Krynoid in their typically explosive fashion.

THE MARA

On two occasions, on two very different worlds, the Fifth Doctor came into contact with the malevolent force known as the Mara. On Deva Loka, the Mara took possession of his companion Tegan in her sleep, causing a mark shaped like a snake to form on her arm. She was controlled by the entity, who sought to spread havoc, and she passed its power on to an inhabitant of the jungle planet. The Doctor eventually removed the snake in a large physical form and destroyed it with mirrors. Tegan, however, was left rattled for some time after the Mara had left her, and after she rejoined the crew, it wasn't too long before the Mara returned to haunt the young traveler. She directed the TARDIS to the Mara's homeworld, Manussa, from where it had been banished some five hundred years previously. The population was celebrating this anniversary but the Mara planned to return using the Great Crystal which gave it life in the beginning. The Doctor was able to use the crystal against the Mara, believing it to be now gone forever.

MACRA

Feeding off poisonous gases and varying life forms, these gigantic crabs managed to travel the universe and bother the Doctor on a couple of occasions ("the scourge of this galaxy," he called them). His second incarnation met the crafty crustaceans on an Earth colony where they had brainwashed the population. An explosion apparently killed the Macra present. Some years later, the Tenth Doctor faced the Macra again on New Earth, where the now mindless gigantic crabs were clawing down cars from the planet's congested sky car lanes and devouring their occupants.

MIGHTY JAGRAFESS OF THE
HOLY HADROJASSIC MAXARODENFOE

This huge creature, nicknamed Max by his servant the Editor (see VILLAINS), was installed by the Daleks to control Satellite 5 in the Fourth Great and Bountiful Human Empire. The Ninth Doctor encountered the huge ceiling-dwelling beast when he and Rose were captured and interrogated by the Editor in the year 200,000. The Jagrafess had lived for thousands of years and required a cool environment to survive. This was used to his disadvantage when the heating was returned to Floor 500, where he lived, exploding the alien spectacularly.

OGRI

To the human eye the Ogri are just large stones, but don't be fooled by these rocks; they are, in fact, sentient beings who feast on blood. The Fourth Doctor and Romana met three Ogri who were stolen by Cessair of Diplos (see Vivien Fay in VILLAINS) to act as her protectors.

OOD

The Doctor met members of this hive-mind race on a number of occasions, and sometimes they were good, but sometimes they were bad…Well, not bad per se but due to their telepathic nature, Ood could be manipulated and brainwashed by more powerful life forms. The Tenth Doctor and Rose Tyler met Ood who were working as slaves for the inhabitants of Sanctuary Base 6 on Krop Tor. Unfortunately, the Beast, who dwelled beneath the planet's surface, took control of every Ood serving the humans, turning them against their masters and making their eyes glow a hate-filled red. After apparently defeating the Beast, the Time Lord expressed deep regret at not being able to save any of the Ood present; all perished when the planet was devoured by a local black hole.

Some time later, when traveling with Donna Noble, the same incarnation visited the Ood home world, the Ood Sphere. The icy planet was witness to the harsh and barbaric treatment of the species, for which Klineman Halpen (see VILLAINS) was chiefly responsible. A revolt, mounted with help from the Friends of the Ood, saw the Ood claim back their rights and also began their friendship with the Doctor. The Ood sang to him as he left their planet, and

used the name "DoctorDonna," prescient of the days to come.

Ood Sigma, who had met the Doctor during their battle on the Ood Sphere, visited the Tenth Doctor in a vision on Earth in the year 2059, immediately after the destruction of Bowie Base One on Mars and the death of Adelaide Brooke (see FRIENDS). Sensing he was being summoned, the Doctor traveled back to the Ood Sphere (eventually) and met with Ood Elders, who sensed the return of the Master on Earth.

During his travels, the Eleventh Doctor bumped into single Oods, meeting one on the mysterious entity House and even in his TARDIS when Albert Einstein came to visit (and where the scientist briefly turned into an Ood too!).

PEG DOLLS

Although these monsters didn't really exist, they certainly frightened the Doctor's companions Rory and Amy who met them. There were the creation of Tenza child George, who had brought them to life by placing his fears into his doll's house. When people were transported within it, they met these grotesque wooden "life-size" dolls, which mimicked their looks and clothing. They attacked those who weren't like them, and could alter humans into Peg Dolls by simply touching them. When George was convinced of his safety, through his father's love for him, the Peg Dolls reverted back to their normal form.

POCKET UNIVERSE CREATURE

Like a number of aliens and beasts, the Doctor has met throughout the galaxy, this particular "monster" was unnamed by those who came into contact with it. When investigating ghost-like disturbances at Caliburn House on Earth in 1974, the Time Lord found himself in a pocket universe searching for Hila Tacorien but also discovered a huge ungainly beast. At first, its intentions seemed sinister, but the Doctor finally deduced that it was trying to pair up with its partner, who had been stuck on Earth. With help from the TARDIS, he was able to reunite the couple.

PRISONER ZERO

Some might call Prisoner Zero a "multi-form" but to the layman, it was another shape-shifter, although it was able to perform the shape-shifting with multiple hosts. It was captured and imprisoned by the Atraxi but managed to escape through a crack in space and time, ending up in Leadworth, England—specifically in Amelia Pond's bedroom. The creature hid in the house for a dozen years or so, using a perception filter to mask its presence. During this time it built up a psychic link with comatose patients in the nearby hospital and was able to use their forms. Eventually the Atraxi located Prisoner Zero and returned it to the inter-dimensional prison, with a little help from the newly regenerated Eleventh Doctor.

PYROVILES

Another stone race of creatures, which terrorized the inhabitants of Pompeii with their size and
fire-breathing escapades. After their home world of
Pyrovillia was stolen by Davros to form his Reality Bomb, some of the species traveled to Earth,
crash-landing at Mount Vesuvius, where their rock
bodies transformed to dust. An initial eruption of
the volcano in the year 62 A.D. acted as a catalyst
for their return, and the dust from their bodies was
breathed in by certain people in Pompeii who thus
became psychic, although they gradually also turned
to stone. Seventeen years later the Tenth Doctor
arrived with Donna Noble and fought off Pyroviles,
sometimes using a water pistol, and partly transformed Pyrovile humans as the stone beasts tried to
make Earth the new Pyrovillia. The Time Lord used
the eruption of Vesuvius to destroy the remaining
Pyroviles and their converts.

REAPERS

These ghastly creatures' activities were often
stopped by the Time Lords but after Gallifrey's
obliteration in the Time War, the Reapers were
free to act as they pleased. The flying beasts fed on
time, seeking out temporal paradoxes where they
sterilized the "wound" (the paradox) by devouring
everything in their path. When the Ninth Doctor and
Rose popped back to 1987 to witness the death of
Pete Tyler (see FRIENDS) the young blonde created
a paradox by saving her father's life, giving an opportunity for the Reapers. After they attacked many
humans near the paradox, the Time Lord took the
survivors inside a church, knowing that the ancient
building would give some respite for a little while.
Sadly, for him, Rose inadvertently gave the Reapers
access by touching her younger self; the Doctor
sacrificed himself to save those present. The aliens
were finally defeated when Pete Tyler reset his own
timeline by allowing his death to happen as it should
have and thus returning all the victims back to reality.

RUTANS

Well known to the Doctor before he encountered one, the Rutans were the sworn enemy of the Sontarans and had battled them for thousands of years in a seemingly unending war, although both the Sixth and Tenth Doctors suggested at various points that the Rutans had the upper hand. Their form was similar to that of an Earth jellyfish, although Rutan bodies glowed a sinister green, as did their numerous tendrils. They could feed off electrical energy and also fire electrical shocks at opponents, a trait the Fourth Doctor and Leela discovered in a lighthouse at Fang Rock on Earth in the early 1900s. The Rutans could shape shift into human form and were defeated on that occasion when the Doctor used the lighthouse lamp and some diamonds to destroy their spacecraft.

SATURNYNES

This fish/crustacean-like species fled from their home world of Saturnyne after the crack in space and time doomed it to non-existence. The Eleventh Doctor, traveling with the Ponds, met a number of Saturnynes in 1580 in Venice, which was desirable because of its watery features. Rosanna Calvierri (see VILLAINS) led this group who tried to convert the local population into Saturnynes with a view to increasing their species' population. Their plan was foiled by the Doctor, and the remaining Saturnynes devoured their leader, living out their days until extinction.

SEA DEVILS

Cousins of the Silurians, the Sea Devils (not their actual name: it was coined by a crewmember who came in contact with them) were an advanced race who lived on Earth in prehistoric times and were reptilian in form. They teamed up with the Master, freeing him from the island prison where he had been incarcerated for his crimes. The Third Doctor believed a truce between the Sea Devils and humanity was possible to allow peaceful coexistence, and he acted as a negotiator. The Master, however, had different plans and forced his fellow Time Lord into helping to build a machine that would awaken the Sea Devil colonies all over the planet so they could conquer the planet. However, the sea creatures betrayed the Master, imprisoning him along with the Doctor. Fortuitously, the Doctor had sabotaged the machine and the Sea Devil colony was destroyed.

A century later, in 2084, on Sea Base 4 the Fifth Doctor, traveling with Tegan and Turlough, faced an army of Sea Devils awoken by a group of Silurians. After a battle began between the humans and their invaders causing many casualties, the Doctor saved the day by releasing hexachromite gas, which killed all the Sea Devils and Silurians. Disappointed at the outcome, he mourned, "There should have been another way."

Alternate Universe Note:
In an alternative time-line, a number of members of the Silence were contained in water tanks in the Area 52 pyramid. Some broke free and attacked Amy and Rory, but were gunned down.

THE SILENCE

We were tempted to leave this entry empty and simply say we couldn't remember anything about the Silence—but we'll leave that gag for others to make. The Eleventh Doctor, Amy, Rory, and River Song first met the forgettable lot in the USA in 1969. Picnicking at Lake Silencio, Amy spotted one from afar and also encountered one at the White House in Washington, where she took a photograph of a Silent on her phone. This enabled the Doctor to help identify them. The species had lived on Earth for thousands of years undetected, since, whenever they were seen, they were immediately forgotten as soon as the person turned away. The Silence shot electrical charges from their hands, disintegrating their targets and also instructed humans through a kind of hypnotism. The Time Lord used a recording filmed by Canton Delaware III of a Silent claiming "You should kill us all on sight," to spark the human race into killing their tall, gray memory-proof aliens, by placing the footage on television into the moment when man landed on the moon, which was seen worldwide.

Members of the Silence teamed up with Madame Kovarian to kidnap River Song and turn her into a weapon to defeat the Doctor although this plan eventually failed.

SILURIANS

The Doctor first met the Silurians (sometimes known, also incorrectly, as Eocenes and, more correctly, homo reptilia) while assisted by Liz Shaw on Wenley Moor, Earth investigating odd occurrences there on behalf of UNIT. The Silurians had been awoken from hibernation because of activity at the research center. They had put themselves to sleep millions of years earlier because they believed a large object was about to hit the Earth, but it turned out to be the arrival of the moon. Used to being the dominant species on the planet, the Silurian leaders disagreed with each other about the future and one of them released a virus to kill humanity. The Doctor and Liz cured the virus, and although the Third Doctor tried to negotiate between the two species, the Brigadier blew up the Silurian base, leaving the Time Lord very disgruntled.

Many years later, another branch of the Silurian race came out of hibernation and awoke an army of Sea Devils to attack Sea Base 4 in 2084. This battle also saw the use of the fearsome Myrka, a huge beast that could sustain prolonged firearms attack. The Silurians' plan to launch nuclear weapons to annihilate the human race was aborted and, faced with no other options, the Fifth Doctor released hexachromite gas, killing them and their aquatic cousins.

In his Eleventh incarnation, the Doctor met another group of Silurians in Wales. Awoken by drilling, some of the underground city dwellers came to the surface, kidnapping humans for experimentation. Ever the peacemaker, the Gallifreyan brought humans and Silurians round a table, but Restac (see VILLAINS) was intent on bringing death to the humans. However, after his rebellion was put down, the Silurians went back into hibernation for one thousand years,

in the hope that humanity would be able to negotiate once more.

A group of Silurians aided in the capture and imprisonment of the Eleventh Doctor in the Pandorica at Stonehenge in 102 A.D. The Gallifreyan came across a Silurian Ark in the twenty-fourth century where he found a trader named Solomon had used robots to destroy a great number of Silurians.

SONTARANS

Another war-loving species! Hailing from Sontar, this clone race were humanoid in shape although their appearance often made them look like walking baked potatoes. Despite being clones, some members of the species had different numbers of fingers and often looked and sounded very different. Their love of war made them fierce competitors, and they took much joy in dying in battle. They were in permanent conflict with the Rutan Host—a war that neither side looked likely ever to win.

The Doctor's first encounter with the species took place in thirteenth century England while in his third incarnation. A Sontaran, named Linx, was using an osmic projector to bring scientists from the twentieth century back in time to help repair his crashed spaceship. He was killed by an arrow which hit him in the probic vent at the back of his head, the Sontarans' one weak spot. Protecting this ensured that all Sontarans faced front at all times when in battle.

Shortly after his next regeneration, the Time Lord found himself on Earth in its far future, thousands of years after solar flares had caused the population to abandon the planet. Field Major Styre had captured some human colonists from a crash-landed ship and had begun experimenting on them, sometimes in horrific fashion, to define their responses, and thus identify their strengths and possible threats to the Sontaran fleet. The Time Lord engaged Styre in physical combat, and, with help from one of the human experiments who sacrificed his life, defeated his alien foe. The same incarnation was Lord President on Gallifrey during a Sontaran invasion, which was defeated with help from his companion Leela.

It was some time before the Doctor crossed paths once more with one of the war-obsessed beings,

with two regenerations teaming together to fight them. Sent by the Time Lords to investigate unauthorized time experiments, the Second Doctor was captured by Sontarans, who wanted the secrets of time travel. The Sixth Doctor came to the aid of his former self, in 1980s Spain, and stopped the plans. It would be many years, and a number of regenerations, before the Sontarans attempted another Earth invasion. Using boy genius Luke Rattigan (see VILLAINS), they sought to rid the world of humanity, leaving Earth as a new breeding-ground for the Sontaran clones. The Tenth Doctor and Donna Noble teamed up with UNIT, for whom Martha Jones was now working, to see off this threat but it was Luke who sacrificed himself to save mankind, by using a bomb to destroy the Sontarans' ship, killing almost all of the Sontaran army on board.

A number of Sontarans were part of the alliance of aliens who imprisoned the Eleventh Doctor in the Pandorica, under Stonehenge on Earth. A member of the species was abducted and made to face their fear with the Creature in his prison ship (disguised as an Earth hotel from the 1980s).

SYCORAX

A war-like, aggressive but proud and almost noble race, the Sycorax attacked Earth one Christmas Day, shortly after the Ninth Doctor regenerated into the Tenth. A great number of the species traveled in their asteroid-like ship, using blood control to intimidate the humans, controlling those with A-positive type blood a sample of which they found on the Guinevere One space probe. After the Sycorax captured the TARDIS, Rose Tyler and Harriet Jones (see FRIENDS), the Doctor challenged the Sycorax Leader to a sword duel where, although he lost his hand (don't worry, it grew back quickly!), he vanquished the duplicitous foe.

The remaining Sycorax left the air space over London, knowing Earth was protected, but shortly afterwards, Harriet Jones ordered Torchwood to use alien technology to destroy the ship, much to the Doctor's anger. The Eleventh Doctor found himself at their mercy when, along with hundreds of other alien species, he was imprisoned in the Pandorica.

TOCLAFANE

In a bid to enslave the human race and become its ruler (which, in fairness, he did succeed in doing for a year), the Master (see TIME LORDS) used a species that he called the Toclafane to attack the Earth, decimate its population, and police it. Spherical in shape, with spikes as accessories, the beings could fire laser bolts and kill with ease. The Toclafane were believed to be a myth, according to the Tenth Doctor, who claimed they were merely the stuff of children's nightmares. This was to prove the case. During the "year that never was" when the Master ruled the Earth, Martha Jones discovered the horrific truth behind the Toclafane: they were the last remains of humanity, their final evolution. Inside the shell, Martha found a shriveled human head, cybernetically connected to the sphere. While still in human form as Professor Yana, the Master had sent the last of humanity from Malcassairo to "Utopia" (a non-existent planet) in 100,000,000,000,000, but then he had returned to save them from their deaths. The Toclafane were the result. They shared race memories, as demonstrated when one recognized Martha. who had met a young boy on Malcassairo. The "year that never was" was reversed by the Doctor and the paradox eliminated.

TRICKSTER'S BRIGADE

Who knew a little Time Beetle could cause so many problems? When Donna Noble and the Tenth Doctor visited Shan Shen, the Chiswick temp was tempted into a fortune teller's stall. During this session, a Time Beetle climbed on her back and forced her to change her past and thus bring into existence an alternative time-line, in which the Doctor died. With a little help from Rose Tyler, who broke into this new universe, Donna broke free; this resulted in the death of the beetle, which fell off her back. It was identified by the Time Lord as a member of the Trickster's Brigade: the Trickster was an entity who thrived on chaos and temporal shifts. The two came face-to-face when the Trickster became involved in the life of the Doctor's friend Sarah Jane Smith, which he did on a number of occasions, including at her wedding when the Doctor had to intervene.

TRACTATORS

These underground-dwelling insectoids were a powerful race, using their antennae to control gravity. Led by the Gravis (the only one of their kind with intelligence), they used their abilities to batter the planet Frontios with meteorites (and the odd TARDIS) and drag the human inhabitants down through the earth to their doom. The Fifth Doctor, traveling with Tegan and Turlough, helped the Earth colony to repel their attacks. Turlough had a race memory of the Tractators from his home planet of Trion.

Alternate Universe Note:
After a beetle climbed on her back and forced Donna Noble to change her past, she brought an alternative time-line into existence…one in which the Doctor dies.

TRITOVORES

This insectoid species are not dissimilar to humans, though they have fly-like heads, speak with clicks and feed on feces. The Tenth Doctor and Lady Christina de Souza met two Tritovores in their crashed ship on the planet San Helios after a group of humans had arrived there on a London bus via a wormhole. The Time Lord quickly became friends with them and offered to help, though their acquaintanceship would not last long; they were killed by a stingray-like alien (see the next entry). A member of the Tritovore species was abducted and made to face their fear with the Creature in his prison ship, disguised as an Earth hotel from the 1980s.

UNNAMED ALIEN SPECIES

These creatures flew around the planet San Helios and bore a striking resemblance to stingrays from Earth, although these could fly and eat through anything, including hard metals. The Tenth Doctor discovered them after traveling through a wormhole on a London bus and landing on the desert planet. The aliens had destroyed an entire civilization, killing millions. The energy created by their swarm started wormholes that gave them access to new planets. Some made their way to Earth after the Time Lord had escaped but were dispatched by UNIT troops.

VASHTA NERADA

More biting killer aliens, although these were very hard to spot. Hiding in the Library, which contained every book ever written, the Vashta Nerada slowly separated and hunted River Song's archaeological team. Like piranhas, they ate the flesh off their victims incredibly cleanly, leaving just a pure white skeleton. They moved through the shadows stalking their prey, and they were able to work together to form a single body and communicate with other species. Once face-to-face with the Doctor, they realized that he was a formidable force, so backed off.

VERVOIDS

These plant creatures were created artificially as a slave race. Humanoid in stature and form, they had the ability to shoot poisonous darts from their "hands" and release gas from their "mouths." The Sixth Doctor, traveling with Mel, encountered them on the Hyperion III starliner in 2986. The species attacked the humans on board, fighting for survival; the Doctor had no choice about destroying them before they could wreak any more damage and death.

VESPIFORM

Another shape-shifting alien, and one with a sting in its tale. In its true form, the Vespiform looked like a giant wasp from Earth. The Tenth Doctor and Donna Noble came across the creature when visiting Agatha Christie in England, 1926. This Vespiform was the cross-species result of a Vespiform that landed in India, 1885 mating with human female Clemency Eddison, and it was hiding under the human identity of a local vicar. He attacked and killed members of the community before the Time Lord figured out what was going on. This Vespiform drowned after Donna threw his Firestone (a Vespiform telepathic recorder) into a river and the creature followed it in.

WEEPING ANGELS

Known throughout the universe and throughout time (even name-checked by Lord President Rassilon himself), the Weeping Angels were one of the most feared aliens in the entire galaxy. A quantum-locked species, they have to cover their eyes (normally with their hands) for fear of seeing another of their kind and thus trapping themselves in petrified form forever. The Angels, sometimes known as the Lonely Assassins, could move when not being seen and quickly attack even in the blink of an eye. When touched by a Weeping Angel, the victim is sent back in time where they lived out the rest of their life while the angel fed off the time energy left.

The Tenth Doctor, traveling with Martha Jones, encountered some Weeping Angels in 2007. They sent the couple back to 1969 and stole the TARDIS. With a little help from Billy Shipton, Larry Nightingale, and Sally Sparrow (see FRIENDS) in a serious of timey-wimey, wibbly-wobbly communications, the Time Lord's ship was returned to him, and four Weeping Angels were rendered harmless.

In his next regeneration, the Gallifreyan came into contact with much more aggressive Weeping Angels. These killed people by snapping their necks, and the Doctor learned much more about their dark talents including their ability to communicate using voices of the dead. After the Byzantium crashed on Alfava Metraxis, a lone Weeping Angel on board sought to reunite with its kind. The Angels had wiped out the indigenous population thousands of years earlier but had starved with no food source. This was to change with the arrival of the Eleventh Doctor, Amy Pond,

River Song, and an army of Clerics. The Time Lord discovered that an image of an angel could itself become a Weeping Angel and infect those who had set their eyes upon it: an unfortunate side effect experienced by Amy Pond after watching a close-circuit video recording of an Angel. The Scot slowly began to turn into an Angel, which controlled her mind and caused her to hallucinate. The army of Angels was eaten by the crack in space and time after the Doctor turned off the gravity in the Byzantium, and the crack was sealed with their energy.

But this was not to be the last meeting for the Eleventh Doctor and his stone enemies. New York in the early 2010s saw the Angels attack, resulting in a trip to 1938, where the city was infested with Angels: even the Statue of Liberty was one (which was rather odd since it was made of bronze). Angels were turning regular everyday statues into Weeping Angels, but they were defeated when Amy and Rory created a paradox by killing themselves, although both humans ended up unharmed in modern day New York.

Sadly, for the Doctor, one Weeping Angel remained and sent Amy and Rory back in time, leaving the Doctor certain he would never see them again.

* * *

THE WIRE

Using the burgeoning popularity of television sets in the1950s thanks to the impending Queen's Coronation, the Wire fed off the signals in human brains which it captured when they were watching television. This left the victims without a face. Its physical manifestation came through television screens where it appeared as a polite female television announcer. Using Mr. Magpie (see VILLAINS), the Wire ensured televisions were easily available in order to satiate its hunger but when the Tenth Doctor and Rose Tyler arrived in 1953, its reign of terror was brought to an end. The energy being managed to capture Rose, leaving her disembodied head pleading for help on a television screen, leaving the Time Lord with no option other than to finish the Wire off. He managed to capture the Wire onto video tape and then erased it by recording over it.

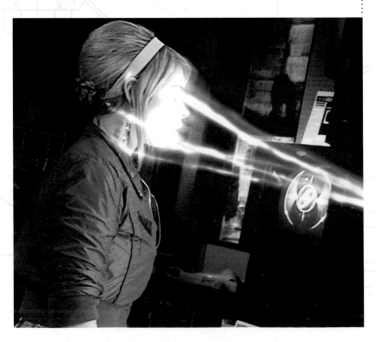

ZYGONS

Sucker-clad and whispery of voice, the Zygons terrorized northern Scotland by kidnapping the local population of Tulloch Moor (not far from Loch Ness). Shape shifters, the Zygons took human body prints and changed their physiques accordingly; the original "source" was kept alive as the metamorphic process had to be renewed periodically. Their ship had crashed in the Scottish highlands centuries earlier where they survived for some years before enacting a place to render the Earth uninhabitable for humans, but perfect for Zygons. With the help of the Skarasen, a huge dinosaur-like cyborg whose milk they required to live, they destroyed oil rigs and attacked London. However the Fourth Doctor, accompanied by Sarah Jane Smith and Harry Sullivan, brought an end to the planned takeover, with some help from UNIT.

Some years later, the Zygons were involved in the alliance of numerous alien races that formed to fight the Eleventh Doctor and imprison him in the Pandorica, located under Stonehenge on Earth. Not long after, while treating his chums Amy and Rory to an anniversary gift, the trio encountered Zygons in the Savoy Hotel in 1890 at its grand opening, where they had shape-shifted into the staff.

But that wasn't the last of the Zygons and their love of the Earth and meetings with the Doctor. In fact, it would be two versions of the Time Lord, the Tenth and Eleventh incarnations, who battled them once more when the Zygons infiltrated UNIT...

PICTURE CREDITS

Page 126, Yvonne Hartman played by Tracy Ann Oberman © WireImage/Getty Images

Page 128, Cyberman © 80eight Photography & Design/Alamy

Page 130, Clockwork Droids © Shaun Finch-Coyote-Photography.co.uk/Alamy

Page 133, Gadget with Tenth Doctor David Tennant and Adelaide Brooke played by Lindsay Duncan © REX USA

Page 134, Gunslinger played by Andrew Brooke © BBC Photo Library

Page 134, Handbots © BBC Photo Library

Page 135, Host © Alastair Balderstone/ Alamy

Page 135, K1 Robot © BBC Photo Library

Page 136, Kamelion © BBC Photo Library

Page 137, K9 © REX USA

Page 138, K9 with the Doctors: Richard Hurndall (as William Hartnell), Peter Davison, a model of Tom Baker, Jon Pertwee, and Patrick Troughton © REX USA

Page 139, Kraal © BBC Photo Library

Page 139, The Daleks and the Mechonoids battle it out © Hulton Images/Getty Images

Page 140, Movellans © BBC Photo Library

Page 141, Quarks © BBC Photo Library

Page 141, Raston Warrior Robot © BBC Photo Library

Page 142, Roboforms © John Robertson/ Alamy

Page 143, Sharaz Jek © BBC Photo Library

Page 144, War Machines © BBC Photo Library

Page 146, Mel played by Bonnie Langford, Seventh Doctor Sylvester McCoy, and the Rani played by Kate O'Mara © REX USA/ South West News Service

Page 148, Borusa © BBC Photo Library

Page 151, Jenny played by Georgia Moffett © WireImage/Getty Images

Page 152, The Master and the Doctor played by Anthony Ainley and Tom Baker © AF archive/Alamy

Page 153, The Master played by John Simm © Allstar Picture Library/Alamy

Page 154, The Master and the Doctor played by Anthony Ainley and Tom Baker © Moviestore collection Ltd/Alamy

Page 156, Morbius © BBC Photo Library

Page 157, Omega © BBC Photo Library

Page 158, Mel played by Bonnie Langford, Seventh Doctor Sylvester McCoy, and the Rani played by Kate O'Mara © REX USA/ South West News Service

Page 159, Rassilon played by Timothy Dalton © Getty Images

Page 160, Romana played by Mary Tamm with Fourth Doctor Tom Baker © Hulton Archive/Getty Images

Page 161, Susan Foreman played by Carol Ann Ford with First Doctor William Hartnell © Moviestore collection Ltd/Alamy

Page 164, A Dalek with Davros ©REX USA/Chris Balcombe

Page 166, Cassandra © Studio9/Alamy

Page 166, Cassandra played by Zoe Wannamaker © Getty Images

Page 168, A Dalek with Davros ©REX USA/Chris Balcombe

Page 169, Mr. Finch played by Anthony Head © epa european pressphoto agency b.v./Alamy

Page 169, Florence Finnegan played by Anne Reid © REX USA/Nick Cunard

Page 170, Gantok played by Rondo Haxton © BBC Photo Library

Page 172, John Lumic played by Roger Lloyd © Trinity Mirror/Mirrorpix/Alamy

Page 173, Joshua & Abigail Naismith played by David Harewood & Tracy Ifeachor © BBC Photo Library

Page 174, Miss Kizlet played by Celia Imrie © Getty Images

Page 174, Klineman Halpen played by Tim McInnerny © REX USA/Ray Tang

Page 175, Lance Bennett played by Don Gilet © REX USA

Page 175, Lucy Saxon played by Alexandra Moen © Mirrorpix

Page 176, Luke Rattigan played by Ryan Sampson © Getty Images

Page 177, Lytton played by Maurice Colbourne © REX USA/Mark Richards/ Associated Newspapers/Rex

Page 179, Margaret Blaine played by Annette Badland © REX USA/Jonathan Hordle

Page 180, Mawdryn played by David Collings © BBC Photo Library

Page 181, Rosanna Calvierri played by Helen McCrory © Getty Images

Page 183, Sharaz Jek © BBC Photo Library

Page 184, Sky Silvestry played by Lesley Sharp © Hulton Archive/Getty Images

Page 185, The Black Guardian © BBC Photo Library

Page 185, The Siren played by Lily Cole © WireImage/Getty Images

Page 187, The Editor played by Simon Pegg © REX USA

Page 187, Vivien Fay © BBC Photo Library

Page 188, Dr. Walter Simeon played by Richard E. Grant © REX USA/Rex

Page 190, Cyberman © John Cairns/Alamy

Page 191, Abzorbaloff © BBC Photo Library

A NOTE FROM THE BLOGTOR

Being a *Doctor Who* fan can be an odd pastime. An odd and time-consuming pastime. With so many stories, planets, characters and Doctors, coming to grips with the show and fully understanding its 50-year history can be intimidating, infuriating, and, on numerous occasions, contradictory.

As a longtime fan, I recognize these varying emotions all too well. From my earliest memories of Scaroth, last of the Jaggaroth, revealing his horrific face at the end of "City of Death, Part One" to the cancellation of the show at the end of the 1980s to its glorious return in 1996 with Paul McGann, and to the even more glorious regeneration in 2005, courtesy of Russell T Davies and Christopher Eccleston.

It's no wonder that *Doctor Who* fans are such an amazing and eclectic bunch. After all, what other fandom has had to deal with so much trauma and uncertainty!

Despite the uncertainty, however, my love for *Doctor Who* has only grown over the years. I loved it as a child, never missing an episode on original transmission and even sending my own fan art to the BBC children's program *Saturday Superstore* (though, sadly, they never displayed it on screen). Now, as an adult, I celebrate the world's greatest television series with my own website, *Blogtor Who*.

The popularity of the site (there are days it gets over eighty thousand page views) has allowed for so many incredible opportunities, including meeting and chatting with some of the biggest stars in *Doctor Who* history. I feel very lucky to have had the opportunity to sit down and have a sociable drink with people like lovely Murray Gold (*Doctor Who's* sublime composer); cheery Chris Chibnall (writer of a number of brilliant stories like "Dinosaurs on a Spaceship"); beautiful Torchwood actress Eve Myles (who plays Gwen Cooper); current showrunner, Steven "SteeMo" Moffat; outgoing TARDIS pilot Matt Smith, who is both a true gentleman and affable in the extreme; and many more from in front of and behind the camera.

When I met the man who brought *Doctor Who* back in 2005, Russell T Davies, he was not only aware of *Blogtor Who*, but he even gave me a big hug in thanks for my support as did the Tenth Doctor himself, David Tennant (a fellow Scot)! I can't explain the joy of knowing that the ramblings typed out in my kitchen were also being read by those who were involved in the making of my favorite show—well, my heart nearly burst with glee.

It's also the popularity of the site that led to the writing of *The Who's Who of Doctor Who*, a dream of mine for many, many years. This book celebrates the joyous collection of companions, aliens, monsters, villains and even robots over the past fifty years—but by no means is this an exhaustive look at the heroes and villains of *Doctor Who*. Not everyone (or everything) is included. Not even nearly everything. But you've probably noticed I included the main players in the "Whoniverse"—some big, some small, but all notable.

Here's to 50 more years!

– Cam

ACKNOWLEDGMENTS

Dedicated to my mum Carol, gone but never forgotten.

Special thanks to:
My Dad Angus, for supporting me so heartily over the years.

Raul Ruiz, now sadly no longer with us, and Dr. Alan Marcus, for their invaluable help and positive support during my time at the University of Aberdeen.

I'd also like to thank the following people for their general support and wonderful help over the last five years or so (and in no particular order!): Joy Abella and Erika Tsang (without whom this book would not have happened); Jeannine Dillon, Paul Simpson, Caroline Wong, Danielle Rhodes, Heidi North and the team at Race Point Publishing for all their work on the book; Andrew Skilleter for his wonderful illustrations; Richard Starkings; Simon Brew and Will Martin (for letting me write for their sites; Mark Machado (for being so kind on my move to London); Lisa Gifford and Elisar Cabrera (and their comfy couch); Chris Chapman; Frank Collins; Nick "Ampersand-Whelks" Fraser; Jack Bowman; Emrys Matthews; Gavin Dunbar; Alun Preece; Daren Thomas; Dick Fiddy; Edward Russell, Chris Hicks, Emma Cooney, Christopher Allen, Reetu Kabra and all the lovely people at BBC Worldwide; Gary Russell; Murray Gold; Stephen P Kelly; Dan Martin; and to everyone who's visited and assisted with the *Blogtor Who* site since 2008.

ABOUT THE AUTHOR

CAMERON K. McEWAN is the man behind *Blogtor Who*, a fan site dedicated to *Doctor Who*. Started in 2008, *Blogtor Who* is now one of the most popular *Doctor Who* blogs in the world, on some days receiving over 80,000 page views with nearly 40,000 followers on Twitter.

Its popularity and success have gained Blogtor Who access to the production team, and he is regularly invited to press events (such as the Official Convention in 2012, the Official Celebration in 2013, and the opening of the Doctor Who Experience). He has interviewed Matt Smith, Steven Moffat, Mark Gatiss, Murray Gold, and many others involved in the production of *Doctor Who*. Cameron also makes appearances at conventions, hosting panels and interviews across Europe while also making the odd television appearance on the BBC and in the United States.

While studying film at the University of Aberdeen, Cameron obtained a First Class Degree and worked alongside maverick filmmakers such as Alex Cox and Raul Ruiz. In 2013, he was part of the team that released the *Doctor Who* documentary, *Who's Changing*, all about the fans.

Cameron also writes for sites like *Den of Geek, Cult Box*, and *The Huffington Post*, and reviews television weekly on BBC London. Not content with writing and filmmaking, he was also seen on the stage last year at the RSC in Stratford-upon-Avon (Twelfth Night) and at the Edinburgh Fringe Festival (Who Do You Think You Are?).

He currently lives in London with his three trousers.

www.blogtorwho.com

ABOUT THE ILLUSTRATOR

ANDREW SKILLETER has worked as an illustrator, publisher and occasional writer. Best known for his professional association with *Doctor Who* between 1979 and 1995 and a long creative partnership with the BBC, he has painted hundreds of covers across numerous genres and media. His work has also encompassed the illustration of many books and magazines. *Blacklight : The Art of Andrew Skilleter*, a large format, color hardback written by the artist was published by *Virgin* in 1995, showcasing his *Doctor Who* work. Living in England with his artist and writer wife, he continues to work on a variety of commissions and is currently developing a new range of stylish work combining digitally his traditional art and figurative photography.

www.andrewskilleter.com